CHOICES

CHOICES
AN INTRODUCTION TO DECISION THEORY

‖‖‖‖‖‖‖‖‖‖‖‖‖‖‖‖‖‖‖‖‖‖

Michael D. Resnik

Professor of Philosophy
University of North Carolina
at Chapel Hill

University of Minnesota Press, Minneapolis

Published by the University of Minnesota Press,
2037 University Avenue Southeast, Minneapolis, MN 55414.
Published simultaneously in Canada
by Fitzhenry & Whiteside Limited, Markham.
Printed in the United States of America.

Library of Congress Cataloging-in-Publication Data

Resnik, Michael D.
  Choices : an introduction to decision theory.
  Includes bibliographies and index.
  1. Decision-making.   2.Statistical decision.
I. Title.
T57.95.R45   1986   001.53'8   86-11307
ISBN 0-8166-1439-3
ISBN 0-8166-1440-7 (pbk.)

The University of Minnesota is
an equal-opportunity educator and employer.

In Memoriam
Beatrice Salzman Spitzer Katz
Mary Edwards Holt

CONTENTS

PREFACE

I CALL DECISION THEORY the collection of mathematical, logical, and philosophical theories of decision making by rational individuals — taken alone, in competition, and in groups. For me it includes utility theory, game theory, and social choice theory. By whatever name, it has become an integral part of important approaches to the philosophy of science, the theory of rationality, and ethics. The debate between John Rawls and John Harsanyi about the proper decision method to use behind the "veil of ignorance" is perhaps the best-known instance of the use of decision theory in philosophy. But the use of epistemic utility maximization is equally important in the philosophy of science, and the prisoner's dilemma of game theory and Arrow's theorem of social choice theory recently have stimulated ethical thought.

Not only is decision theory useful to philosophers in other fields; it also provides philosophers with philosophical perplexities of its own, such as the well-known Newcomb's paradox. (I call it the Predictor paradox.) These and a host of other paradoxes raise serious questions for our accepted view of rationality, probability, and value.

Decision theory has been taught largely by statisticians, economists, and management scientists. Their expositions reflect their interests in applications of the theory to their own domains. My purpose here is to put forward an exposition of the theory that pays particular attention to matters of logical and philosophical interest. Thus I present a number of proofs and philosophical commentaries that are absent from other introductions to the subject. However, my presentation presupposes no more than elementary logic and high school algebra. In keeping with the introductory nature of the book, I have left open many of the philosophical questions I address.

The first four chapters are concerned with decision making by a single agent. In chapter 1, I set out the standard act-state-outcome approach and then turn in chapter 2 to decision making under ignorance. Here I discuss several of the well-known rules, such as the maximin rule and the principle of insufficient reason. In this chapter I also discuss types of scales for measuring utilities and demonstrate which type of scale each rule presupposes. With each rule I give a brief account of its philosophical and practical advantages and disadvantages.

I then turn to the question of which rule, if any, is the correct one and illustrate this with an account of the Rawls-Harsanyi dispute.

Chapters 3 and 4 deal with individual decisions under risk. After presenting the rule of expected utility maximization, I turn to the component theories associated with it—probability theory and utility theory. My account of probability begins with a development of the probability calculus through Bayes's theorem. I then discuss several interpretations of probability, proving the Dutch Book theorem during the course of my account of subjective probability. Turning to utility theory, I develop the Von Neumann-Morgenstern approach and prove a representation theorem. I take pains to explain how this theorem shows that all agents who satisfy certain conditions of rationality must have preference orderings that can be represented as if they maximize expected utility. I explain why this shows that it is rational to maximize expected utility even when one is taking a one-shot gamble. The discussion of utility concludes with a review of paradoxes—Allais's, Ellsberg's, the Predictor, and the St. Petersburg—and an examination of causal decision theory.

Chapter 5 is devoted to game theory with a focus on two-person zero sum games. I develop the standard account and prove the maximin theorem for two-by-two games. This requires some fancy factoring but no higher mathematics. I then turn to two-person nonzero sum games and the failure of the equilibrium concept to provide satisfactory solutions. This leads into the prisoner's dilemma and the challenge it poses to the theory of rationality. I discuss Gauthier's attempt to show that it can be rational to cooperate with one's partners when caught in a prisoner's dilemma. I pass from this to bargaining games and the solutions proposed by John Nash and David Gauthier. This part of the book concludes with a discussion of multiperson games and coalition theories.

Chapter 6 is devoted to social choice theory. I prove Arrow's theorem, after exploring the nature of its conditions. Then I turn to majority rule and prove May's theorem. Last, I turn to utilitarianism and prove a theorem of Harsanyi's, which can be stated dramatically as to the effect that in a rational and impartial society of rational agents the social ordering must be the utilitarian one. The book concludes with a critique of this theorem and a discussion of the problem of interpersonal comparisons of utility.

Although I intend this book for use by philosophers (as well as social and management scientists and others) seeking an introduction to decision theory, I also have found it suitable for a one-semester undergraduate course enrolling students with a variety of interests and majors. Most of my students have had a semester of symbolic logic, but able students with no previous work in logic have done quite well in the course. The logical and mathematical exercises given throughout the book have formed the basis for much of the written work in my course, but I have also assigned, with good results, a number of philosophical essay questions on the material covered.

M. D. R.

ACKNOWLEDGMENTS

ANYONE WHO KNOWS the subject will recognize that I owe a large debt to those who have already worked on and written about decision theory. I have drawn heavily on the material in Luce and Raiffa's *Games and Decisions*, Raiffa's *Decision Analysis*, and Sen's *Collective Choice and Social Welfare*. I was also fortunate enough to have seen parts of Gauthier's *Morals by Agreement* before its publication and have included an account of his views on game theory. The idea for a book of this sort and the topics to be included goes back to a conversation about courses in decision theory that Ned McClennen and I had one morning almost ten years ago.

Daniel Albert started my serious interest in decision theory when, as a Robert Woods Johnson Clinical Scholar, he asked me to teach him "the logic of medicine." I have been grateful for his friendship and encouragement ever since. I am also grateful for the stipend I received as Albert's mentor under the Clinical Scholar's program. Duncan MacRae, director of the University of North Carolina Program in Public Policy Analysis, included me in a Sloan Foundation grant, which funded me for a summer to work on this book.

Henry Kyburg and Ellery Eells sent me comments on the book in their capacity as referees for the University of Minnesota Press, as did an anonymous political scientist. They did much to improve the book. Obviously they are not responsible for any remaining faults.

I am also grateful for comments, conversations, moral support, and editorial assistance from James Fetzer, Susan Hale, John Harsanyi, Philip Kitcher, Arthur Kuflick, Barry Loewer, Claire Miller, Richard Nunan, Joe Pitt, David Resnik, Janet Resnik, Jay Rosenberg, Carolyn Shearin, Brian Skyrms, Henry West, and Bill Wright. I would also like to thank my undergraduate students for questions and comments. Their struggles to understand the material forced me to improve my exposition. I neglected to note most of their names, but one stands out quite vividly: Sheldon Coleman, whose reactions caused me to rewrite several exercises.

CHOICES

1-1. What Is Decision Theory?

Decision theory is the product of the joint efforts of economists, mathematicians, philosophers, social scientists, and statisticians toward making sense of how individuals and groups make or should make decisions. The applications of decision theory range from very abstract speculations by philosophers about ideally rational agents to practical advice from decision analysts trained in business schools. Research in decision theory is just as varied. Decision theorists with a strong mathematical bent prefer to investigate the logical consequences of different rules for decision making or to explore the mathematical features of different descriptions of rational behavior. On the other hand, social scientists interested in decision theory often conduct experiments or social surveys aimed at discovering how real people (as opposed to "ideally rational agents") actually behave in decision-making situations.

It is thus usual to divide decision theory into two main branches: normative (or prescriptive) decision theory and descriptive decision theory. Descriptive decision theorists seek to find out how decisions *are* made—they investigate us ordinary mortals; their colleagues in normative decision theory are supposed to prescribe how decisions *ought* to be made—they study ideally rational agents. This distinction is somewhat artificial since information about our actual decision-making behavior may be relevant to prescriptions about how decisions should be made. No sane decision analyst would tell a successful basketball coach that he ought to conduct a statistical survey every time he considers substituting players—even if an ideally rational agent acting as a coach would. We can even imagine conducting research with both normative and descriptive ends in mind: For instance, we might study how expert business executives make decisions in order to find rules for prescribing how ordinary folk should make their business decisions.

Recently some philosophers have argued that all branches of the theory of rationality should pay attention to studies by social scientists of related behavior by human beings. Their point is that most prescriptions formulated in terms of ideally rational agents have little or no bearing on the question of how humans should behave. This is because logicians, mathematicians, and philosophers usually assume that ideally rational agents can acquire, store, and process unlimited amounts of information, never make logical or mathematical mistakes, and know all the logical consequences of their beliefs. Of course, no humans — not even geniuses — come close to such ideals. This may favor studying more realistic models of rational agents, but I do not think that we have grounds for dismissing the usual theories of rationality altogether. The ideals they describe, although unattainable in practice, still serve to guide and correct our thinking. For example, we know that perfect memories would help us make better decisions. Instead of settling for poor decisions, we have tried to overcome our limitations by programming computers — which have larger and better memories than we do — to assist us in those tasks whose success depends on storing and retrieving large quantities of information.

Another problem with putting much weight on the distinction between normative and descriptive decision theory is that some abstract decision models have been introduced with neither normative nor descriptive ends in mind. I am thinking of the concept of *rational economic man* used in economics. This hypothetical being is an ideally rational agent whose choices always are the most likely to maximize his personal profit. By appealing to a hypothetical society of rational economic men economists can derive laws of supply and demand and other important principles of economic theory. Yet economists admit that the notion of rational economic man is not a descriptive model. Even people with the coolest heads and greatest business sense fail to conform to this ideal. Sometimes we forget the profit motive. Or we aim at making a profit but miscalculate. Nor do economists recommend that we emulate economic man: Maximizing personal profit is not necessarily the highest good for human beings. Thus the model is intended neither normatively nor descriptively, it is an explanatory idealization. Like physicists speculating about perfect vacuums, frictionless surfaces, or ideal gases, economists ignore real-life complications in the hope of erecting a theory that will be simple enough to yield insights and understanding while still applying to the phenomena that prompted it.

For these reasons I favor dropping the normative-descriptive distinction in favor of a terminology that recognizes the gradation from experimental and survey research toward the more speculative discussions of those interested in either explanatory or normative idealizations. With the caveat that there is really a spectrum rather than a hard-and-fast division, I propose the terms "experimental" and "abstract" to cover these two types of decision-theoretic research.

This book will be concerned exclusively with abstract decision theory and will focus on its logical and philosophical foundations. This does not mean that readers will find nothing here of practical value. Some of the concepts and methods I will expound are also found in business school textbooks. My hope is that readers will come to appreciate the assumptions such texts often make and some of the perplexities they generate.

Another important division within decision theory is that between decisions made by individuals and those made by groups. For the purposes of this division an individual need not be a single human being (or other animal). Corporations, clubs, nations, states, and universities make decisions *as individuals* (and can be held responsible for them) when they attempt to realize some organizational goal, such as enhancing their reputation or bettering last year's sales figures. However, when several individuals who belong to the same club, corporation, or university adjudicate differences about group goals or priorities, they are involved in making a *group decision*. We can illustrate the difference between group and individual decisions by looking at the role of United States presidents. By electing a Republican rather than a Democratic president, voters can decide general social and economic policy. Elections are thus one way for United States citizens to make group decisions. Once elected the president also makes decisions. They are in the first instance his own choices, to be sure; but, insofar as he incorporates the national will, they may be decisions of the United States as well. Thus when President Reagan elected to invade Grenada, this also became a decision of the United States. This was in effect an individual decision by a nation.

When we turn to game theory we will deal with individual decisions that at first sight look like group decisions. Games are decision-making situations that always involve more than one individual, but they do not count as group decisions because each individual chooses an action with the aim of furthering his or her own goals. This decision will be based on expectations concerning how other participants will decide, but, unlike a group decision, no effort will be made to develop a policy applying to all the participants. For example, two neighboring department stores are involved in a game when they independently consider having a post-Christmas sale. Each knows that if one has the sale and the other does not, the latter will get little business. Yet each store is forced to decide by itself while anticipating what the other will do. On the other hand, if the two stores could find a way to choose a schedule for having sales, their choice would ordinarily count as a group decision. Unfortunately, it is frequently difficult to tell whether a given situation involves an individual or a group decision, or, when several individuals are choosing, whether they are involved in a game or in a group decision.

Most of the work in group decision theory has concerned the development of common policies for governing group members and with the just distribution of resources throughout a group. Individual decision theory, by contrast, has concentrated on the problem of how individuals may best further their personal interests, whatever these interests may be. In particular, individual decision theory has, to this point, made no proposals concerning rational or ethical ends. Individual decision theory recognizes no distinction—either moral or rational—between the goals of killing oneself, being a sadist, making a million dollars, or being a missionary. Because of this it might be possible for ideally rational agents to be better off violating the policies of the groups to which they belong. Some group decision theorists have tried to deny this possibility and have even gone so far as to offer proofs that it is rational to abide by rationally obtained group policies.

It should be no surprise, then, that some philosophers have become fascinated with decision theory. Not only does the theory promise applications to traditional philosophical problems but it too is replete with its own philosophical problems. We have already touched on two in attempting to draw the distinctions between the various branches of decision theory, and we will encounter more as we continue. However, philosophers have paid more attention to applications of decision theory in philosophy than they have to problems within decision theory. The notion of a rational agent is of primary importance to philosophy at large. Since Socrates, moral philosophers have tried to show that moral actions are rational actions, in other words, that it is in one's own best interest to be moral. Political philosophers have similarly tried to establish that rational agents will form just societies. Such arguments remained vague until modern decision theory supplied precise models of rationality and exact principles of social choice. It is now possible to formulate with nearly mathematical exactness modern versions of traditional arguments in ethics and social philosophy. The techniques of decision theory have also suggested new approaches to old ethical and moral problems.

Statisticians use decision theory to prescribe both how to choose between hypotheses and how to determine the best action in the face of the outcome of a statistical experiment. Philosophers of science have turned these techniques with good results on the problems in rational theory choice, hypothesis acceptance, and inductive methods. Again this has led to significant advances in the philosophy of science.

Decision theory is thus philosophically important as well as important to philosophy. After we have developed more of its particulars we can discuss some of its philosophical applications and problems in greater detail.

PROBLEMS

1. Classify the following as individual or group decisions. Which are games? Explain your classifications.
   a. Two people decide to marry each other.
   b. The members of a club decide that the annual dues will be $5.
   c. The members of a club decide to pay their dues.
   d. The citizens of the United States decide to amend the Constitution.
   e. Two gas stations decide to start a price war.
2. If it turned out that *everyone* believed that $1 + 1 = 3$, would that make it rational to believe that $1 + 1 = 3$?
3. Although decision theory declares no goals to be irrational in and of themselves, do you think there are goals no rational being could adopt, for example, the goal of ceasing to be rational?

1-2. The Basic Framework

A decision, whether individual or group, involves a choice between two or more options or *acts*, each of which will produce one of several *outcomes*. For example, suppose I have just entered a dark garage that smells of gasoline. After groping to no avail for a light switch, I consider lighting a match, but I hesitate because I know that doing so might cause an explosion. The acts I am considering are *light a match, do not light a match*. As I see it, if I do not light the match, there will be only one outcome, namely, *no explosion results*. On the other hand, if I do light the match, two outcomes are possible: *an explosion results, no ex-*

plosion results. My decision is not clear-cut because it is not certain that an explosion will result if I light the match. That will depend on the amount and distribution of the gasoline vapor in the garage. In other words, the outcome of my act will depend on the *state* of the environment in which the act takes place.

As this example illustrates, decisions involve three components—*acts*, *states*, and *outcomes*, with the latter being ordinarily determined by the act and the state under which it takes place. (Some outcomes are certain, no matter what the state or act. For instance, that I will either live through the day or die during it is certain whether or not I light the match and regardless of the presence of gasoline in the garage.) In decision theory we also construe the term "state" in a very broad sense to include nonphysical as well as physical conditions. If you and a friend bet on the correct statement of the fundamental theorem of calculus, the outcome (your winning or losing) is determined by a mathematical state, that is, by whether your version really formulates the fundamental theorem.

When analyzing a decision problem, the decision analyst (who may be the decision maker himself) must determine the relevant set of acts, states, and outcomes for characterizing the decision problem. In the match example, the act *do not light a match* might have been specified further as *use a flashlight*, *return in an hour*, *ventilate the garage*, all of which involve doing something other than lighting the match. Similarly, I might have described the outcomes differently by using *explosion* (*no damage*), *explosion* (*light damage*), *explosion* (*moderate damage*), *explosion* (*severe damage*). Finally, the states in the example could have been analyzed in terms of the gasoline-to-air ratio in the garage. This in turn could give rise to an infinity of states, since there are infinitely many ratios between zero and one. As I have described the example, however, the relevant acts, states, and outcomes are best taken as the simpler ones. We can represent this analysis in a *decision table*. (See table 1-1.)

1-1

		States	
		Explosive Gas Level	Nonexplosive
Acts	Light a Match	Explosion	No Explosion
	Do Not Light a Match	No Explosion	No Explosion

In general, a decision table contains a row corresponding to each act, a column for each state, and an entry in each square corresponding to the outcome for the act of that row and state of that column.

Suppose we change the match example. Now I want to cause an explosion to scare some friends who are with me. But I am a practical joker, not a murderer, so I want the explosion to be nondamaging. Then in analyzing this decision problem we would be forced to break down the explosive outcome into *damaging/nondamaging*. But the magnitude of the explosion would depend on the amount of vapor in the garage, so our new analysis would also require a different division of the environment into states. This might yield a decision table such as 1-2.

1-2

		States Amount of Gas Present	
	X	Y	Z
Light	No Explosion	Explosion No Damage	Explosion Damage
Do Not Light	No Explosion	No Explosion	No Explosion

(left label: **Acts**)

In specifying a set of acts, states, and outcomes, or in drawing a decision table, we determine a *problem specification*. A moral to be drawn from the match example is that several problem specifications may pertain to the same decision situation. In such cases the decision analyst must determine the proper specification or specifications to apply. This is a problem in applied decision theory yet it may be absolutely crucial. In 1975, government health experts conducted an elaborate analysis prior to deciding to issue the swine influenza vaccine to the general public. But according to newspaper accounts, they simply never considered the outcome that actually resulted—that the vaccine would paralyze a number of people. Thus they failed to use the proper problem specification in making their decision.

For a problem specification to be definite and complete, its states must be mutually exclusive and exhaustive; that is, one and only one of the states must obtain. In the match example, it would not do to specify the states as *no vapor*, *some vapor*, *much vapor*, since the second two do not exclude each other. Lighting a match under the middle state might or might not cause an explosion. On the other hand, if we used the states *no vapor*, *much vapor*, we would neglect to consider what happens when there is some but not much vapor.

Securing mutually exclusive state specifications may require careful analysis, but we can easily guarantee exhaustiveness by adding to a list of nonexhaustive states the description *none of the previous states obtain*. Like the cover answer "none of the above" used to complete multiple-choice questions, this easy move can lead a decision analyst to overlook relevant possibilities. Perhaps something like this was at work in the swine flu vaccine case.

1-2a. Some Philosophical Problems about Problem Specifications

Selecting a problem specification is really an issue that arises in applying decision theory. We will eschew such problems in this book and, henceforth, assume that we are dealing with problem specifications whose states are mutually exclusive and exhaustive. Yet there are several interesting philosophical issues related to the choice of problem specifications. Three merit mention here.

The first concerns the proper description of states. Any decision problem involves some outcomes the decision maker regards as better than others. Otherwise there would be no choice worth making. Thus any decision might be specified in terms of the state descriptions *things turn out well*, *they do not*. Suppose, for example, that you are offered a choice between betting on the American or National League teams in the All-Star Game. A winning bet on the American League pays $5 and one on the National League pays $3. A loss on either bet costs $2. We would usually represent this decision problem with table 1-3.

1-3	American League Wins	National League Wins
Bet American	+ $5	− $2
Bet National	− $2	+ $3

Given that you are not a totally loyal fan of either league, this way of looking at the choice would lead you to choose between the bets on the basis of how probable you thought the American League to win. (Later we will see that you should bet on the American League if you think its chances are better than 5 in 12.) But suppose you use table 1-4 instead. Then you would simply bet Amer-

1-4	I Win My Bet	I Lose It
Bet American	+ $5	− $2
Bet National	+ $3	− $2

ican on the grounds that that bet pays better. You might even argue to yourself as follows: I will either win or lose. If I win, betting American is better, and if I lose, my bet does not matter. So whatever happens, I do at least as well by betting American.

The principle illustrated in this reasoning is called *the dominance principle*. We say that an act *A dominates* another act *B* if, in a state-by-state comparison, *A* yields outcomes that are at least as good as those yielded by *B* and in some states they are even better. *The dominance principle tells us to rule out dominated acts.* If there is an act that dominates all others, the principle has us choose it.

However, we cannot always rely on the dominance principle — as an example from the disarmament debate demonstrates. Doves argue that disarmament is preferable whether or not a war occurs. For, they claim, if there is no war and we disarm, more funds will be available for social programs; if there is a war and we disarm, well, better Red than dead. This produces decision table 1-5.

1-5	War	No War
Arm	Dead	Status Quo
Disarm	Red	Improved Society

Given the view that it is better to be Red than dead, disarming dominates.

Hawks need not question anything that has transpired. They can simply respond that disarming makes it virtually certain that the other side will attack us but that continuing to arm makes war very unlikely. Doves have not taken this into account. They have not considered that in this case the act we choose affects the probabilities of the states. The example shows that the dominance principle applies only when the acts do not affect the probability of the states.

The same problem arises in the betting example. The probability of winning varies with the bet chosen. So reasoning according to the dominance principle does not apply to the choice between betting American or National.

One might think that all that is wrong with the betting example is a misapplication of the dominance principle, but I think there is a deeper problem here. It is a case of an *illegitimate problem specification*. In any decision table that uses states such as *I win*, or *things turn out well*, we can substitute the state description *I make the right choice* without having to change the outcomes or the effect of the various acts on the states. But it is surely pointless to use a decision table with the state headings *I make the right choice*, *I fail to make the right choice* to make that very choice. If you already knew the right choice, why bother setting up a decision table? Actually, this is a bit flippant. The real problem is that the designation of the term "right choice" varies with the act. If I bet American, I make the right choice if and only if the American League wins. Correspondingly for betting National. So the phrases *I make the right choice*, *I fail to make the right choice* cannot serve as state descriptions, since they do not pick out one and the same state no matter what the act. The same point obviously applies to descriptions such as *I win* or *things turn out well*.

It is not always clear, however, when a state description is proper. Suppose, for example, that you are trying to choose between going to law school and going to business school. It is tempting to use state descriptions such as *I am a success* or *opportunities are good*, but a moment's thought should convince you that these are variants of *I make the right choice* and, thus, improper. Unfortunately there is no algorithm for determining whether a state description is proper.

Nor are there algorithms for deciding whether a set of states is relevant. Suppose again that you are deciding between law school and business school. The states *the rainfall is above average for the next three years*, *it is not* are plainly irrelevant to your decision. But how about *there is an economic depression three years from now*, *there is not*? Perhaps lawyers will do well during a depression whereas business school graduates will remain unemployed; those states might then be relevant to consider.

I will leave the problem of state descriptions to proceed to another one, which also involves the choice of problem specifications. In this instance, however, the state descriptions involved may be entirely proper and relevant. To illustrate the problem I have in mind let us suppose that you want to buy a car whose asking price is $4,000. How much should you bid? Before you can answer that question, you must consider several alternative bids, say, $3,000, $3,500, and $4,000. Those three bids would generate a three-act problem specification. But is this the best specification for your problem? How about using a wider range of bids? Or bids with smaller increments? Those are clearly relevant questions and they bear on which decision table you ultimately use. Now if we think of the various answers to these questions as giving rise to different decision tables (e.g., the three-bid table first mentioned, another with the bids $2,500, $3,000, $3,500, $3,750, etc.), choosing the best problem specification amounts to choosing between decision tables. We are thus involved in a *second-order* decision, that is, a decision about decision problem specifications. We can apply decision theory to this decision too. For example, if the best act according to any of the specifications under consideration is *bid $4,000*, it would not matter which table you choose. And if all the tables use the same states, we can combine them into one big table whose rows consist of all the bids used in any of the smaller tables and whose columns are the states in question. The best bid according to that table will be the best for your decision. If the states vary too, the solution is not so clear. But that is a technical problem for decision theory. Let us continue with the philosophical problem. We have now formulated a second-order decision problem concerning the choice of tables for your original bidding problem. But questions may arise concerning our choice of a second-order problem specification. Should we have considered other first-order tables with additional bids or other sets of states? Should we have used different methods for evaluating the acts in our first-order tables? Approaching these questions through decision theory will lead us to generate a set of second-order tables and attempt to pick the best of these to use. But now we have a third-order decision problem. An infinite regress of decision problems is off and running!

The difficulty here can be put succinctly by observing that *whenever we apply decision theory we must make some choices*: At the least, we must pick the acts, states, and outcomes to be used in our problem specification. But if we use decision theory to make those choices, we must make yet another set of choices.

This does not show that it is impossible to apply decision theory. But it does show that to avoid an infinite regress of decision analyses any application of the theory must be based ultimately on choices that are made without its benefit. Let us call such decisions *immediate decisions*. Now someone might object that insofar as decision theory defines rational decision making, only those decisions made with its benefit should count as rational. Thus immediate decisions are not rational, and because all decisions depend ultimately on these, no decisions are rational.

Should we give up decision theory? I think not. The objection I have just rehearsed assumes that decision theory has cornered the market on rational decision making, that a decision made without its benefits is irrational. In fact, it is frequently irrational to use decision theory; the costs in time or money may be too high. If an angry bear is chasing you, it would not make sense to use decision theory to pick which tree to climb. On the other hand, it is not always rational to make an immediate decision either. You would not (or should not) choose your career, college, or professional school without weighing the pros and cons of a few alternatives.

But then how do we decide when to do a decision analysis and when to make an immediate decision? Well, we do not do it on a case-by-case basis. Each time I see a car coming at me in my lane, I do not ask myself, Should I do a decision analysis to decide between braking, pulling off the road, or continuing as I am or should I make an immediate decision? If I did I would have been killed years ago. (I would also have trapped myself in an infinite regress.) Instead, I follow an unstated policy of letting my "gut reactions" make the choice. And that is plainly the rational thing to do, since a sober, healthy, and experienced driver usually does the right thing in such situations. We live by many policies that tell us when we should make an immediate decision and when a decision analysis of some kind is required. Some of those policies are more rational than others; they lead in general to better lives. This means that it may be appropriate from time to time to reassess one or more of our policies. Of course, decision theory may help with that task.

A persistent skeptic might object that now we need a policy for reassessing policies, and another regress of decisions is in the offing. But I will leave the matter as it stands.

A final preliminary philosophical issue is illustrated by this fanciful example. Baker and Smith, competitors in the oil business, are both considering leasing an oil field. Baker hires a decision analyst to advise him, and Smith decides to base his decision on the flip of a coin. The decision analyst obtains extensive geological surveys, spends hours reviewing Baker's balance sheets, and finally concludes that the risks are so great that Baker should not bid on the lease at all. Letting the flip of a coin decide for him, Smith pays dearly for the lease. Yet, to everyone's surprise, a year later he finds one of the largest oil reserves in his state and makes piles of money. Something seems to have gone wrong. Smith never gave the matter any consideration and became a billionaire, whereas the thoughtful Baker remained a struggling oilman. Does this turn of events show that Baker's use of decision theory was irrational?

We can resolve some of our discomfort with this example by distinguishing between *right decisions* and *rational decisions*. Agents' decisions are *right* if they eventuate in outcomes the agents like at least as well as any of the other possibilities that might have occurred after they had acted. According to our story Smith made the right decision and Baker did not. If we had complete foreknowledge, individual decision theory would need only one principle, namely, *make the right decision*. Unfortunately, most of our decisions must be based on what we think *might* happen or on what we think is *likely* to happen, and we cannot be certain they will result in the best outcomes possible. Yet we still should try to make choices based on the information we do have and our best assessments of the risks involved, because that is clearly the rational approach to decision making. Furthermore, once we appreciate the unfavorable circumstances under which most of our decisions must be made, we can see that a rational decision can be entirely praiseworthy even though it did not turn out to be the right decision. (How often have you heard people remark that although it was true they had hoped for a better outcome, they made the only rational choice open to them at the time? Or that despite having made a stupid decision, some-one "lucked out"?)

PROBLEMS

1. Set up a decision table for the following decision situation. Jack, who is now twenty, must decide whether to marry his true love Jill immediately or not see her again until he is twenty-one. If he marries her now then he will lose the million dollars his uncle has left him in trust. If he waits to see her until he is twenty-one, he will receive the money and can marry Jill at that time—*if* she still loves him. (Part of your problem is selecting an appropriate set of acts, states, and outcomes.)
2. Pascal reasoned that it was better to lead the life of a religious Christian than to be a pagan, because if God exists, religious Christians go to Heaven and everyone else goes to Hell, whereas if God does not exist, the life of the religious Christian is at least as good as that of the pagan. Set up a decision table for this argument and explain why the dominance principle supports Pascal's reasoning.

1-3. Certainty, Ignorance, and Risk

Sometimes we can be quite certain that our acts will result in given outcomes. If you are in a cafeteria and select a glass of tomato juice as your only drink then, ingenious pranksters and uncoordinated oafs aside, that is the drink you will bring to your table. Sometimes, however, you can know only that your choice will result in a given outcome with a certain probability. If, for instance, you bet on getting a 10 in one roll of a pair of unloaded dice, you cannot be certain of winning, but you can know that your chances are 1 in 12. Finally, sometimes you may have no earthly idea about the relationship between an act open to you and a possible outcome. If you have a chance to date a potential mate, a possible outcome is that the two of you will someday together pose for a photo with your great-grandchildren. But, offhand, it would seem impossible for you to estimate the chances of that happening if you make the date.

If you are making a decision in which you can be certain that all your acts are like the first example, decision theorists call your choice a *decision under certainty*. Here all you need to do is determine which outcome you like best, since you know which act (or acts) is certain to produce it. That is not always easy. Even a student who could be certain of getting all her courses might have a hard time deciding whether to sign up for logic and physics this term or for music and physics this term, postponing logic until next term. Or suppose you are planning an auto trip from New York to Los Angeles with stops in Chicago, St. Louis, New Orleans, and Las Vegas. You can use one of many routes, but they will differ in mileage, driving conditions, traffic, chances for bad weather, and scenery. Even supposing that everything concerning these attributes is certain, which will you choose?

The mathematical theory of linear programming has been applied to many problems concerning decisions under certainty with quantitative outcomes.

However, neither decision theorists nor philosophers have paid this subject much attention, so we will not cover it further in this book.

When, in a given decision problem, it is possible to assign probabilities to all the outcomes arising from each act, the problem is called *a decision under risk*. Choices between bets on fair coins, roulette wheels, or dice are paradigms of decisions under risk. But it is usual to classify investment decisions, bets on horse races, marketing decisions, choices of crops to plant, and many others like them as decisions under risk, because even when we cannot assign an exact probability, say, to the stock market rising or to a drought, it often pays to treat those decisions as if they were decisions under risk, pure and simple.

Finally, when it makes no sense to assign probabilities to the outcomes emanating from one or more of the acts (as in your date resulting in great-grandchildren), the decision problem is called a *decision under ignorance*. (Some decision theorists call it a decision under uncertainty.) Ignorance may be partial or total; it may be possible to assign probabilities to some of the outcomes emanating from some of the acts, but to none emanating from the other acts. We will turn shortly to techniques for dealing with decisions under ignorance, but we will treat only decisions under total ignorance in this book.

This classification of decisions as under certainty, risk, and ignorance is plainly an idealization. Many decisions do not fall neatly into one category or another. Yet if the uncertainties in a decision are negligible, such as an uncertainty as to whether the world will exist tomorrow, the problem is fairly treated as one under certainty. And if we can estimate upper and lower bounds on probabilities, we can break a decision problem into several problems under risk, solve each, and compare the results. If each solution yields the same recommendation, our inability to assign exact probabilities will not matter. On the other hand, if the range of probabilities is very wide, it might be better to treat the problem as a decision under ignorance.

The classification is philosophically controversial too. Some philosophers think the only certainties are mathematical and logical. For them there are few true decisions under certainty. Other philosophers—not necessarily disjoint from the first group—think we are never totally ignorant of the probabilities of the outcomes resultant from an act. Thus for them there are no true decisions under ignorance. We will learn more about this later when we study subjective probability.

1-3a. Some Details of Formulation

Suppose you are deciding whether to eat at Greasy Pete's and are concerned that the food will make you sick. The relevant outcomes associated with your act are *you get sick* and *you do not get sick*. Now if you take the states to be *Pete's food is spoiled*, *it is not*, the act of eating at Greasy Pete's under the state that his food is spoiled is *not* certain to result in your getting sick. (Perhaps you eat very little of the spoiled food or have a very strong stomach.) Yet, our use of decision tables presupposes that we can find exactly one outcome for each act-state pair. So how can we use decision tables to represent your simple problem?

We could introduce outcomes that themselves involve elements of uncertainty. For example, we could replace the outcomes of your getting (not getting) sick with the outcomes *you have a chance of getting sick*, *you do not*. This would ensure no more than one outcome per square. Or we could introduce a more refined division of the environment into states, using, for instance, *the food is spoiled but you can handle it*, *the food is spoiled and you cannot handle it*, and *the food is not spoiled* for the last example. Different decision problems will call for different combinations of these approaches. In any case, because these are problems with applying decision theory, we will assume henceforth that each act-state pair determines a unique outcome.

In view of this assumption, we can focus all the uncertainty in a decision on the states involved. If you do not know whether eating at Greasy Pete's will make you sick, we will take that to be because you do not know whether the food is spoiled or whether you can handle it. A further consequence is that, in the case of decisions under risk, probabilities will be assigned to states rather than outcomes. Again, if you eat at Greasy Pete's, the only way you can get sick is for the food to be spoiled and you to be unable to handle it. So to treat your problem as a decision under risk we must assign probabilities to that compound state and the other states. Suppose the probability of the food being spoiled is 70% and that of your being unable to handle spoiled food is 50%. Then (as we will learn later) the probability of your getting rotten food at Greasy Pete's and being unable to handle it is 35%, whereas the probability that you will get bad food but will be able to handle it is 35% and the probability that your food will be fine is 30%.

Unless some malevolent demon hates you, your choosing to eat at Greasy Pete's should not affect his food or your ability to handle it. Thus the probabilities assigned to the states need not reflect the acts chosen. This means that we can use the unqualified probability that Greasy Pete's food will be spoiled rather than the probability that it will be spoiled *given* that you eat there. On the other hand, if you are deciding whether to smoke and are worried about dying of lung cancer, your acts will affect your chances of entering a state yielding that dreaded outcome. As you know, the lung cancer rate is much higher among smokers than among the total population of smokers and nonsmokers. Consequently, the probability of getting lung cancer *given* that you smoke is much higher than the probability that you will get lung cancer no matter what you do. The latter probability is called the *unconditional* probability, the former the *conditional* probability of getting lung cancer. Plainly, in deciding whether to smoke, the conditional probabilities are the ones to use.

We say that a state is *independent* of an act when the conditional probability of the state given the act is the same as the unconditional probability of that state. Getting heads on the flip of a fair coin is independent of betting on heads. There being rotten food at Pete's is independent of your eating there. But contracting lung cancer is not independent of smoking, earning good grades is not independent of studying, and surviving a marathon is not independent of training for it.

When some of the states fail to be independent of the acts in a decision

·under risk, we should use the probabilities of the states conditional on the acts. When all of the states are independent of the acts, it does not matter which probabilities we use; for, by the definition of independence, there is no difference between them. Since there is no harm in always using conditional probabilities, for the sake of uniformity, we will do so.

Those who prefer unconditional probabilities may find it possible to reformulate their decision problems using new states that are independent of the acts. Consider the smoking decision again. Not everyone who smokes gets lung cancer—not even those who have been very heavy smokers since their teens. It ·is plausible, then, that those who avoid cancer have some protective factor that shields them from smoking's cancer-inducing effects. If there is such a factor, smoking is unlikely to be responsible for its presence or absence. With this in mind, we can reformulate the smoking decision in terms of states involving this new factor. We replace the two states *you (do not) get lung cancer* with four states: *you have the protective factor and do (do not) get terminal lung cancer from nonsmoking causes*, *you do not have the protective factor and you do (do not) get terminal lung cancer from nonsmoking causes*. Then your smoking will not affect your chances of being in one state rather than another. In the original formulation, you saw smoking as actually determining whether you entered a state leading to your death from lung cancer; thus you saw smoking as affecting the probability of being in that state. On the new formulation, you are already in a state that can lead to your death from lung cancer or you are not. If you are in the unlucky state, your not smoking cannot alter that; but if you smoke you are certain to die, since you lack the protective factor. You do not know what state you are in, but if you knew enough about lung cancer and the factors that protect those exposed to carcinogens from getting cancer, you could assign *unconditional* probabilities to the four new states. For those states would be independent of the acts of smoking or not smoking.

For a final bit on reformulations, consider Joan's problem. She is pregnant and cannot take care of a baby. She can abort the fetus and thereby avoid having to take care of a baby, or she can have the baby and give it up for adoption. Either course prevents the outcome *Joan takes care of a baby*, but Joan (and we) sense a real difference between the means used to achieve that outcome. There is a simple method for formulating Joan's choice so that it becomes the true dilemma that she sees it to be. We simply include act descriptions in the outcome descriptions. We no longer have a single outcome but two: *Joan has an abortion and does not take care of a baby*, *Joan gives her baby up for adoption and does not take care of it*.

PROBLEMS

1. Classify the following as decisions under certainty, risk, or ignorance. Justify your classifications.
   a. Jones chooses his bet in a roulette game.
   b. Smith decides between seeking and not seeking a spouse.

c. A veterinarian decides whether to put a healthy stray dog to sleep or to adopt it as his own pet.

d. A student trying to satisfy degree requirements chooses among the courses currently available.

e. A lawyer decides whether to accept an out-of-court settlement or to take her client's case to trial.

2. Set up a decision table for the last version of the Greasy Pete problem. Why is the outcome description *you do not get sick* in more than one square? What is the *total* probability that you will get an outcome so described?

1-4. Decision Trees

It is often more expeditious to analyze a decision problem as a sequence of decisions taking place over time than to treat it as a single one-time decision. To do this we use a *decision tree* instead of a table. A decision tree is a diagram consisting of branching lines connected to boxes and circles. The boxes are called *decision nodes* and represent decisions to be made at given points in the decision sequences. The circles are called *chance nodes* and represent the states relevant to that point of the decision. Each line projecting to the right of a node represents one of the acts or states associated with it and is usually labeled with an appropriate act or state description. To demonstrate these ideas, let us use the decision tree (shown in figure 1-1) to represent the disarmament problem discussed earlier. As the tree illustrates, outcomes are written at the tips of the

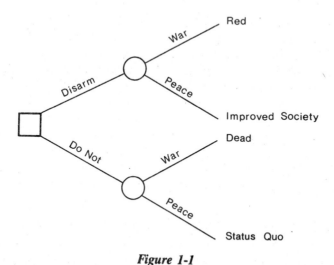

Figure 1-1

tree. This permits us to assess the possible consequences of a choice by following each of the branches it generates to its tip. Disarming, for instance, leads to an improved society if there is no war, but it leads to life as a Red if there is one.

INTRODUCTION

The practical advantage of trees over tables can be appreciated by considering the following example. Suppose you must first choose between going to the seashore or staying at home. If you go to the seashore, you will wait to determine whether it is raining. If it rains, you will decide whether to fish or stay inside. If you fish and the fishing is good, you will be happy; if the fishing is not good, you will be disappointed. If you stay in, you will feel so-so. On the other hand, if there is no rain, you will sunbathe and be happy. Finally if you stay home, you will feel so-so. Figure 1-2 presents the tree for this decision.

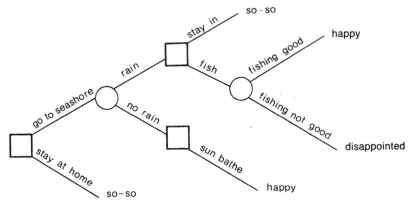

Figure 1-2

It is easy to go from a decision table to a decision tree. Start the tree with a box with one line emanating from it for each row of the table. At the end of each line place a circle with one line coming from it for each column of the table. Then at the tips of each of these lines write the outcome entries for the square to which that tip corresponds.

It is by far more interesting and important that the decision tree for any problem can be transformed into an equivalent decision table. We accomplish this by collapsing sequences of decisions into one-time choices of *strategies*. A strategy (S) is a plan that determines an agent's choices under all relevant circumstances. For example, the plan

S_1: I will go to the shore; if it rains, I will fish; if it does not rain, I will sunbathe

is a strategy appropriate for the problem analyzed by the preceding tree. The other appropriate strategies are:

S_2: I will go to the shore; if it rains, I will stay in; if it does not, I will sunbathe;

S_3: I will stay at home (under all circumstances).

We can similarly find a set of strategies that will enable us to represent any other sequential decision as a choice between strategies. This representation generally necessitates using more complicated states, as table 1-6 illustrates for the seashore problem. In case you are wondering how we obtain the entries in the second row of this table, notice that in this row S_2 is adopted. So if it rains you

1-6	Rain & Good Fishing	Rain & Bad Fishing	No Rain
S_1	Happy	Disappointed	Happy
S_2	So-so	So-so	Happy
S_3	So-so	So-so	So-so

will stay in, and whether or not the fishing is good (for anyone), you will feel so-so. If it does not rain, you will sunbathe and be happy.

Decision theorists have presented mathematically rigorous formulations of the technique illustrated here and have proved that any decision tree can be reduced to a decision table in which the choices are between strategies. Since our interest in this book is more theoretical than practical, we will stick with decision tables and not pursue the study of decision trees further.

PROBLEMS
1. Formulate the following decision problem using a decision tree. Danny, who has been injured by Manny in an automobile accident, has applied to Manny's insurance company for compensation. The company has responded with an offer of $10,000, Danny is considering hiring a lawyer to demand $50,000. If Danny hires a lawyer to demand $50,000, Manny's insurance company will respond by either offering $10,000 again or offering $25,000. If they offer $25,000, Danny plans to take it. If they offer $10,000, Danny will decide whether or not to sue. If he decides not to sue, he will get $10,000. If he decides to sue, he will win or lose. If he wins, he can expect $50,000. If he loses, he will get nothing. (To simplify this problem, ignore Danny's legal fees, and the emotional, temporal, and other costs of not settling for $10,000.)
2. Mimicking the method used at the end of this section, reformulate Danny's decision problem using a decision table.

1-5. References
In giving references at the end of each chapter, I will refer to works by means of the names of their authors. Thus *Luce and Raiffa* refers to the book *Games and Decisions* by R. D. Luce and H. Raiffa. When I cite two works by the same author, I will either use a brief title or give the author's name and the publication date of the work in question.

The classic general treatise on decision theory is *Luce and Raiffa*. It not only surveys several of the topics not covered in this book but also contains an extensive bibliography. The reader wishing to do more advanced study in decision theory should begin with this work. *Von Neumann and Morgenstern* was the first major book on the subject and set the agenda for much of the field. A number of journals publish articles on decision theory, but *Theory and Decision* is the principal interdisciplinary journal devoted to the subject.

Raiffa is an excellent introduction to individual decision theory for those interested in applications of the theory to business problems. This book also makes extensive use of decision trees. *Eells*, *Jeffrey*, and *Levi* are more advanced works in the subject for those with a philosophical bent. *Savage* and *Chernoff and Moses* approach the subject from the point of view of statistics.

Davis is a popular introduction to game theory, and *Sen* is a classic treatise on social choice theory. Both books contain extensive bibliographies.

For more on problem specifications, see Jeffrey's "Savage's Omelet," and *Nozick*.

Chapter 2

DECISIONS UNDER IGNORANCE

KATHRYN LAMBI is a brilliant graduate student in physics. She is also happily married to Paul Lambi and they want children. Kathryn has a difficult decision to make because her ideas about mothering are rather traditional; she believes that she ought to care for her children herself during their preschool years. But she cannot do that and perform long and delicate experiments. Each day resolving her dilemma becomes more urgent. Should she have her children now and postpone her career? Or should she capitalize now on her brilliant start in order to establish herself as a physicist and raise her family later? As Kathryn sees her decision, the relevant states concern her ability seven years from now to establish a career or to be a good mother. (She believes that the latter depends on her fertility and psychic energy and that both decrease with age.) We can thus represent her problem as choosing between two acts: *have children now and postpone career* and *pursue career now and postpone children*. This choice is made against the background of four states:

> *In seven years K. L. will be able to be a good mother and have a good career.*
>
> *In seven years K. L. will not be able to be a good mother but will be able to have a good career.*
>
> *In seven years K. L. will be able to be a good mother but will not be able to have a good career.*
>
> *In seven years K. L. will be able neither to be a good mother nor to have a good career.*

Kathryn has read several articles and books about delayed motherhood and feels that she can confidently assign a probability (or range of probabilities) to her being able to be a good mother seven years hence. But she simply has no idea of how to assign a probability to her being able successfully to start over as a physicist.

Kathryn's is a decision under ignorance. Decision theorists have debated long and hard about how to handle such decisions, and today many issues concerning them remain unresolved. In this chapter I will present four of the alternatives decision theorists have proposed, discuss their advantages and limitations, and briefly explore the matter of determining which approach to decisions under ignorance is correct.

Kathryn's decision is one of partial ignorance, since she can assign some probabilities to the states relative to her acts. For instance, she can appeal to the literature she has read to assign a probability to her being able to be both a good mother and a good physicist if she pursues her career now. Despite this I will restrict my treatment to decisions under complete ignorance.

2-1. Preference Orderings

There is another complication to Kathryn's decision. She would rather be a good mother and a good physicist, but when she contemplates the prospect of not being able to be both, she finds herself wavering between preferring to be a good mother and preferring to be a good physicist. Of course, she cannot even begin to resolve her original dilemma until she gets her preferences straight. Decision theory has very little to say about how Kathryn should do this. Rather it concentrates on describing what her preferences must be like if she is to apply decision theory to her problem. That will be our focus here.

For convenience, I will use the expression "xPy" to mean "the agent prefers x to y" and "xIy" to mean "the agent is indifferent between x and y." I will also use these abbreviations in discussing Kathryn's preferences:

"$m \& p$" for "K. L. is a good mother and a good physicist."
"$m \& -p$" for "K. L. is a good mother but not a good physicist."
"$-m \& p$" for "K. L. is not a good mother but is a good physicist."
"$-m \& -p$" for "K. L. is neither a good mother nor a good physicist."

(We may presume that these are the outcomes Kathryn considers.) We know that $(m \& p)P(m \& -p)$, $(m \& p)P(-m \& p)$, that is, Kathryn prefers being both a good mother and a good physicist to being only one of the two. Do we not also know that $(m \& -p)I(-m \& p)$; namely, she is indifferent between being, on the one hand, a good mother while not a good physicist and, on the other hand, being a good physicist while not a good mother? No, that does not follow from her wavering. In decision theory, an agent is considered to be indifferent between two alternatives only if she has considered them and is completely willing to trade one for the other. Kathryn has arrived at no such conclusion. Decision theorists think that she should, and this is reflected in the requirement that given any two acts, the agent prefers one to the other or is indifferent between them (in the sense just stated).

To be more explicit, decision theorists have proposed a minimal set of conditions that the preferences of an ideally rational agent must satisfy. (Such conditions have been called variously conditions of coherence, consistency, and rationality, but we will see that it is debatable whether rational, consistent, or coherent agents must conform their preferences to *each* of these conditions.) I will refer to these conditions collectively as the *ordering condition*.

Let us start with three uncontroversial components of the ordering condition. They require the agent not to prefer a thing x to one y while also being indifferent between them or preferring y to x. These hold for all outcomes x and y that the agent has under consideration:

O1. If xPy, then not yPx.

O2. If xPy, then not xIy.

O3. If xIy, then not xPy and also not yPx.

In more mathematical terms, these conditions state that various *asymmetries* hold among the agent's preferences.

Of course, agents change their minds and may be quite rational in doing so. Condition O1, for instance, is not meant to preclude my now preferring writing a book to traveling around the world and having the opposite preferences in ten years. The ordering condition deals only with an agent's preferences at a moment.

The next condition requires that any two outcomes be *connected* to each other via the agent's preferences.

O4. xPy or yPx or xIy, for any relevant outcomes x and y.

This is the condition that requires Kathryn to make up her mind. (Note: I am following the practice, customary in mathematics and logic, of interpreting "or" as meaning "at least one and possibly both." That is why I need both the asymmetry and connectivity conditions. If I had interpreted "or" as "at least one but not both" then I could have used just a reinterpreted condition O4 instead of my conditions O1–O4. Exercise: Prove my last claim.)

The next components of the ordering condition are called the *transitivity* conditions.

O5. If xPy and yPz, then xPz.

O6. If xPy and xIz, then zPy.

O7. If xPy and yIz, then xPz.

O8. If xIy and yIz, then xIz.

These are to hold for all relevant outcomes x, y, and z. Condition O5, for example, requires you to prefer apples to ice cream if you prefer apples to peaches and peaches to ice cream; condition O7 requires you to prefer cars to boats if you prefer cars to horses and are indifferent between horses and boats.

Experiments can easily demonstrate that humans are not always able to have transitive preferences. By adding small amounts of sugar to successive cups of coffee, one can set up a sequence of cups of coffee with this property: People will be indifferent between adjacent cups, but not between the first and last. This shows that sometimes we violate condition O8. But a carefully designed version of this experiment can show more, namely, that we cannot help ourselves. All we need do is make sure that the increments in sugar levels between adjacent cups are below the level of human detectability. Does this mean that our biology forces us to be irrational? Or that condition O8's claim to be a condition of rationality is a fraud?

Speaking for myself (for there is no consensus among the experts on this issue), neither alternative is quite correct. Surely we should try for transitive preference orderings when and where we can. For transitive preference orderings organize our preferences into a simple and tractable structure. Yet the coffee cups do not signal an irrational blind spot. The transitivity conditions characterize the preferences of an ideally rational agent. We fall short of that ideal by lacking tastes sufficiently refined to avoid being "tricked" into a transitivity failure. But rather than dismiss a powerful decision theory based on transitivity, we should take steps, when a decision is important, to emulate ideal agents more closely. For instance, if some very important matter turned on a transitive ranking of the cups of coffee, we could use chemical tests to determine their relative "sweetness."

We also fail from time to time to have connected preferences—especially when many things must be evaluated at once and our attention spans become overtaxed. Again I regard the connectivity condition as an ideal whose importance increases in proportion to the importance of the decision at hand.

Those depressed by our failures at ideal rationality might take comfort in the fact that we can often make a rational choice without satisfying all the ordering conditions. For instance, if you know that you can have your first choice for dessert, you need not completely rank ice cream, cake, fruit, and pie against each other. It is enough that you decide that cake, say, is better than all the rest. You can leave the rest unconnected or with failed transitivities, since, as far as getting dessert goes, the effort of ranking them is wasted.

If an agent's preferences meet conditions O1–O8, items ordered by his preferences divide into classes called *indifference classes*. They are so called because the agent is indifferent between items in the same classes but prefers items one way or the other in one class to those in a different class. (Economists, who usually restrict themselves to graphable preferences, speak of indifference curves rather than indifference classes. Our concept is a generalization of theirs.) We will rank an agent's indifference classes according to the preference relations that hold between their members: One indifference class ranks above another just in case its members are preferred to those of the other. To illustrate this, let us suppose that an agent's preferences among ten items—a, b, c, d, e, f, g, h, i, and j—are as follows:

aIb, aPc, cPd, dIe, eIf, fIg, dPh, hIi, iPj.

The ordering condition permits us to derive additional information from the preferences given. For example, condition O8 yields dIf and dIg and condition O6 yields bPc. This additional information tells us that the ten items divide into ranked indifference classes as follows:

a, b	[5]
c	[4]
d, e, f, g	[3]
h, i	[2]
j	[1]

Once we have divided a set of alternatives into ranked indifference classes, we can assign a number to each class that will reflect the relative importance or *utility* of items in the class to the agent. (Note: This may not be possible when the number of indifference classes is infinite. See exercise 6 in the next Problems section.) The convention used in decision theory is to assign higher numbers to higher-ranked items. Other than that we are free to choose whatever numbers we wish. We have used the numbers 1–5 but we could have used 5–10, or even $-1, 0, 1/2, 1, 3$. Any increasing sequence of five numbers will do. All that is required is that the number assigned to an item x—called *the utility of* x and written "$u(x)$"—be such that

      a. $u(x) > u(y)$ if and only if xPy
      b. $u(x) = u(y)$ if and only if xIy

for all ranked items x and y.

    Decision theorists call the various ways of numbering the items in a preference ordering *utility functions* or *utility scales*. (More precisely, the functions are the various *ways* of associating numbers with preference orderings and the scales are the *sequences* of numbers used. But no harm will result from our using the terms "utility function" and "utility scale" interchangeably.) Utility functions (scales) that satisfy conditions (a) and (b) are called *ordinal* utility functions (scales) because they represent only the ordering of an agent's preferences. Any change or *transformation* of an ordinal scale that preserves this representation gives rise to an equally acceptable ordinal scale for the agent's preferences. Suppose $t[u(x)]$ is the transformation of the utility of x on the u-scale into a utility number on the $t(u)$-scale. Then the new scale will be an acceptable ordinal utility scale for the agent just in case

      c. $w \geq v$ if and only if $t(w) \geq t(v)$, for all w and v on the u-scale.

For then the $t(u)$-scale will satisfy conditions (a) and (b) too. We will call transformations that satisfy condition (c) *ordinal transformations*.

    Ordinal scales represent only the relative ordering of the items falling within the scope of an agent's preferences; they do not furnish information about how many items fall between two items or about the intensity of an agent's preferences. Yet they do allow us to formulate some decision methods more conveniently. One example is the dominance principle. We can now define dominance in terms of utilities: An act A *dominates* an act B if each utility number in row A is greater than or equal to its correspondent in row B and at least one of these numbers is strictly greater.

    Example. In table 2-1, with three acts and four states, act A_2 dominates the others.

2-1	S_1	S_2	S_3	S_4
A_1	1	0	3	0
A_2	2	1	3	1
A_3	2	−1	3	0

DECISIONS UNDER IGNORANCE

PROBLEMS

1. Convert the 1 to 5 scale used to rank a–j into a 20 to 25 scale, into a -5 to 0 scale, and into a scale whose numbers are all between 0 and 1.
2. What happens to an ordinal scale when it is transformed by multiplying each number by -1? By 0? Are these acceptable transformations of the original scale? Why or why not?
3. Show that the transformation t of an ordinal utility scale u into a scale, $t(u)$, produces a scale that also satisfies conditions (a) and (b), provided t satisfies condition (c).
4. Show that the following are ordinal transformations:

    a. $t(x) = x - 2$.
    b. $t(x) = 3x + 5$.

5. Is the transformation $t(x) = x^2$ an ordinal transformation when applied to a scale whose numbers are greater than or equal to 0? What if some of the numbers are negative?
6. Suppose an agent has preferences for paired items $(x; y)$ where item x is the amount of time she has to live and y is the amount of time she will go through her death throes. Let us suppose that x varies continuously between 0 moments and 20 years and y between 0 moments and 2 weeks. The agent always prefers to live longer and suffer less but puts an absolute priority on living longer. This means, for instance, that she prefers the pair (18 years; 2 weeks) to (17 years; 11 months and 28 days; 25 minutes). Explain why it is impossible to use an ordinary finite number scale to represent the agent's preferences, although she does satisfy the ordering condition. Explain why it is possible to represent this preference using the real numbers if we concern ourselves with only preferences for moments of life or for moments of death throes.

2-2. The Maximin Rule

Using ordinal utility functions we can formulate a very simple rule for making decisions under ignorance. The rule is known as the *maximin rule*, because it tells the agent to compare the minimum utilities provided by each act and choose an act whose minimum is the maximum value for all the minimums. In brief, the rule says *maximize the minimum*.

Example. In table 2-2 the minimums for each act are starred and the act whose minimum is maximal is double starred.

2-2	S_1	S_2	S_3	S_4
A_1	5	0*	0*	2
A_2	-1*	4	3	7
A_3	6	4	4	1*
**A_4	5	6	4	3*

When there are two or more acts whose minimums are maximal, the maximin rule counts them as equally good. We can break some ties by going to the *lexical maximin* rule. This tells us to first eliminate all the rows except the tied ones and then cross out the minimum numbers and compare the next lowest entries. If the maximum of these still leaves two or more acts tied, we repeat the process until the tie is broken or the table is exhausted.

Example. Applying the lexical maximin rule still leaves A_1 and A_4 tied in table 2-3.

2-3	S_1	S_2	S_3	S_4	S_5
A_1	0	3	5	4	1
A_2	0	3	2	1	1
A_3	0	1	2	3	3
A_4	3	0	4	1	5

Conservatism underlies the maximin approach to decisions under ignorance. Assuming that whatever one does the worst will happen, the maximin rules pick the best of the worst. Perhaps this is the best stance to take when one's potential losses are enormous. Being no James Bond, I suspect I would follow the maximin rule were I to contemplate jumping from a plane without a parachute.

Despite examples like these, the maximin rules are easily criticized on the grounds that they prohibit us from taking advantage of opportunities involving slight losses and great gains. For example, in table 2-4 the maximin act is A_1;

2-4	S_1	S_2
A_1	\$1.50	\$1.75
A_2	\$1.00	\$10,000

but choosing A_2 would mean giving up at most \$.50 for a chance at \$10,000. (I am assuming here that the agent's attitude toward money is fairly typical.)

PROBLEMS

1. Find the maximin acts for tables 2-5 and 2-6. Use the lexical maximin rule to break ties.

2-5

A_1	1	− 3	5	6
A_2	2	2	3	3
A_3	4	6	− 10	5

2-6

A_1	0	1	1	3
A_2	0	4	2	1
A_3	3	0	0	1

2. Some students of medical decision making have alleged that doctors always use the maximin rule. Do you think that when most plastic surgeons decide to do a facelift (rather than not do it), they follow the maximin rule? Explain your reasoning.

3. My criticism of the maximin rule based on table 2-4 tacitly presupposes that we know more than the fact that the agent prefers more money to less. What more must we know for my criticism to work?

4. Present decision tables that show that neither the maximin nor the lexical maximin rule always excludes a dominated act.

2-3. The Minimax Regret Rule

Examples such as the last, where the agent rejected a chance at $10,000 to avoid a potential loss of $.50, suggest that in some situations it may be relevant to focus on missed opportunities rather than on the worst possibilities. In table 2-4, the agent misses an opportunity to gain an additional $9998.25 if he chooses A_1 and S_2 turns out to be the true state, whereas he only misses an opportunity to gain an additional $.50 if he does A_2 when the true state is S_1. Let us call the amount of missed opportunity for an act under a state the *regret* for that act-state pair. Then the maximum regret for A_1 is $9998.25 and that for A_2 is only $.50. (The regret for the pairs (A_1, S_1) and (A_2, S_2) is zero, since these are the best acts to have chosen under the respective states.)

   To extract a general rule from our example, we must first explain how to derive *regret numbers* and a *regret table* from a decision table. We first obtain a regret number R corresponding to the utility number U in each square in the decision table by subtracting U from the maximum number in its column. Notice that although we can use the formula

$$R = \text{MAX} - U,$$

where MAX is the largest entry in R's column, the number MAX may vary from column to column, and thus R may vary even while U is fixed. MAX represents the best outcome under its state. Thus the value $\text{MAX} - U$ represents the amount of regret for the act-state pair corresponding to R's square. To obtain the regret table corresponding to a decision table, we simply replace each entry U with its corresponding regret number R (tables 2-7 and 2-8).

2-7   Decision Table

	S_1	S_2	S_3
A_1	5	−2	10
A_2	−1	−1	20
A_3	−3	−1	5
A_4	0	−4	1

2-8   Regret Table

	S_1	S_2	S_3
A_1	0	1	10∗
∗∗A_2	6∗	0	0
A_3	8	0	15∗
A_4	5	3	19∗

Example. Maximum regrets are starred; the act with the minimum maximum regret is double starred.

The minimax regret rule states that we should pick an act whose *maximum regret is minimal*. The maximum regrets in table 2-8 are 10, 6, 15, and 19 for A_1, A_2, A_3, and A_4, respectively. So the rule picks A_2. To handle ties one can introduce a lexical version of the minimax regret rule, but we will not bother with that here.

Given two decision tables the two maximin rules pick the same acts as long as the utility scales used in the two tables are ordinal transformations of each other. Not so for the minimax regret rule. Consider decision and regret tables 2-9 and 2-10. The maximin act is A_1 and the minimax regret rule ties A_1 and

2-9	Decision Table		2-10	Regret Table	
A_1	3	5	A_1	0	2
A_2	1	7	A_2	2	0

A_2. Next consider the two new tables (2-11 and 2-12) that we can obtain from the original two by first performing an ordinal transformation on the decision table and then forming a regret table from the new decision table. (The ordinal transformation converts 1 to 3, 3 to 7, 5 to 11, and 7 to 16.)

2-11	Decision Table		2-12	Regret Table	
A_1	7	11	A_1	0	5
A_2	3	16	A_2	4	0

The maximin act remains the same—it is still A_1; but the only minimax act is now A_2. Thus *the minimax regret rule need not pick the same act when an ordinal utility transformation is applied to a decision table.* This means that the minimax regret rule operates on more information than is encoded in a simple ordinal utility scale. Otherwise, applying an ordinal transformation should never affect the choice yielded by the rule, since ordinal transformations preserve all the information contained on an ordinal scale.

Go back to the new decision table (2-11) and replace 16 with 15. Now calculate the new regrets. You will see that the maximum regrets for A_1 and A_2 are both 4 and that the minimax regret rule again ties the two acts. Both times we transformed the decision tables using an ordinal transformation, but the second time we operated in accordance with a special type of ordinal transformation. For notice that the conversion of 1 to 3, 3 to 7, 5 to 11, and 7 to 15 takes place according to the formula

$$u' = 2u + 1.$$

This is a special case of the formula

$$u' = au + b,$$

which is known as a linear transformation because the graph of u' against u is a line. When $a > 0$, as happens above, the transformation is called a *positive linear transformation*. As we will see, positive linear transformations are of great importance in decision theory.

To see that positive linear transformations are special types of ordinal transformations, suppose that (with $a > 0$)

$$u'(x) = au(x) + b$$
$$u'(y) = au(y) + b.$$

Then $u(x) \geq u(y)$ if and only if $au(x) \geq au(y)$, since $a > 0$. But for any b, $au(x) \geq au(y)$ if and only if $au(x) + b \geq au(y) + b$. Putting this together yields $u(x) \geq u(y)$ if and only if $u'(x) \geq u'(y)$, which is the condition for u' to be an ordinal transformation of u.

Not every ordinal transformation is a positive linear transformation. Not every ordinal transformation preserves the ordering of the acts given by the minimax regret rule, but *positive linear transformations do*. The last example illustrated this, but let us see why it holds in general. When we form a regret table we calculate the numbers $R = \text{MAX} - U$, where MAX is the largest number in the column containing U. Now suppose we perform a positive linear transformation on a decision table to obtain $aU + b$ in place of the old U. The old MAX was one of the old U's; the new MAX will now have the form $a\text{MAX} + b$. Since positive linear transformations are order preserving, the new MAX will still be the largest number in its column. Thus when we form the new regret table we will calculate $R' = (a\text{MAX} + b) - (aU + b)$. But a little algebra shows that $R' = aR$. Recall that $a > 0$. This implies that our transformation of the decision table has brought about an order-preserving transformation on the old regret table. That in turn means that the new maximum regrets are located in the same squares as were the old ones and that the minimums of these are located in the same rows. Thus the same acts are picked by the minimax regret rule as were picked prior to the transformation.

We have seen that positive linear transformations of a utility scale preserve more information than is preserved by ordinal transformations in general. But what is that additional information? Algebra shows that (where $a > 0$)

$$x - y \geq z - w \text{ if and only if } (ax + b) - (ay + b) \geq (az + b) - (aw + b).$$

This means that the distance or *interval* between two utility numbers is preserved under a positive linear transformation. For this reason utility scales that admit only positive linear transformations are called *interval scales*. Accordingly, we can summarize our examination of the various decision and regret tables as follows: Although the maximin rules presuppose merely that the agent's preferences can be represented by an ordinal utility scale, *the minimax regret rule presupposes that they can be represented by one that is also an interval scale*.

However, satisfying the ordering condition (O1–O8) does not suffice to generate an interval utility scale. Thus to use the minimax regret rule agents must have more refined preference structures than are needed to use the maximin rules. This is considered a definite disadvantage of the minimax regret rule. (In chapter 4 we will prove that if agents satisfy certain conditions over and above the ordering condition, their preferences are representable on an interval scale.)

There is another feature of the minimax regret rule that disadvantages it in comparison with the maximin rules. It is illustrated in tables 2-13 through

2-13   Decision Table

A_1	0	10	4
A_2	5	2	10

2-14   Regret Table

A_1	5	0	6
A_2	0	8	0

2-15

A_1	0	10	4
A_2	5	2	10
A_3	10	5	1

2-16

A_1	10	0	6
A_2	5	8	0
A_3	0	5	9

2-16. Tables 2-15 and 2-16 have been obtained by adding a new act, A_3. In the first set A_1 is the minimax regret act, in the second A_2 is. Thus, although A_3 is not a "better" act than A_1 or A_2 according to the rule, its very presence changes the choice between A_1 and A_2. Of course, the reason is that A_3 provides a new maximum utility in the first column, which in turn changes the regrets for A_1 and A_2. Yet it seems objectionable that the addition of an act (i.e., A_3), which will not be chosen anyway, is capable of changing the decision.

A final objection to the minimax regret rule is that, as with the maximin rule, there are situations in which it seems inappropriate. Consider, for example, tables 2-17 and 2-18. The minimax regret act is A_2. Despite this it appears that

2-17   Decision Table

	S_1	S_2	S_3	. . .	S_{100}
A_1	0	99.9	99.9	. . .	99.9
A_2	100	0	0	. . .	0

2-18   Regret Table

	S_1	S_2	S_3	. . .	S_{100}
A_1	100	0	0	. . .	0
A_2	0	99.9	99.9	. . .	99.9

we actually have a greater chance of suffering regret if we pick A_2, since there are ninety-nine states under A_1 in which we will have no regrets and only one under A_2.

There is a standard reply to this sort of objection, however. It consists in pointing out that the 99 to 1 ratio of the A_1 zero regret to the one A_2 zero regret is no reason to conclude that states with zero regrets are more *probable*. After all, the decision is supposedly made under ignorance; so, for all we know, state S_1 is a billion times more probable than all the other states together.

Despite this reply, many people would feel uncomfortable with applying the minimax regret rule to decisions such as that illustrated in table 2-18. A full account of this would lead us to an examination of the subjective theory of probability. That must be postponed until the next chapter.

PROBLEMS

1. Form the regret tables and find the minimax regret acts for decision tables 2-19 and 2-20.

2-19

A_1	7	0	4
A_2	5	21	11
A_3	10	-5	-1

2-20

A_1	5	20	6
A_2	-3	8	10
A_3	4	5	9

2. Prove that the minimax regret rule does not exclude all dominated acts.
3. What happens to a decision table when we apply a nonpositive linear transformation (i.e., one in which $a \leq 0$)?
4. Show that if we can convert one decision table into another by means of a positive linear transformation, we can convert the regret table for the former into that of the latter by means of a transformation of the form $u' = au$ with $a \geq 0$.
5. Show that if the scale u is convertible to the scale u' by means of a positive linear transformation and u' is similarly convertible to the scale u'', then u can be similarly converted into u''.
6. Show that any decision table can be converted by means of a positive linear transformation into one whose maximum entry is 1 and whose minimum entry is zero.

2-4. The Optimism-Pessimism Rule

The maximin rule reflects the thinking of a conservative pessimist. An unbridled optimist, by contrast, would tell us to maximize maximums. He would assume that no matter which act we choose the best outcome compatible with it will eventuate, and accordingly, he would urge us to aim for the best of the best. This thinking would give rise to what one could call the *maximax* rule. But that rule surely would have few adherents. Still, perhaps the heavy conservatism of the maximin rule could be lightened by combining it with the maximax rule. The former operates only on the minimum of each act, the latter only on the maximum. Because these are represented by numbers, it is possible to "compromise" between them by using numbers that themselves fall between the two extremes. For example, if the maximum for an act is 10 and the minimum is zero, then

5 can represent a halfway compromise, 8 can represent one favoring the maximum, and 3 one favoring the minimum. To be consistent, we should at least use the same weighting factor throughout a decision problem. Thus letting MAX be the maximum for an act and min its minimum, we want a weighting of MAX and min that yields a number somewhere in between. The formula

$$aMAX + (1 - a)\text{min},$$

where $0 \leq a \leq 1$, produces such a number, and it yields MAX and min themselves as special cases (by taking a as 1 and 0, respectively). We will call the number a an *optimism index*. The optimism-pessimism rule then tells us to calculate the number $aMAX + (1 - a)\text{min}$ for each act (this is the act's a-index) and then pick an act whose a-index is maximal.

Example. In table 2-21, if we let $a = 1/2$, the a-index for A_1 will be 5 and that for A_2 will be 4, and A_1 will be chosen. Letting $a = .2$ yields a-indexes of 2 for A_1 and 2.8 for A_2, and causes A_2 to be chosen. Notice that the interme-

2-21

A_1	10	4	0
A_2	2	6	6

diate utilities have no effect on which act is chosen.

Where do the optimism indexes come from? Each agent must choose an optimism index for each decision situation (or collection of decision situations). The closer the optimism index is to 1, the more "optimistic" the agent is. When the index equals 1, the agent's use of the optimism-pessimism rule is equivalent to using the maximax rule. Similarly, an agent with an index of 0 will in effect use the maximin rule.

Agents can determine just how "optimistic" they are by performing the following thought experiment. They think of a decision problem under ignorance whose utility table has the form of table 2-22, where they are indifferent between

2-22

A_1	0	1
A_2	$c*$	$c*$

the acts A_1 and A_2 and where $0 \leq c* \leq 1$. Since the agents are indifferent between A_1 and A_2, and since we may assume (in this section) that they use the optimism-pessimism rule, we may conclude that the acts have identical a-indexes. Hence

$$1a + 0(1 - a) = c*a + c*(1 - a),$$

which implies that $a = c*$.

This method is, perhaps, better than just guessing at one's optimism index without the benefit of further reflection, and using a simple decision problem to find one's optimism index is a useful preparation for approaching more complex problems. Nevertheless, this method accents a rather deep conceptual difficulty with optimism indexes and the rule based on them. Since it is left to the agent to determine an optimism index, it is to be expected that different agents will have different indexes. Furthermore, we could hardly require that an agent pick an optimism index once and for all time, since even rational people change their attitudes toward uncertainties as their living circumstances or experiences change. Consequently, the optimism-pessimism rule imposes no consistency on the decisions under ignorance made by a group of individuals or even by a single individual over time. How can we find a paradigm of rationality in an agent who rejects yesterday's well-wrought decision for no reason other than feeling more pessimistic today? Indeed, by going over their prior reasons, we can persuade friends who get "cold feet" to go ahead with their decisions. That avenue will be closed to us if we permit agents to change their minds by merely changing their optimism indexes.

Worse, we could often get away with making snap decisions and "rationalizing" them by declaring an appropriate optimism index. Given any two-act problem in which the maximum for A_1 is greater than that for A_2 while the minimum for A_1 is less than that for A_2, we can "rationalize" the choice of either act by appropriately moving our optimism index closer to 1 (to justify A_1) or to 0 (to justify A_2).

Finally, let us also note that the optimism-pessimism rule presupposes an interval utility scale. To see this consider decision table 2-23. Letting the opti-

2-23

A_1	0	4
A_2	2	1

mism index be 1/2, the rule picks A_1. But now let us hold the optimism index constant and apply an ordinal transformation to obtain table 2-24. Now the rule

2-24

A_1	0	10
A_2	8	7

picks A_2. Hence the rule presupposes more than an ordinal utility scale. On the other hand, it can be proven that positive linear transformations do not change the acts picked by the rule; so it presupposes no more than an interval utility scale.

PROBLEMS

1. Find the a-indexes for all the acts presented in tables 2-23 and 2-24.
2. Show that in the last example the transformation of table 2-23 into table 2-24 is ordinal but not positive linear.
3. Give an example of a decision table for which the optimism-pessimism rule fails to exclude a dominated act no matter what the agent's optimism index is.
4. Prove that if the a-index for an act A is greater than or equal to that for an act B ($0 \leq a \leq 1$), it remains so when the utilities for the acts A and B are subjected to the same positive linear transformation. (Hint: MAX_A is transformed to $c\text{MAX}_A + b$.)
5. Do you think that the canons of rational decision making should require more consistency among various agents than the optimism-pessimism rule requires?

2-5. The Principle of Insufficient Reason

The rules we have considered so far focus on maximums and minimums while ignoring the intermediate values and the number of states in a decision problem. The two acts of table 2-25, for example, appear to be quite different, yet all the rules introduced so far in this chapter treat them as indifferent. The next rule

2-25

A_1	10	9	9	9	9	9	9	9	0
A_2	10	9	0	0	0	0	0	0	9

takes account of both these neglected features of decision tables.

In a decision problem under ignorance there is no reason for viewing one state as more probable than another. Thus, it has been argued, if we are truly ignorant, we should treat all states as equally probable and independent of our choices. For example, suppose we are presented with a coin about which we know nothing and are asked to choose between the two bets given in table 2-26.

2-26

	H	T
B_1	-1	5
B_2	8	-2

Then, or so it is suggested, we should assume that no matter which bet we choose the chance of heads equals that of tails, the explanation offered being that there is *insufficient reason* for any other assignment of probabilities. (Notice that this is different from the claim that the probabilities should be taken as equal because we have *good reasons for believing* that the coin is fair—a condition that never holds when the decision is made under ignorance.)

Let us grant the probability assignment proposed. Then what should we expect if the coin is flipped time after time and we choose B_1 each time? Half the time we would lose 1, half the time we would gain 5. Thus our average gain would come close to $1/2(-1) + 1/2(5)$ or 2. Similarly our average gain from taking B_2 time after time would be 3. Thus it seems more rational to pick B_2 since it provides a greater long-term expectation.

This argument for B_2 is not completely tight, since we may not intend to take the bets more than once and in any given flip we gain neither 3 nor 2. To deal with this objection we need to introduce the concept of the *expected utility* of an act and argue that we should maximize expected utilities. Doing this will take us almost completely through the next two chapters. For the moment, let me simply introduce the formula for the expected utility of an act for a two-state problem. It is

$$u_1 p + u_2(1 - p),$$

where u_1 and u_2 are the outcome utilities, p is the probability of S_1 and $1 - p$ is the probability of S_2. Although this formula also fits the calculation of the average gains for the two bets, expected utilities (and not average gains) are defined for choices that are made only once and they represent the agent's evaluation of an *act* (not just an outcome) in terms of *its* utility. These may seem unnecessary subtleties right now, but when we have completed our study of utility theory they will fall into place.

The rule illustrated by means of the two-bets example is known as the *principle of insufficient reason*. It tells us to calculate the expected utilities for each act under the assumption that each state is equally probable and then pick an act whose expected utility is maximal. For each row this amounts to dividing the utilities by the number of states and summing the results. We then compare the resulting sums and pick an act whose sum is maximal. There is a shortcut, however, since the fractions obtained for each row have the same denominator: We simply add the entries across each row and pick an act whose resulting sum is maximal.

Example. In table 2-27 the expected utilities for each act (under the principle of insufficient reason) are given at the right of each row. The principle chooses A_2.

2-27	S_1	S_2	S_3	S_4	S_5	
A_1	5	7	2	1	10	5
A_2	10	2	3	5	20	8
A_3	1	4	6	4	0	3

Like the minimax regret and the optimism-pessimism rules, the principle of insufficient reason demands that the agent's utility scale be invariant under positive linear transformations. No mere ordinal utility scale will suffice; it must be an interval scale as well. In this respect the maximin rule has the upper hand on the other rules.

There is also an important philosophical objection to the rationale given earlier for the principle of insufficient reason. It is this: If there is no reason for assigning one set of probabilities rather than another, *there is no justification for assuming that the states are equiprobable either*. I find this point compelling. If every probability assignment is groundless, the only rational alternative is to assign none at all. Unless some other rationale can be provided for the principle of insufficient reason, that means that we should turn to some other rule for making decisions under ignorance.

Another objection to the principle is that it could lead to bad results. For all we know, when we make a decision under ignorance, one state with a terrible outcome or that produces a large regret has the greatest chance of being the true one. Thus the principle of insufficient reason could lead us to disaster. The point is illustrated by table 2-28. The principle recommends A_1. Yet, if unbeknown

2-28	S_1	S_2	
A_1	-100	300	100
A_2	10	30	20

to us, the probability of S_1 were, say, .9, the expected utility of A_1 (being $[-100].9 + [300].1$ or -60) would be significantly less than that of A_2 (being 12). In a life-or-death situation the principle could be totally disastrous.

This is not an objection to the rationale for the principle of insufficient reason; it is rather an attempt to move us toward a more conservative approach to decisions under ignorance. In evaluating it we should remember that even the maximin rule is no guarantee against disaster. If one of the outcomes of the maximin act is terrible, that rule can do nothing further to avoid it. It can only ensure that even worse outcomes (if there are any) are avoided.

PROBLEMS

1. Prove that the principle of insufficient reason never recommends a dominated act.
2. Present a decision table and an ordinal transformation of it that shows that some ordinal transformations fail to preserve the acts picked by the principle of insufficient reason.
3. Show that the shortcut version of the principle (i.e., summing across the rows) is equivalent to the original formulation.

2-6. Too Many Rules?

Suppose we were to exclude the principle of insufficient reason on the grounds that we would be unjustified in a decision under ignorance in treating each state as equally probable. Would that help us determine which of the remaining rules is the correct one? No, for we have seen that strong considerations can be offered for and against each of the rules that have been proposed. The result is that it is simply not clear which is preferable to the others.

To make matters worse, there are even decision problems in which the maximin, minimax regret, and optimism-pessimism rules make contradictory recommendations. In table 2-29 maximin picks A_1, minimax regret picks A_2, and the optimism-pessimism rule picks A_3 (for an optimism index of 1/2).

2-29

A_1	1	14	13
A_2	-1	17	11
A_3	0	20	6

We might try to resolve this by using "majority rule." The "votes" are given in table 2-30. (Note that in applying the minimax regret rule we cannot

2-30

	A_1 vs. A_2	A_2 vs. A_3	A_1 vs. A_3
Maximin	A_1	A_3	A_1
Minimax	A_2	A_2	A_1
Opt.-Pess.	A_2	A_3	A_3

use the original three-act table but must use three two-act tables, since the three-act table would illegitimately affect *pairwise* comparisons of the acts.) Majority rule will not work, as table 2-30 shows. Two out of three rank A_2 over A_1, two out of three rank A_3 over A_2, and two out of three rank A_1 over A_3. Thus we have a cycle: A_1 over A_3, A_3 over A_2, A_2 over A_1, A_1 over A_3, and so on. There is no first, second, or third choice, since any candidate for any position has others ranked above and below it. (The generation of cycles such as this by majority rule is known as the *voting paradox*. We will return to it in our treatment of group decision making.)

With majority rule eliminated, there appears to be no easy or plausible method for combining conflicting recommendations from the rules into a single decision. Indeed, even if majority rule did not produce cycles or other anomalies, there is little reason to view it as a plausible solution to the problem. After all, the rules are not *persons* with conflicting points of view whose interests should be respected and adjudicated. The rules instead embody alternative proposals concerning the rational approach to decision making under ignorance. Is it not more reasonable to judge each proposal on its merits and try to determine whether one rule is the best?

Some decision theorists have attempted to do this by proposing conditions that purport to describe how an ideally rational agent would rank acts when making decisions under ignorance. They hoped to find a set of conditions that would eliminate all the rules but one. The survivor could then be declared to be the only rational rule to use.

One of the proposed conditions is the following *mixture condition*:

If a rational agent is indifferent between two acts, the agent will be indifferent between them and the third act of flipping a fair coin and doing the first on heads and the second on tails.

This eliminates the optimism-pessimism rule. For in table 2-31, A_1 and A_2 are indifferent according to that rule for any index of optimism. But if we add the

2-31

A_1	1	0
A_2	0	1

"mixed" act of flipping a fair coin and doing A_1 on heads and A_2 on tails, we obtain table 2-32. And the only way for an agent to be indifferent between its three acts is to have an optimism index equal to 1/2. (The values for A_3 are

2-32

A_1	1	0
A_2	0	1
A_3	½	½

computed by noting that its utility under either state is the expected utility of a bet on a fair coin that pays 0 and 1.) A rational agent using the optimism-pessimism rule with an optimism index of, say 5/8, would fail to be indifferent between all three acts in this table. This would contradict the mixture condition. But since we cannot restrict an agent's optimism index, this means that many rational agents would be unable both to conform to the requirements of the mixture condition and to use the rule. The mixture condition thus eliminates the optimism-pessimism rule.

The next condition eliminates the minimax regret rule. I will call it the *irrelevant expansion condition*. You may remember it from our previous discussion.

The addition of a new act, which is not regarded as better than the original ones, will not change a rational agent's ranking of the old acts.

If you do not recall how this affects the minimax rule, return to section 2-3 where you will find two sets of tables (2-13, 2-14 and 2-15, 2-16) demonstrating why an agent cannot use the minimax rule while respecting this condition.

As it turns out, the sole survivor of a seemingly reasonable set of conditions is none other than the principle of insufficient reason. Yet earlier we argued against that rule! One way out of this situation is to attack the conditions that have pushed this principle to the forefront. For instance, we could object to the irrelevant expansion condition on the grounds that the addition of a new act—even one that would not be chosen—could lead a rational agent to reevaluate a decision. To take an illustration well known to decision theorists, suppose you sat down in an apparently seedy restaurant and were offered a choice between hamburger and roast duck. Ordinarily you prefer roast duck but you fear that this cook will ruin it. So you silently opt for the hamburger. Then the waiter returns to tells you that today you can also have frog legs sautéed in wine. The thought revolts you, but the new choice informs you that the cook has skill; so you change your mind and order the duck.

Alas, there are counterarguments to this counterargument. For example, somebody could argue that the addition of the new act has caused such a radical change in the decision situation that the old acts are no longer options. For the old acts were *order hamburger at a seedy place*, *order roast duck at the same seedy place*. But the new acts do not include these since you no longer think of the restaurant as seedy. Hence the restaurant example fails to call the condition into question.

The debate could go back and forth over the conditions in this fashion with results no more conclusive than our previous discussions of the rules themselves. The situation is likely to remain this way, I think, until we have amassed a rich backlog of studies of genuine real-life examples of good decision making under ignorance. My hope is that these would help us sharpen our judgments concerning the various rules. I would also conjecture that we will ultimately conclude that no rule is always the rational one to use but rather that different rules are appropriate to different situations. If this is so, it would be more profitable to seek conditions delimiting the applicability of the various rules rather than to seek ones that will declare in favor of a single rule.

PROBLEMS

1. With respect to table 2-32, show that A_1, A_2, and A_3 are indifferent only if the agent's optimism index is 1/2.
2. Also with respect to table 2-32, show that A_1 and A_2 are both picked if the index is greater than 1/2 and that A_3 is picked when the index is less than 1/2.
3. Show that the maximin rules are excluded by the condition that a rational agent always excludes dominated acts.
4. If you had to choose one rule for making all decisions under ignorance for the rest of your life, which would you choose? Why?

2-7. An Application in Social Philosophy: Rawls vs. Harsanyi

One of the most interesting and important recent debates in social philosophy is that between John Rawls, a moral philosopher, and John Harsanyi, a decision theorist with strong philosophical interests. Although the stated issue of their debate concerns conflicting conceptions of the just society, crucial points in their reasoning turn on the choice of a rule for making decisions under ignorance. Rawls argues for the maximin rule and principles of social justice that protect the interests of those at the bottom of the social ladder; Harsanyi champions the principle of insufficient reason and principles of justice that tend to promote the average level of well-being in a society.

Rawls calls his principle of justice the *difference principle*. For our purposes, we can take it as declaring one society better than another if the worst-off members of the former do better than the worst-off in the latter. (I have greatly simplified both the difference principle and Rawls's view. The same warning applies to my exposition of Harsanyi's view.) According to Rawls, contemporary North American society, for all its ills, is superior to medieval European society, because the destitute in North America today fare better than did their medieval European counterparts.

Harsanyi counters Rawls by claiming that we should not focus on the worst-off in societies when determining which is more just but instead should compare societies in terms of the average amount of utility realized in them. His position is a form of *utilitarianism*, a view that originated with Jeremy Bentham and John Stuart Mill. If we assume that we can measure utility in purely monetary terms—and that is a big assumption—then certain oil-rich Middle Eastern societies will count as more just than contemporary England, since the average wealth in the oil-rich nations is greater than that in England. (Of course, using the difference principle the ranking might be just the opposite.)

Even if we do not measure happiness in terms of wealth, it is clear that, in theory at least, the difference principle and utilitarianism can lead to different rankings. To see how, let us imagine two societies. The first consists of 1,000 people, with 100 being workers and the rest free to engage in any pleasure they wish. We can easily imagine the workers being able to produce enough goods and services to take care of the needs of the entire society. Let us also think of the workers as quite poor and unhappy and the nonworkers as flourishing and happy. To be more specific, using a 0 to 100 utility scale, let us suppose that the workers each receive 1 unit of utility while the others get 90 units each. Then the average utility is 81.1. Next let us imagine a society technologically quite similar to the first, but let us suppose that under some reasonable rotational scheme, everyone takes a fair turn at being a worker. This now causes everyone to realize the same utility of, let us say, 35 units. Thus utilitarianism would count the first society as more just, but the difference principle would favor the second.

(One way to get a feel for this example is to think of the first society as a resort community and the second as a rural commune. Which do you think is more just? If you might end up having any role in the society you happen to belong to, but do not know which role, to which society would you rather belong?)

Now it might be that the difference principle and utilitarianism will never ' conflict in practice, despite the theoretical conflicts we can easily derive from them. One reason is that it is very difficult to determine whether a given social policy really promotes average utility or the interests of the worst-off, and thus it is difficult to determine whether the policy accords with either utilitarianism or the difference principle.

Whether or not utilitarianism and the difference principle conflict in practice is not crucial to our present concern. What is important is the differing arguments Rawls and Harsanyi use to support their views. Both start from common ground: Principles of social justice must pass a special test of *fairness*. The test is that they be principles that rational, self-interested agents would choose when behind a "veil of ignorance." This veil of ignorance would prevent them from knowing who they are, their social status, their ancestry, or their talents. In short, behind the veil of ignorance individuals know neither their place in society nor their ability to change it. For all they know, they can be movie stars, beloved politicians, uneducated dishwashers, or inmates of a Nazi concentration camp. Their society might be a modern democratic welfare state or a despotism.

To test a proposed principle of social justice, Harsanyi and Rawls tell us to ask ourselves this question: Would rational agents, placed behind the veil of ignorance and given a list of proposed principles of justice from which to choose, pick this principle? (The list will include not only the candidate but also both the difference principle and the principle of maximizing average utility [utilitarianism]. Agents are to think of themselves as choosing the principle that will regulate whichever society they happen to find themselves in when the veil is lifted.) Rawls and Harsanyi believe that principles chosen under these circumstances should count as just and fair, since they are ones that would be chosen by rational self-interested agents under conditions of choice in which everyone is treated fairly and impartially. They also agree that the decision in question is made under ignorance.

But here their agreement ends. Harsanyi claims that all rational individuals placed behind the veil of ignorance will use the principle of insufficient reason as their decision rule. Although an agent will not know which person she will be in a given society or to which society she will belong, she can be expected to know (or so Harsanyi claims) the amount of utility she would receive if she were a given person in a given position in a given society. It would simply be the amount of utility that person enjoys. Furthermore, using the principle of insufficient reason, an agent will infer that she has an equal chance of being *any* given person in a given society. She will thereby conclude that the utility of belonging to a given society is the same as the utility of a gamble or lottery in which she has an equal chance of being any given person in that society. But that utility is simply the average of the utilities available in that society. Given all this, the principle of insufficient reason will enjoin an agent to pick a society for which the average utility is maximal. It follows from all this that when Harsanyi's rational agents ask themselves, What sort of society would I want to be in when the veil is lifted? they will answer, One in which the principle of maximizing expected utility holds sway. Thus Harsanyi's rational agents will be utilitarians.

Not so for Rawls. He claims that the proper principle for rational agents to use behind the veil of ignorance is the maximin rule. Given this, rational agents will compare societies by looking at the positions of the worst-off persons in them—because occupying one of these positions is the minimum of the outcomes they can expect. And they will favor one society over another if the worst-off in the former do better than in the latter. That means that rational agents will rank societies in accordance with the difference principle, and thus will choose that principle when placed behind the veil of ignorance.

Rawls also presents an interesting case for the use of the maximin rule behind the veil of ignorance. He points out that since we have no reason for choosing one probability assignment over another, there are no grounds for the equiprobable assignment implicit in the principle of insufficient reason. This does not lead us directly to the maximin rule, but Rawls believes that the particular decision at hand mandates its use. First, the consequences of making a bad choice are extremely serious. One could end up being the only serf in a society of nobles. Second, we do not need great amounts of wealth or power to lead happy lives. Realizing this, rational individuals will hardly regret missing a chance to be rich or powerful. This excludes the considerations that support the minimax regret rule. Finally, Harsanyi's approach requires agents behind the veil of ignorance to rank the lives of members of various societies on a common interval utility scale. As we will see in chapter 6 (section *6-4c*), there are reasons to doubt that such interpersonal comparisons of utility are possible. By contrast, Rawls's proposal requires only that agents behind the veil be able to generate an ordinal ranking of the worst-off individuals in the various societies.

This argument for the maximin rule on the grounds of its appropriateness and lack of presuppositions will not favor the maximin approach to all decisions under ignorance. However, it suggests a way for resolving our problem of having too many rules: When making a decision under ignorance, we should look for circumstances connected with the decision at hand that favor some rules and exclude others.

The debate over the difference principle and utilitarianism is far from settled, as is the debate about the correct rule for making decisions under ignorance. For the time being let us take notice of how one debate has advanced the other. Rawls and Harsanyi have borrowed from decision theory to argue for positions in social philosophy. Yet their debate has helped us better understand some of the issues in decision theory. For Rawls has pinpointed the conditions under which the best case can be made for the maximin rule and has sharpened some of the objections to the principle of insufficient reason.

PROBLEMS

1. Set up in schematic form a decision table for picking societies behind the veil of ignorance.
2. Explain in detail how in the Rawls-Harsanyi framework rational agents behind the veil of ignorance can replace the choice of *principles* to regulate their society by the choice of *societies* to which to belong.
3. Do you think there are circumstances under which utilitarianism could sup-

port oppression? Are there circumstances under which the difference principle could support it?

4. In my discussion of Rawls's case for the maximin rule, I failed to rule out the optimism-pessimism rule. Can Rawls exclude it? How?

2-8. References

My treatment of decisions under ignorance draws heavily from *Luce and Raiffa*. *Levi* presents an approach to partial ignorance. For the Rawls-Harsanyi dispute see both *Rawls* and *Harsanyi*.

Chapter 3
DECISIONS UNDER RISK:
PROBABILITY

3-1. Maximizing Expected Values

When Michael Smith applied to Peoples Insurance Company for a life insurance policy in the amount of $25,000 at a premium of $100 for one year, he was required to fill out a lengthy health and occupation questionnaire and submit to an examination by a physician. According to the results, Smith fell into the category of persons with a 5% death rate for the coming year. This enabled Peoples to assign a probability of .05 to Smith's dying within the year, and thus the decision whether or not to insure him became one *under risk*.

I will represent this decision problem by means of decision table 3-1. Notice that I have put both outcome values and probabilities in the same square.

3-1	Smith Dies		Smith Lives	
Insure Smith	− $25,000	.05	$100	.95
Do Not	$0	.05	$0	.95

Let us leave the Peoples example for a moment and turn to Sally Harding's decision. She needs a car and has a choice of buying an old heap for $400 or a four-year-old car for $3,000. Harding plans to leave the country at the end of the year, so either car need serve her for only the year. That is why she is considering the old heap. On the other hand, if either car breaks down before the end of the year, she intends to rent one at an estimated cost of $200. Harding would pay cash for the older car and junk it at the end of the year. If, on the other hand, she buys the newer car, she will finance it and sell it when she leaves. She believes that her net cost for the newer car would come to $500. Being an experienced mechanic, Harding estimates that the chances of the old heap surviving the year are 5 in 10 and that the newer car's chances are 9 in 10.

Harding's decision is again one under risk and can be represented by table 3-2.

3-2	No Need to Rent	Must Rent
Buy New	− $500 .90	− $700 .10
Buy Old	− $400 .50	− $600 .50

You might be tempted to solve Harding's problem by appealing to the dominance principle, for buying the old heap costs less no matter what happens. But remember, the chances of Harding having to rent a car are a function of which car she buys. Buying the older car increases her chances of having to rent by a factor of 5. This is exactly the sort of case where the dominance principle should not be applied.

In Harding's decision problem, the probabilities of the states vary with the acts. Writing different probability numbers in different rows reflects this. In the insurance problem the acts do not affect the probabilities of the states; hence, the probabilities of the states conditional on the acts collapse to absolute probabilities. That is why the same probability numbers are written in each row.

Peoples Insurance Company came to a decision quite easily. They decided they could not afford to insure Smith — at least not at a $100 premium. They reasoned that if they were to insure a hundred people like Smith, five would die. That would cost the company $125,000 in death benefits and would be counterbalanced by only $10,000. So the net loss would be $115,000. Peoples concluded that, whether they insured a hundred, a thousand, or a million people similar to Smith, their losses would average close to $1,150 per person. On the other hand, they would neither gain nor lose by not insuring Smith and others like him.

Peoples proceeded as insurance companies are wont to do. They calculated the *expected monetary value* (EMV) of each option and chose the one with the highest EMV. You can calculate the EMV for an act from a decision table quite easily: Multiply the monetary value in each square by the probability number in that square and sum across the row. Do this for Sally Harding's decision. You will see that the EMV of buying the newer car is − $520 and the EMV of buying the older one is − $500.

Should Sally Harding buy the older car? On the average, that would save her the most money. But what about the pleasures of riding in a newer car? And what of the worry that the older one will break down? These relevant factors have been neglected. But perhaps these could be assigned a monetary value and the decision could be made on the basis of a revised set of EMVs. There remains another problem. Sally Harding will buy a car only once this year, and to the best of our knowledge, no one else has been confronted with a very similar decision. So how can we speak of what happens "on the average" here? This is a one-shot deal so there is nothing to average out. And even if there were, Sally

Harding should be concerned with what happens to her, not to the average person like her.

We can deal with these problems by replacing monetary values with utility values and showing that maximizing expected utility does not suffer from the drawbacks of maximizing EMVs. Utility is thus one of the chief ingredients of the theory of decisions under risk. But before we can attend to it we must achieve a better understanding of the other major ingredient, namely, probability.

3-2. Probability Theory

Probability judgments are now a commonplace of our daily life. Every time we turn on the radio or pick up a newspaper we are apt to encounter a weather, economic, or political forecast framed in probabilistic terms. Probability is also essential to theoretical science since it is the backbone of certain areas of physics, genetics, and the social sciences. Despite its pervasiveness in our culture, there is still much debate among philosophers, statisticians, and scientists concerning what probability statements mean and how they may be justified or applied. Some believe, for instance, that it is not proper to assign probabilities to single events, and hence that probability judgments inform us only of proportions. They claim that, strictly speaking, we should not say that the chances are 1 in 10 that Jackson will die within the year; rather, we should say that in a large group of people like Jackson, 10% will die. Others believe that single events or statements can be assigned probabilities by simply refining our best hunches. Some believe that probability is a measure of the *strength of beliefs* or lack thereof; others think it is a property of reality.

There is, however, a common focal point for the study of probability—*the probability calculus*. This is a mathematical theory that enables us to calculate additional probabilities from those we already know. For instance, if I know that the probability that it will rain tomorrow is 50% and that there is a 10% probability that the price of gold will drop tomorrow, the calculus allows me to conclude that the probability that both will occur tomorrow is 5%. The beauty of the probability calculus is that it can be used with almost all the interpretations of probability that have been proposed. Furthermore, much of the superstructure of the theory of decision under risk depends on the probability calculus. Let us then turn to this calculus before we plunge into the more philosophical questions about probability.

There are a number of alternative presentations of the probability calculus. I will use a formulation in which probabilities are assigned to simple and compound statement forms, since this will enable many philosophical readers to draw on their training in symbolic logic.

The basic formulas of the calculus will take the form

$$P(S) = a.$$

Here S represents a statement form, such as "p or q," "p & q," or "p & (q or r)," and a represents a numeral. The entire expression "$P(S) = a$" should be read as: "the probability of S is a." Some examples are

$P(p) = 1/2$, $P(p$ or $q) = 2/3$, $P($not q or $r) = .9$.

In applications the letters will be replaced with sentences or sentence abbreviations. Thus we can have:

$P($the coin comes up heads$) = 1/2$
$P($heart or diamond$) = 1/2$
$P($ace and spade$) = 1/52$.

These statements are all *absolute* probability statements.

We will also need *conditional* probability statements, which we will write as

$P(S/W) = a$

and read as "the probability of S given $W = a$." Because it is essential to appreciate the difference between conditional and absolute probability statements, let us reflect on an example. The probability of drawing a heart at random from a fair deck is 1/4, but if all the black cards were removed and only red cards remained, the probability in question would be the probability of drawing a heart *given* that the card to be drawn is red. That would be 1/2. We express the first probability judgment as an absolute probability statement

$P($heart$) = 1/4$,

but the second should be formulated as the conditional probability

$P($heart/red$) = 1/2$.

Now one might think that the conditional probability of a heart given a red card is just the absolute probability of the conditional "If the card is red, then it is a heart." But that will not work, given our current methods for treating conditionals in logic and mathematics. For the conditional in question is equivalent to "either the card is not red or it is a heart," and

$P($not red or heart$) = 3/4$

since thirty-nine out of fifty-two cards are either not red or hearts.

Another important point: $P(S/W)$ and $P(W/S)$ are generally distinct. Thus $P($heart/red$) = 1/2$ but $P($red/heart$) = 1$, since every heart is red.

Conditional and absolute probability are related, however, through a number of laws of probability. This is one of the most important of those laws: $P(p$ & $q) = P(p) \times P(q/p)$. It says that the probability of a conjunction is the probability of the first component times the probability of the second given the first. The idea here is that it is less probable that two things will be true together than that either one will be true separately. Since probabilities are less than or equal to 1, multiplying them will produce a number smaller than or equal to either. But in general we cannot simply multiply the probabilities of the two conjuncts, since their truth and falsity might be linked. There is, for instance, no chance for a coin to come up both heads and tails, yet the simple product of the probabilities that it does is 1/4. On the other hand, multiplying by the conditional probability of the second component given the first avoids this difficulty:

P[heads and tails (on the same toss)] $= 0 = P$(heads) $\times P$(tails/heads) $= 1/2 \times 0$.

Example. What is the probability of drawing two aces in a row from an ordinary deck of fifty-two cards when the first card is not put back into the deck? This is the probability of drawing an ace on the first draw and then again on the second draw. So we must calculate as follows:

P(ace on draw 1 and ace on draw 2) $= P$(ace on draw 1) $\times$
P(ace on draw 2/ace on draw 1) $= 4/52 \times 3/51 = 3/663$.

The first probability is simply the ratio of the aces to the total number of cards in the deck. The second is figured by noting that if an ace is drawn on the first draw and not replaced, three aces out of a total of fifty-one cards remain.

This example illustrates another important concept of probability theory. Because the first card is not put back into the deck, the outcome of the first draw affects the outcome of the second draw: There are fifty-one cards to draw after the first draw, and one less ace if the first card drawn was an ace. On the other hand, if the first card drawn is replaced and the deck reshuffled, the outcome of the first draw has no effect on the outcome of the second draw. In this case, we say that the outcomes are *independent*. When we replace and reshuffle the cards

P(ace on draw 2) $= P$(ace on draw 2/ace on draw 1).

This leads to the following definition.

Definition 1. p is *independent* of q if and only if $P(p) = P(p/q)$.

Another important concept we will need is that of *mutual exclusiveness*. If a single card is drawn, then drawing an ace and simultaneously drawing a king are mutually exclusive. But drawing an ace and drawing a spade are not; one can draw the ace of spades. Generalizing we have:

Definition 2. p and q are mutually exclusive if and only if it is impossible for both to be true.

If p and q are *mutually exclusive*, if one is true the other must be false. So if p and q are mutually exclusive, $P(p/q)$ and $P(q/p)$ are 0. Consequently, if p and q are mutually exclusive, p and q will not be independent of each other—unless each already has a probability of 0.

With these definitions in hand we can now lay down the basic laws or *axioms* of the probability calculus. All the other laws of the calculus can be derived from these using purely logical and mathematical reasoning.

A (logically or mathematically) impossible statement has no probability of being true; so 0 is a natural lower bound for probabilities. On the other hand, the probability of a certainty being true is 100%; so 1 is a natural upper bound for probabilities. Statements that are neither impossible nor certain have proba-, bilities between 0 and 1. These considerations motivate the first two axioms of the calculus.

AXIOM 1. a. $0 \le P(p) \le 1$.
   b. $0 \le P(p/q) \le 1$.
AXIOM 2. If p is certain, then $P(p) = 1$.

What is the probability of drawing a face card or an ace? Four cards out of fifty-two are aces and twelve are face cards. So the probability of drawing an ace or a face card is 16/52 or 5/13. This example illustrates the next axiom.

AXIOM 3. If p and q are mutually exclusive, then
   $P(p \text{ or } q) = P(p) + P(q)$.

We can immediately apply these axioms to derive this law.

THEOREM 1. $P(p) + P(\text{not } p) = 1$.

PROOF. "p" and "not p" are mutually exclusive, and their disjunction is certain. Thus by axioms 2 and 3 we have:

   $1 = P(p \text{ or not } p) = P(p) + P(\text{not } p)$.

Theorem 1 yields a rule for calculating negated statements. If we already know $P(p)$, we can find $P(\text{not } p)$ by subtracting $P(p)$ from 1.

Example. What is the probability of taking more than one roll of a fair die to get a 6? Since taking more than one roll to get a 6 is the same as not getting a 6 on the first roll, $P(\text{not } 6)$ is the probability we want. But it must equal 5/6, since $P(6) = 1/6$.

We can also generalize the proof of theorem 1 to establish that the probabilities of any set of mutually exclusive and exhaustive alternatives sum to 1. (Alternatives are exhaustive if and only if it is certain that at least one of them is true.) This is important for decision theory, since it tells us that the probabilities in each row of a properly specified decision table must total 1.

Two equivalent statements must both be true together or both be false together. Thus there is no chance for the one to be true when the other is not. This leads to the following theorem.

THEOREM 2. If p and q are equivalent, then $P(p) = P(q)$.

PROOF. Suppose that p and q are equivalent. Then one is true just in case the other is. But then (a) "either not p or q" is certain and (b) q and not p are mutually exclusive. From (a) and axiom 2, we conclude that

   $P(\text{not } p \text{ or } q) = 1$.

From (b) and axiom 3, we get

   $P(\text{not } p \text{ or } q) = P(\text{not } p) + P(q)$.

Putting this together with an application of theorem 1 yields

   $1 = 1 - P(p) + P(q)$

from which $P(p) = P(q)$ follows immediately by algebra.

This theorem lets us draw on mathematics and logic to show that certain statements or statement forms are equiprobable. (In applying this and axioms 2 and 3 to examples outside mathematics and logic, we may also use those equivalences, certainties, and impossibilities that are part of the background assumptions of the application. For example, we may ordinarily assume that it is certain that a coin will land either heads or tails, though one tossed onto a sand pile need not.) The next theorem appeals to logical equivalences.

THEOREM 3. $P(p \text{ or } q) = P(p) + P(q) - P(p \text{ \& } q)$.

PROOF. "p or q" is logically equivalent to "either p & q or p & not q or else not p & q"; so their probabilities must be equal. But the first two disjuncts are mutually exclusive with the third. Thus by substituting in axiom 3, we obtain

(1) $P(\text{either } p \text{ \& } q \text{ or } p \text{ \& not } q \text{ or else not } p \text{ \& } q) = P(\text{either } p \text{ \& } q \text{ or } p \text{ \& not } q) + P(\text{not } p \text{ \& } q)$.

But "either p & q or p & not q" is equivalent to "p"; so if we apply theorem 2 and substitute in equation (1) we get:

(2) $P(\text{either } p \text{ \& } q \text{ or } p \text{ \& not } q \text{ or else not } p \text{ \& } q) = P(p) + P(\text{not } p \text{ \& } q)$.

But, remember, the left side of equation (1) equals $P(p \text{ or } q)$; so we may get

(3) $P(p \text{ or } q) = P(p) + P(\text{not } p \text{ \& } q)$.

Adding $P(p \text{ \& } q)$ to both sides of equation (3) we get

(4) $P(p \text{ or } q) + P(p \text{ \& } q) = P(p) + P(\text{not } p \text{ \& } q) + P(p \text{ \& } q)$.

Noting that "not p & q or else p & q" is equivalent to "q" and that its disjuncts are mutually exclusive, we may apply axioms 3 and 4 to equation (4) to obtain:

(5) $P(p \text{ or } q) + P(p \text{ \& } q) = P(p) + P(q)$.

The theorem then follows by subtracting $P(p \text{ \& } q)$ from both sides of this equation.

Theorem 3 and axiom 3 can both be used to calculate the probabilities of disjunctions from the probabilities of their components. Axiom 3 is simpler to use, but it does not always apply, whereas there is no restriction on theorem 3. (Note that theorem 3 has axiom 3 as a special case; for when p and q are mutually exclusive $P(p \text{ \& } q) = 0$.) The more complicated appearance of theorem 3 is to prevent double counting when calculating probabilities of disjunctions whose components do not exclude each other. For example, the probability of a heart or a king is *not* $1/4 + 1/13$ because the king of hearts would be counted twice; rather the probability is $1/4 + 1/13 - 1/52$ where the double count has been subtracted. Notice that this follows the model of theorem 3.

Example. What is the probability of getting exactly two heads on three tosses of a fair coin? The two heads might occur in any one of three mutually exclusive ways: *HHT, HTH,* and *THH.* Each of these has a probability of 1/8 since each is one of the eight possibilities. Thus the answer is 3/8.

Example. What is the probability of getting a heart or an ace on at least one of two draws from a deck of cards, where the card drawn is replaced and the deck reshuffled after the first draw? The probability of getting a heart or an ace on the first draw is $13/52 + 4/52 - 1/52$ or $4/13$. But the probabilities are the same for the second draw. Furthermore, the question allows for the possibility that a heart or an ace is drawn both times; so the probability in question is $8/13$.

We still lack methods for calculating the probability of conjunctions. This is remedied by the next axiom, which we discussed in connection with conditional probability.

AXIOM 4. $P(p \ \& \ q) = P(p) \times P(q/p)$.

If $P(p) \neq 0$, we can divide both sides of axiom 4 by it, obtaining the formula of the next theorem.

THEOREM 4. If $P(p) \neq 0$, then
$P(q/p) = P(p \ \& \ q)/P(p)$.

(In many presentations theorem 4 is taken as the definition of conditional probability.)

According to definition 1, if q is independent of p, $P(q) = P(q/p)$. Thus, by axiom 4, we have:

THEOREM 5. If q is independent of p, then
$P(p \ \& \ q) = P(p) \times P(q)$.

Theorem 5 and axiom 4 let us calculate the probabilities of conjunctions in terms of their components. This is illustrated in the next example.

Example. What is the probability of getting twenty heads on twenty tosses of a fair coin? This is the probability of getting heads on the first toss and on the second toss and . . . and on the twentieth toss. But each toss is independent of the others, so the probability of getting twenty heads is the probability of getting one head multiplied by itself nineteen more times, i.e., $(1/2)^{20}$.

The next theorem shows that independence is almost always mutual.

THEOREM 6. p is independent of q if and only if q is independent of p, provided that $P(p)$ and $P(q)$ are both nonzero.

PROOF. Suppose that both $P(p)$ and $P(q)$ are not zero. Suppose that p is independent of q. Then $P(p) = P(p/q)$. Then, by theorem 4,

$P(q/p) = P(q \ \& \ p)/P(p) = [P(q) \times P(p/q)]/P(p)$
$\qquad = [P(q) \times P(p)]/P(p) = P(q)$.

That means that q is independent of p. By interchanging "q" and "p" in this proof we can show that p is independent of q if q is independent of p.

The next theorem relates independence and mutual exclusiveness.

THEOREM 7. If p and q are mutually exclusive and both $P(p)$ and $P(q)$ are nonzero, then p and q are not independent.

PROOF. If p and q are mutually exclusive, then the negation of their conjunction is certain; so by theorem 1 and axiom 2, we have $P(p \ \& \ q) = 0$. On the other hand, if either p or q is independent of the other, then

$$P(p \ \& \ q) = 0 = P(p) \times P(q),$$

which implies that one of $P(p)$ or $P(q)$ is 0. That would contradict the hypothesis of the theorem.

Notice that the converse of theorem 7 does not hold: Independent statements need not be mutually exclusive. Getting heads on the second toss of a coin is independent of getting heads on the first toss, but they do not exclude each other.

The next pair of theorems, known as the inverse probability law and Bayes's Theorem, respectively, have been of fundamental importance in decision theory, statistics, and the philosophy of science.

THEOREM 8 (the inverse probability law). If $P(q) \neq 0$, then
$P(p/q) = [P(p) \times P(q/p)]/P(q)$.

PROOF. Since "$p \ \& \ q$" and "$q \ \& \ p$" are equivalent, theorem 2 and axiom 4 yield

$$P(q) \times P(p/q) = P(p) \times P(q/p),$$

and the theorem follows by dividing by $P(q)$.

THEOREM 9 (Bayes's theorem). If $P(q) \neq 0$, then

$$P(p/q) = \frac{P(p) \times P(q/p)}{[P(p) \times P(q/p)] + [P(\text{not } p) \times P(q/\text{not } p)]}$$

PROOF. By theorem 8 we have

$$(1) \ P(p/q) = \frac{P(p) \times P(q/p)}{P(q)} \ .$$

But "q" is equivalent to "either $p \ \& \ q$ or not $p \ \& \ q$." The probability of this disjunction is equal, by axioms 3 and 4, to the denominator of the theorem. Thus the theorem follows from equation (1) and theorem 2.

To give these theorems some meaning, let us consider the situation of a physician who has just observed a spot on an X ray of some patient's lung. Let us assume that the physician knows the probability of observing such spots *given* that the patient has tuberculosis and that she also knows the incidence of TB and the incidence of lung spots. Letting "S" stand for "the patient has a lung spot," the known probabilities are $P(S)$, $P(TB)$, and $P(S/TB)$. By applying the inverse probability law our physician can calculate the probability that the patient has TB *given* that he has a lung spot. This is

$$P(TB/S) = [P(TB) \times P(S/TB)]/P(S).$$

Having observed the lung spot, it would be legitimate for our physician to take $P(TB/S)$ as the probability that the patient has TB and to base her decisions on it.

The probability assigned to TB before the spot was observed—$P(TB)$—is called the *prior* probability of TB. The conditional probability, $P(TB/S)$, the physician uses after observing the spot is called the *posterior* probability of TB. (The physician also uses a prior probability for lung spots, but does not obtain a posterior probability for them in this example.) Posterior probabilities can also be used as new priors in further applications of the inverse probability law. For example, if the physician now tests her patient with a TB skin test and obtains a positive reading, she can apply the formula again using the posterior probability for TB as her new prior.

It is likely that a physician will know or can easily find out the probability of observing lung spots *given* that a patient has TB, and it is likely that she can find the probability of a patient's having TB, since there are much medical data concerning these matters. But it is less likely that a physician will have access to data concerning the probability of observing lung spots per se. Then the inverse probability law will not apply, but Bayes's theorem might. For suppose the physician knows that the patient has TB or lung cancer but not both. Then lung cancer (LC) can play the role of not TB in Bayes's Theorem and we obtain:

$$P(TB/S) = \frac{[P(TB) \times P(S/TB)]}{[P(TB) \times P(S/TB)] + [P(LC) \times P(S/LC)]} .$$

Example. Suppose that on any given day the probability of rain (R) is .25, that of clouds (C) is .4, and that of clouds given rain is 1. You observe a cloudy sky. Now what are the chances of rain? Using the inverse probability law we obtain:

$$P(R/C) = [P(R) \times P(C/R)]/P(C) = [1/4 \times 1]/(4/10) = 5/8.$$

PROBLEMS

1. Assume a card is drawn at random from an ordinary fifty-two card deck.
    a. What is the probability of drawing an ace?
    b. The ace of hearts?
    c. The ace of hearts or the king of hearts?
    d. An ace or a heart?
2. A card is drawn and not replaced, then another card is drawn.
    a. What is the probability of the ace of hearts on the first draw and the king of hearts on the second?
    b. What is the probability of two aces?
    c. What is the probability of no ace on either draw?
    d. What is the probability of at least one ace and at least one heart for the two draws?
3. $P(p) = 1/2$, $P(q) = 1/2$, $P(p \ \& \ q) = 1/4$. Are p and q mutually exclusive? What is $P(p \text{ or } q)$?
4. A die is loaded so that the probability of rolling a 2 is twice that of a 1, that of a 3 three times that of a 1, that of a 4 four times that of a 1, etc. What is the probability of rolling an odd number?

5. Prove that if "*p*" implies "*q*" and $P(p) \neq 0$, then $P(q/p) = 1$. (Hint: "*p*" implies "*q*" just in case "*p*" is equivalent to "*p & q*.")
6. Prove that $P(p \ \& \ q) \leq P(p)$.
7. Suppose that $P(p) = 1/4$, $P(q/p) = 1$, $P(q/\text{not } p) = 1/5$. Find $P(p/q)$.
8. There is a room filled with urns of two types. Type I urns contain six blue balls and four red balls; urns of type II contain nine red balls and one blue ball. There are 800 type I urns and 200 type II urns in the room. They are distributed randomly and look alike. An urn is selected from the room and a ball drawn from it.
   a. What is the (prior) probability of the urn's being type I?
   b. What is the probability that the ball drawn is red?
   c. What is the probability that the ball drawn is blue?
   d. If a blue ball is drawn, what is the (posterior) probability that the urn is of type I?
   e. What is it if a red ball is drawn?
9. Suppose you could be certain that the urn in the last example is of type II. Explain why seeing a blue ball drawn from the urn would not produce a lower posterior probability for the urn being of type II.

3-2a. Bayes's Theorem without Priors

Suppose you are traveling in a somewhat magical land where some of the coins are biased to land tails 75% of the time. You find a coin and you and a friend try to determine whether the coin is biased. There is a certain test using magnets that will tell whether the coin is biased, but you do not have any magnets. So you flip the coin ten times. Each time the coin lands tails up. Can you conclude that the coin is more likely to be biased than not?

It would seem natural to try to apply Bayes's theorem (or the inverse probability law) here. But what is the prior probability that the coin is biased? Of course, if you knew that, say, 70% of the coins in this land are biased and that your coin was "randomly" selected, it would be reasonable for you to use .7 as your prior. However, as far as the story goes, you know no such thing.

Some statisticians and decision theorists claim that in a situation such as this you should take your best hunch as the prior probability and use it to apply Bayes's theorem. These people are known as *Bayesians*. This is not only because they desire to use Bayes's theorem (when other statisticians believe it should not be applied), but also because they have constructed an argument in support of their position that is itself based on Bayes's theorem.

In brief, their argument is this. Suppose you (or a group of individuals) come to a situation in which you use your best hunch (or hunches) to estimate the prior probability that some statement *p* is true. Next suppose you are exposed to a large amount of data bearing on the truth of *p* and you use Bayes's theorem or the inverse probability law to generate posterior probabilities for the truth of *p*, taking the posterior probabilities so yielded as their new priors, and repeat this process each time you receive new data. Then as you are exposed to more and more data your probability estimates will come closer and closer to the "objective" or statistically based probability – if there is one. Furthermore, if several individuals are involved, their several (and possibly quite different) personal probability estimates will converge to each other. The claim is that, in effect, large amounts of data bearing on the truth of p can "wash out" poor initial probability estimates.

I have put this argument in an overbold and imprecise form. Unfortunately, a careful formulation would require more mathematics than is appropriate for this book. Perhaps we can illustrate the phenomenon with which the argument is concerned by returning to our example. Recall that you have flipped the coin ten times and each time it has come up tails. These data favor the biased coin, since it is biased to produce tails on three tosses out of four. Now suppose that before you decided to toss the coin you assigned a probability of .01 to its being biased (B) and a probability of .99 to its being not biased (not B). Each toss of the coin is independent of the others, so the probabilities of ten tails in a row conditional on either coin are:

$$P(10 \text{ tails}/B) = (3/4)^{10}$$
$$P(10 \text{ tails/not } B) = (1/2)^{10}.$$

Now instead of calculating $P(B/10 \text{ tails})$ and $P(\text{not } B/10 \text{ tails})$, let us calculate the ratio of the latter to the former. Using the inverse probability law we obtain:

$$\frac{P(B/10 \text{ tails})}{P(\text{not } B/10 \text{ tails})} = \frac{[P(B) \times P(10 \text{ tails}/B)]/P(10 \text{ tails})}{[P(\text{not } B) \times P(10 \text{ tails/not } B)]/P(10 \text{ tails})}$$

$$= \frac{P(B) \times P(10 \text{ tails}/B)}{P(\text{not } B) \times P(10 \text{ tails/not } B)}$$

$$= (.01 \times (3/4)^{10})/(.99 \times (1/2)^{10})$$

$$= (1/99)(3/2)^{10}.$$

This is approximately 57.7, which means that the probability you assigned to the coin's being biased has gone from ninety-nine times smaller than that of its being unbiased to almost fifty-eight times larger. If you had flipped it a hundred times and had gotten a hundred tails, the probability of its being biased would be over 3,000 times larger than its being not biased.

Of course, we have looked at one of the simplest and most favorable cases. More complicated mathematics is required to analyze the cases in which some proportion of the tosses are heads while the balance are tails. It is not hard to show, for example, that if 1/4 of the tosses turned out to be heads, that you would assign a higher probability to the coin's being biased, and that the probability would increase as the number of tosses did.

PROBLEMS

1. Calculate the posterior probability that the coin is biased given that you flip the coin ten times and observe eight tails followed by two heads. [$P(B) = .01$.]

2. Calculate the posterior probability that the coin is biased given that you flip

it ten times and observe any combination of eight tails and two heads. [$P(B) = .01$.]

3. Suppose you assigned a probability of 0 to the coin's being biased. Show that, no matter how many tails in a row you observed, neither Bayes's theorem nor the inverse probability law would lead to a nonzero posterior probability for the coin's being biased.

3-2b. Bayes's Theorem and the Value of Additional Information

Another important application of Bayes's theorem and the inverse probability law in decision theory is their use to determine the value of additional information. It is a commonplace that having more facts on which to base a decision can make a radical difference to our choices. But how can we determine how much those facts are worth? The basic idea for a decision theoretic answer is this. In decisions under risk the choices we make are a function of the values we assign to outcomes and the probabilities we assign to states. As we obtain more information we often revise our probability assignments and, consequently, the choices made on that basis. Additional information may save us from serious mistakes, or it may leave our decisions unchanged. Often, by using Bayes's theorem or the inverse probability law, we can calculate how our probabilities and decisions would change if we had an additional piece of information and how much our expectations would be raised. The latter may be used to determine upper bounds on the value of that information. There are many applications of this technique ranging from evaluating diagnostic tests in medicine to designing surveys for business and politics to the evaluation of scientific research programs. The following example is a simple illustration of the method used.

Clark is deciding whether to invest $50,000 in the Daltex Oil Company. The company is a small one owned by some acquaintances of his, and Clark has heard a rumor that Daltex will sell shares of stock publicly within the year. If that happens he will double his money; otherwise he will earn only the unattractive return of 5% for the year and would be better off taking his other choice— buying a 10% savings certificate. He believes there is about an even chance that Daltex will go public. This has led him to decision table 3-3. Clark makes his

3-3	Daltex Goes Public	Does Not
Invest in Daltex	$100,000 .5	$52,500 .5
Buy a Savings Certificate	$55,000 .5	$55,000 .5

decisions on the basis of expected monetary values; so he has tentatively decided to invest in Daltex since that has an EMV of $76,250. Suppose he could pay some completely reliable person to tell him now whether Daltex will go public.

As things now stand, he is looking at an EMV of $76,250. But if he learned that Daltex was certain to go public, his EMV would increase to $100,000, whereas if he learned that it was certain not to go public, he would buy the savings certificate and decrease his EMV to $55,000. As of now, he believes that he has an even chance of learning either piece of information. Thus his expectations prior to paying the completely reliable person for the truth about Daltex are $100,000(.5) + $55,000(.5) or $77,500. This is an increase of $1,250 over his current expectation of $76,250. Learning the truth about Daltex in order to revise his decision is thus not worth more to him than $1,250.

So far we have not used Bayes's theorem or the inverse probability law, so let us change the example. Now let us suppose that Clark knows Daltex is preparing a confidential annual report and he also knows that if they are going public there is a chance of .9 that they will say so in the report and only a .1 chance that they will deny it. On the other hand, if they are not going public there is a chance of .5 that they will say that they are not and .5 chance that they will lie and say they are.

Clark knows someone in Daltex who will show him a copy of the report—for a price. So he decides to use Bayes's theorem to calculate the probabilities that Daltex will (will not) go public given that they say (deny) that they will in the report. Where P stands for their going public, Y stands for their saying they will, and D stands for their denying it, he obtains

$$P(P/Y) = \frac{P(P) \times P(Y/P)}{P(P) \times P(Y/P) + P(\text{not } P) \times P(Y/\text{not } P)}$$

$$= \frac{.5 \times .9}{.5 \times .9 + .5 \times .5} = .64 + .$$

Similarly, $P(\text{not } P/Y) = .35 +$; $P(P/N) = .16 +$; $P(\text{not } P/N) = .83 +$. Clark then considers two revised decision tables—one based on the probabilities he would use after reading an affirmation of going public, the other based on those he would use after reading a denial. He finds that on either version the EMV of investing in Daltex would still be higher than that of buying the savings certificate. So he decides not to offer the bribe.

By changing the example appropriately we can arrange for Clark to discover that reading a denial in the report would change his original decision. He would then proceed as in the first version of the example to calculate the gains he can expect under the two scenarios and average these to find the maximum price he should pay to see the report.

As the example illustrates, applications of this method can become quite complicated. When nonmonetary values are involved, as happens in medicine or science, it may also be necessary to enlist some advanced ideas in utility theory. So I will not discuss the topic of the value of additional information further in this book.

PROBLEMS

1. Suppose $P(Y/P) = .01$, $P(N/P) = .99$, $P(Y/$ not $P) = .5$, and $P(N/$ not $P) = .5$. How much should Clark be willing to pay to see the report?
2. A closet contains 800 type I urns and 200 type two urns. Urns of both types appear identical but type I urns contain six blue balls and four red ones; type II urns contain one blue ball and nine red ones. An urn is drawn at random from the closet and you must bet on the type of the urn. If you bet on type I and it is one, you win $20, otherwise you lose $10. If you bet on type II and it is one, you win $80, otherwise you lose $10. Assume that you maximize expected monetary values.
   a. Set up a decision table for the choice between the two bets and calculate the EMVs of the two bets. Which one would you choose?
   b. Prior to making your choice, what is the maximum amount you should pay to learn the type of the urn?
   c. Assume that a blue ball has been drawn from the urn. Appropriately revise your table and calculate the new EMVs. Which bet would you choose now?
   d. Assume that the ball drawn is red and and then follow the rest of the instructions for c.
   e. Prior to seeing the ball and making your choice, what is the maximum amount that you should pay to see it?

3-2c. Statistical Decision Theory and Decisions under Ignorance

Several of the rules for making decisions under ignorance were originally developed by statisticians for handling statistical problems in which some of the data necessary for applying Bayes's theorem are unavailable. I will illustrate their thinking with a typical problem in applied statistics – the predicament faced by a drug company that needs to test a new batch of pills prior to marketing them. Let us suppose that we own such a company and our laboratory staff has just manufactured a new batch of pills. Their usual practice is to test new lots by feeding some of the pills to a hundred rats and observing how many die. From their previous experience with this and similar drugs, they have developed good estimates of the percentage of rats that will die if the batch is defective. Unfortunately, due to an irregularity in making this particular batch, our staff has no idea of the probability of its being defective. Suppose the test is run and five rats die. Since the rats in our laboratory die from time to time from various other causes, the staff cannot be certain that the pills are defective. Can they use the test results to calculate the probability of the batch's being defective? They could use Bayes's theorem if they could assign a probability to the batch's being defective *prior* to running the test. But that is exactly the probability they cannot assign.

Bayesian statisticians would urge our staff to try to use their best hunches as the prior probability that the batch is defective. And they could even offer some methods for refining and checking these hunches.

Many statisticians dissent from this recommendation and urge that the problem be treated as one under ignorance. But it is not as simple as a two-act/two-state choice of marketing or not marketing the pills against the possibilities of the batch's being fine or being defective for that would not respond to the test results. They have proposed that prior to running the test we should choose between various strategies for responding to the test results. For instance, we might adopt the strategy of marketing the pills no matter how many rats die or marketing them if no more than two die or not marketing them at all. Then after the test is run we market or withhold the pills according to the prescriptions of the strategy we have selected. This allows the test results to influence our actions without depending on guesses as to the prior probability that the batch is defective.

But how do we choose a strategy? We presumably know the value of marketing defective (or good) pills and the value of withholding them. Also we can use the probabilities that various percentages of the rats die given that the batch is defective (or fine) to calculate the various expected values of our strategies under the assumption that the batch is defective, and we can make similar calculations under the assumption that it is fine. Using this we can form decision table 3-4. Finally, we can apply one of the rules for making decisions under ignorance to this table.

3-4	Batch Defective	Batch Fine
Strategy 1	x	y
Strategy 2	z	w
	⋮	⋮
Strategy n	u	v

Now this certainly does not settle the philosophical and methodological issues raised by the absence of prior probabilities. For we must once again face the question of the proper rule to use for making our decision under ignorance. We will not pursue that question further here, although we will examine more closely the Bayesian case for the use of subjective priors.

PROBLEMS

1. Suppose you formulate strategies as depending on whether fewer than ten rats die or whether ten or more die. This yields four strategies. Two are: (1) market if fewer than ten die; market if ten or more die; (2) market if fewer than ten die; withhold if ten or more die. List the remaining two.

2. Suppose that the probability that ten or more rats die given that the batch is defective is .5 and that it is .01 given that the batch is fine. Construct two tables—one assuming that the batch is defective, the other that it is fine—that

will tabulate your probabilities of marketing and withholding the pills under each strategy. (For example, in the row for strategy 2 of the first table there is a probability of .5 that you will market and one of .5 that you will withhold.) These tables give your *action probabilities*.

3. Now assume that your value for marketing a defective batch is $-1,000$, for marketing a fine one is 100, for withholding a defective one is 0, and for withholding a fine one is -100. Use these values and your action probabilities to calculate the expected values for each strategy under the assumption that the batch is defective. Do the same under the assumption that it is fine. (For example, the first value for the second strategy is -500 or $[.5][-1000] + [.5][0]$.) This should enable you to complete table 3-5. If

3-5	Batch Defective	Batch Fine
Strategy 1		
Strategy 2	-500	
Strategy 3		
Strategy 4		

you use the maximin rule, which strategy do you choose? Do you think this is the only reasonable choice to make in this situation?

3-3. Interpretations of Probability

There are many contending views concerning what probability statements mean, when and how they may be applied, and how their truth may be ascertained. I will not pretend to resolve the complicated and heated debate that surrounds the various views on probability. Here I will only review several of the major views and discuss some of the objections that have been raised against them.

I will classify the interpretations of probability as *objective* or *subjective*. The *objective* interpretations see probability as measuring something independent of human judgments, and constant from person to person. The *subjective* views regard probability as the measure of an individual's belief or confidence in a statement and permit it to vary from person to person. Objective views are further classified as *logical* or *empirical*, according to whether they count probability as a property defined in terms of logical or mathematical structures or as an empirically defined property. To illustrate these distinctions, suppose I assert the statement:

The probability that 2/3 of the next 100 tosses of this coin will land head up is .75.

Subjective views will construe this as meaning that I am reasonably confident that 2/3 of the tosses will result in heads. Logical views will see it as reflecting a logical or mathematical analysis of the various possible tosses and (perhaps) my evidence concerning them. Finally, the empirical views will see my claim as about the behavior of the coin and as testable in terms of it.

Until quite recently probability theorists maintained that a satisfactory interpretation of probability must satisfy the probability calculus. The views I will discuss do, and I will show this by verifying that each interpretation satisfies the axioms of the calculus. Since the theorems of the calculus follow logically from the axioms, any interpretation that makes the latter true must verify the former as well.

3-3a. The Classical View

The classical interpretation of probability, also known as the Laplacean view after one of its founders, is the oldest and simplest view of probability. It is an objective and logical view, which is best applied to games of chance and other clearly specified situations that can be divided into a number of equally likely cases. We have used it implicitly in illustrating the probability calculus, since most of our examples have concerned random card drawings, tosses of fair coins, and rolls of unloaded dice, where one can reasonably assume that each card has an equal chance of being drawn and that each face of the coin or die has an equal chance of landing up.

To state the view in its general form, let us think of each statement as having a finite set of possibilities associated with it. For example, the statement "The coin will land heads in at least one of the next two tosses" is associated with the four possible outcomes of tossing the coin twice (HH, HT, TH, TT). Some of the possibilities associated with a statement verify it, others falsify it. Thus the possibility of getting two heads (HH) verifies the statement about the coin, while the possibility of getting two tails (TT) falsifies it. Given a statement p and the possibilities associated with it, let us call those that verify it the p-cases. Then the classical view may be put as the claim that the probability of p is the ratio of the number of p-cases to the total number of cases or possibilities:

$$P(p) = \#(p\text{-cases})/\#(\text{total possibilities}).$$

We must interpret conditional probability too, since it figures in the axioms of the calculus. Ordinarily, $P(q/p)$ is the number of p-cases that are also q-cases. However, when there are no p-cases, it is zero. This leads to:

$$P(q/p) = \#(p \ \& \ q\text{-cases})/\#(p\text{-cases}) \text{ if } \#(p\text{-cases}) > 0,$$
$$= 0 \text{ if } \#(p\text{-cases}) = 0.$$

To see that this works, consider the probability that the card you have drawn is an ace given that it is a heart. This is just the ratio of the number of aces of hearts to the number of hearts, that is 1/13.

Before discussing the philosophical objections to the classical view let us verify that it does satisfy the probability calculus. That comes to showing that each axiom of the calculus becomes true when interpreted by construing "$P(p)$" and "$P(q/p)$" as previously defined. This is easy to see in the case of axiom 1. For the number of possibilities associated with a statement is never negative and the number of p-cases (p & q-cases) never exceeds the total number of cases (the number of p-cases). Thus $P(p)$ [$P(q/p)$] must be a number between 0 and 1 inclusively.

Axiom 2 is easily verified too. A certainty is true no matter what; thus the cases in which it is true must be identical with all the cases associated with it and the ratio of the number of the one to that of the other must be 1.

Turning now to axiom 3, we must remember that in the probability calculus "p or q" is construed as meaning that either p is true, q is true, or *both* p and q are true. The probability of "p or q" is then the ratio of the number of (p or q)-cases to the total number. If p and q are mutually exclusive (as the condition on axiom 3 states), the (p or q)-cases are simply the cases in which either p or q (but not the other) is true. Thus we have:

$$P(p \text{ or } q) = \#[(p \text{ or } q)\text{-cases}]/\#(\text{total cases})$$
$$= \#(p\text{-cases})/\#(\text{total cases}) + \#(q\text{-cases})/\#(\text{total cases})$$
$$= P(p) + P(q),$$

which verifies axiom 3.

This leaves axiom 4. To verify it let us distinguish two cases: those p for which there are no p-cases and those for which there are some. In the first case, both $P(p)$ and $P(q/p)$ are 0. Furthermore, since every p & q-case is a p-case, $P(p \text{ & } q)$ is 0 too. Thus

$$P(p \text{ & } q) = 0 = P(p) \times P(q/p),$$

which verifies axiom 4 for this case.

In the second case,

$$P(q/p) = \#(p \text{ & } q\text{-cases})/\#(p\text{-cases}),$$

but we also have

$$P(p \text{ & } q) = \#(p \text{ & } q\text{-cases})/\#(\text{total cases})$$
$$P(p) = \#(p\text{-cases})/\#(\text{total cases}).$$

Whence we obtain

$$P(p) \times P(q/p) = \#(p\text{-cases})/\#(\text{total cases}) \times \#(p \text{ & } q\text{-cases})/\#(p\text{-cases})$$
$$= \#(p \text{ & } q\text{-cases})/\#(\text{total cases})$$
$$= P(p \text{ & } q).$$

This establishes that axiom 4 holds for both of the cases we distinguished and completes the demonstration that the classical interpretation satisfies the probability calculus.

PROBLEMS

1. Use the technique of this section to show directly that theorem 1 holds under the classical interpretation.
2. Do the same for theorem 2.

Now let us turn to the objections to this approach. Some can be overcome by enlisting the technical machinery of modern logic and mathematics, but others remain obstacles to the acceptance of even up-dated versions of the classical view.

Taking up a relatively technical problem first, the present version assumes that a definite finite set of possibilities is associated with each statement. That seems a simple enough matter when we are talking about tossing coins, spinning roulette wheels, or drawing cards. But what happens when we are talking about the probability of another world war, being successful in a career or marriage, or even of a drought? What are the relevant possibilities here? And how do we combine the possibilities needed for compound statements? How do we relate the probability that you will have a good career and the probability that you will have a happy marriage to the probability that you will have both? The classical view has no ready answers to these questions.

The situation is worse: The classical view even has problems with the simple questions which it was designed to handle. For example, how do we compute the probability of getting two heads in two tosses of the same fair coin? One computation could run as follows: There are four cases: *HH, HT, TH*, and *TT*; only one is verifying, so the probability is 1/4. *But there is another computation*: There are three cases: *HH, HT*, and *TT*; thus the probability is 1/3. Of course, we all know that the first computation is the right one, because it is based on the relevant set of possibilities. *But the classical view does not tell us that.* (By the way, the possibilities in the second set are mutually exclusive and exhaustive, so we cannot fault it on those grounds.)

In recent years logicians have partially solved the problem of specifying sets of relevant possibilities. They have used precise, limited, and technical languages for formulating those statements to which probabilities are to be assigned and then have defined the associated sets of possibilities in terms of statements within such languages. For example, to describe the tosses of a coin we can introduce a language with two individual constants, "*a*" and "*b*" — one to designate the side that comes up on the first toss, the other to designate the one that comes up on the second toss — and one predicate "*H*" for heads. (Tails can be expressed as "not *H*.") Then the relevant set of possibilities for two tosses of the coin can be specified as those statements of the language that affirm or deny that the coin comes up heads on either toss. These yield the four possibilities: *Ha, Hb*; *Ha*, not *Hb*; not *Ha, Hb*; not *Ha*, not *Hb*.

This method is clearly limited by our ability to construct artificial languages and specify possibilities within them. We would feel that limitation acutely were we to try to use the classical approach to assign probabilities to statements involving an indefinite or infinite number of cases. Try, for instance, to assign a probability to the statement that there will be an atomic holocaust *sometime*. It is not inconceivable, however, that technical developments in logic will solve such problems eventually.

There is another objection that technical developments cannot avert. The classical approach and its modern descendants depend on the assumption that each of the possibilities associated with a statement is *equally likely*. This is used, for example, in assigning a probability of 1/2 to getting heads on a toss of a fair coin, since the calculation assumes that we should give equal weight to getting heads and to getting tails. But how do we know that each case is equally likely? And what does "equally likely" mean in this context? We cannot appeal to the classical view and say " 'equally likely' means that they have the same probability" without involving ourselves in a circle.

Two courses are open to the classical view. The first consists in invoking some other conception of probability to explain and justify the assumption that each case is equally likely. Thus one might state that the claim that getting heads is just as likely as getting tails means that in a long series of tosses of the coin, the proportion of heads will be approximately the same as the proportion of tails. Somebody who took this position might then continue by adding that the classical view is, strictly speaking, an idealization of a more properly experimental approach to probability. Since ratios determined experimentally are often "messy," the classical approach is to be used as a shortcut approximation.

Some adherents of the classical view have offered a second response. They have claimed that the assignment of the same weight to each possibility is simply an assumption that is so fundamental that further attempts to justify it are fruitless. Some have even gone so far as to claim that this assumption—which they have dubbed the *principle of insufficient reason*—is self-evident. I hope that the relationship of this principle to the homonymous rule for decisions under ignorance is clear. I find the principle no more compelling in the context of probability theory than I found its relative in the earlier context.

3-3b. *The Relative Frequency View*

One trouble with the classical view is that it is devoid of empirical content. Because its probabilities are ultimately ratios involving abstract possibilities, a classically interpreted probability statement has no implications concerning actual events and can be neither confirmed nor refuted by them. The relative frequency view is an objective and empirical view that was developed in response to this need; it defines probability in terms of actual events.

To state this view with some precision we must assign probabilities to either classes, kinds, or properties of events rather than to statements. Furthermore, we must view all probabilities as implicitly conditional. This entails modifying our presentation of the probability calculus by replacing statements of the respective forms

$$P(S) = a \text{ and } P(S/W) = b$$

with ones of the forms

$$P_R(S) = a \text{ and } P_R(S/W) = b,$$

and reading these as

the probability that an R is an S equals a;
the probability that an R is an S given that it is a W equals b.

With this modification probability statements no longer make assertions about statements but instead make assertions about classes, properties, or kinds of events. For example, instead of saying the probability assigned to the statement that this coin will land heads on the next toss is 1/2, the frequentist says the probability that a toss of this coin (an event) is one in which it lands heads (another event) is 1/2. This variation on our original approach to the probability calculus is not sufficient to count for or against the frequency approach.

Relative frequentists hold that probabilities are proportions or relative frequencies of events of one kind to those of others. Their interpretation of probability is thus

$P_R(P) = a$ means the proportion of Rs that are Ps is a,
  i.e., $\#(P \ \& \ Rs)/\#(Rs) = a$.

The interpretation of conditional probability is just

$P_R(Q/P) = \#(P \ \& \ Q \ \& \ Rs)/\#(P \ \& \ Rs)$.
  $= 0$ if nothing is both a P and an R.

To illustrate this conception of probability consider the statements:

1. The probability that an airplane flying from New York to London crashes is 1/1,000,000
2. The probability that an airplane flying from New York to London crashes given that it has engine failure is 1/10.

The first predicts that if we were to inspect the record of flights from New York to London we would find that only one in a million crashes, while the second predicts that if we were to keep a record of those flights from New York to London that also experienced engine failures, we would find that the crash rate increased to 1 in 10. Plainly, this approach to probability is very different from the classical approach.

Verifying that the relative frequency interpretation satisfies the axioms of the probability calculus follows the model set earlier for the classical view. The relative frequency interpretation of $P_R(P)$ is concerned with the proportion of events of kind P among those of kind R; it is thus a ratio between 0 and 1 inclusively. Since the same is easily shown for $P_R(Q/P)$ as well, the interpretation satisfies axiom 1. Turning to axiom 2, if every R is certain to be a P, then the ratio of Ps to Rs is 1 and $P_R(P) = 1$.

To verify axiom 3 we must show that

$P_R(P \text{ or } Q) = P_R(P) + P_R(Q)$

when no event can be both a P and a Q. But this just means showing that the proportion of Ps among the Rs plus the proportion of Qs among the Rs is just the proportion of the $(P \text{ or } Q)$s among the Rs. And that must certainly be the case when no R can be both P and Q.

The verification of axiom 4 parallels the verification of the classical interpretation of that axiom. I leave it as an exercise.

PROBLEMS

1. Verify axiom 4.
2. Do the same for theorem 2.

Given the way in which it has been specified, the relative frequency view is bound to have problems with indefinite and infinite totalities. Even determining the frequency of heads in the tosses of the dime on my desk presents difficulties, for no one can currently specify its total number of tosses. However, mathematical improvements on the relative frequency view can handle cases like this one and give them empirical content. Very roughly, we toss the coin again and again and after each toss note the proportion of heads among the tosses to that point. If these ratios appear to be tending to a limit point, then that limit is identified with the probability of getting heads on a given toss of the coin. We might call this "the long-run frequency" approach to probability.

Either frequency approach has the obvious advantage over the classical view of not being circular. Nor does the frequency approach require dubious assumptions, such as the principle of insufficient reason, and it extends to the indefinite/infinite case with greater ease than does the classical approach. On the other hand, the relative frequency approach has a less firm grip on "true" probabilities than the classical approach. To see what I mean, consider the question again of the frequency of heads in tosses of the dime on my desk. A theorem of the probability calculus entails that if the probability of heads is 1/2, the frequencies of these tosses will converge to 1/2 in the long run. However, another theorem entails that ultimate convergence to 1/2 is compatible with any initial finite sequence of tosses consisting entirely of *heads*. Now suppose my dime were tossed 10,000 times and it came up heads 90% of the time. Most relative frequentists would be willing to stop the tossing, proclaim that the coin is most probably biased and that the true probability of heads is close to 9/10. But it could turn out that after the first 10,000 tosses heads start to appear so often that the long-run frequency is 1/2. On the frequency view, 1/2 would be the true probability, although the initial observations belied it. Putting the point more generally, *there is simply no guarantee that the frequencies observed to date are even close to the long-run frequency.*

The classical view does not face this problem because it cuts itself off from observation. But that does not seem to be much of an advantage either; for if my dime did turn up heads on every one of 10,000 tosses, even fans of the classical view would be hard pressed to justify taking 1/2 as the probability of getting heads. (But they would not be without any defense. They could recheck their analyses and stand fast, since on any view of probability such a run of heads on tosses of a fair coin is *possible* though not very probable.)

Since the frequency view specifies probabilities in terms of proportions, it cannot make sense of assigning probabilities to single events or statements. Thus if you ask a frequentist what is the probability that you will pass your final exam in English, he will respond that he can only speak to you of the percentage of students in the course that will pass, or of the percentage of those tests you take that you pass, or of the percentage of those like you in certain relevant respects who will pass, and so on. But he will refuse to assign a probability to the single case of your passing.

Several of these problems can be averted while retaining an empirical account of probability by turning to the *propensity* interpretations of probability. One version of this view construes probabilities as the frequencies predicted by the relevant theoretical laws. Since predicted frequencies may differ from those actually observed, this account is not thrown by my dime coming up heads on the first 10,000 tosses. Of course, that happening with most dimes would strongly signal something wrong with any theory that predicts a frequency of 1/2, and we would take steps to revise it. The propensity view responds to observation without following it slavishly.

The so-called *single-case propensity* interpretation even countenances assigning probabilities to single events. Consider my dime again. By taking advantage of its symmetry and the laws of physics one should be able to design a device for tossing it that would favor neither heads nor tails. Such a device would, we might say, have a propensity of 1/2 to yield heads on its tosses. More important, however, it would have a propensity of 1/2 to yield a head *on any particular toss*. By identifying probabilities with such single-case propensities we could make sense of assigning probabilities to single events.

Unfortunately, there are limits to the applicability of the propensity approach too. Often we do not know enough to discern propensities. Physicians, for instance, know that heart disease is much more frequent among heavy smokers, but currently they have no way of knowing whether any individual heavy smoker has a higher propensity for developing heart disease than some other one does. Also it does not always make sense to speak of propensities where we can significantly speak of probabilities. Thus wondering about the probability of the truth of the theory of relativity seems to make sense, but wondering about its propensity to be true does not.

3-3c. Subjective Views

The logical approach to probability fails in situations where we lack the analytic resources it presupposes. The frequency approach breaks down on single-case probabilities, whereas the propensity approach fails to cover cases where propensities are not known or do not make sense. The subjective approach to probability is an attempt to develop a notion of probability that meets all these challenges. Subjective probabilities are personal assessments. Since we can have and often do have our own estimates of the probability that something is true even when that thing is a single case or when we lack any theory or logical analysis concerning it, the subjective approach bypasses the impediments to the previous views.

Offhand, however, it would seem that a subjective view of probability would immediately encounter insurmountable difficulties. How can personal assessments be subjected to critical evaluation? How can they produce a concept of probability of use to scientists and decision makers? How can they be measured—at all—or with enough accuracy to furnish appropriate numerical inputs for the probability calculus? In the last sixty years logicians, mathematicians, and statisticians have made remarkable progress toward dealing with these questions.

The connection between belief, desire, and action is well known to psychologists and philosophers. There are boundless illustrations. If you believe your water supply has been poisoned, you will resist attempts to make you drink from it even though you may be quite thirsty. If you cross a street, we can reasonably infer that you want to get to the other side and believe it is safe to cross. Frank Ramsey was the first theorist to use these connections to construct a subjective theory of probability. Ramsey realized that our degrees of belief (or confidence) in statements are connected with certain of our actions—the bets we make. If, for example, you believe a certain horse is very likely to win a race, you are likely to accept a bet at less than even money. The more likely you think the horse is to win, the less favorable odds you will accept. Now if we identify your personal probabilities with the odds you are willing to accept, by asking you about the various odds you would accept, we may be able to measure your personal probabilities. Ramsey managed to parlay this into a full case for subjective probabilities.

We are used to betting on the outcome of events, such as races, football games, or elections. But there is no reason in principle why we cannot bet on the truth of statements too. For instance, instead of betting on Fancy Dancer to win in the third race, I can bet that the statement *Fancy Dancer wins the third race* is true. If I am willing to set odds on enough statements and do so in a certain way, it can be shown that my odds constitute probability assignments to those statements and obey the probability calculus. I will present Bruno DeFinetti's proof of this rather than Ramsey's, since the latter's is intertwined with his treatment of utility.

DeFinetti's reasoning deals with an agent in a situation in which he must place a series of bets on a certain set of initial statements as well as all negations, conjunctions, disjunctions, and conditional bets that can be formed using these statements. Let us suppose, for example, that you are the agent in question and the initial statements are

Jones will win the match.
Smith will win the match.
The crowd will be large.

Then you will be expected to bet not only on those three statements but also on the statements

Jones will not win the match.
Smith will win the match or Jones will win the match.
Jones will win the match and the crowd will not be large.

In addition you will be expected to take conditional bets such as

Jones will win given that the crowd is large,

Jones will not win given that the crowd is large and Smith does not win,

and so on, for all of the infinitely many bets that are constructible from the initial set.

For future reference, let us call the set of statements on which the agent is expected to bet the *DeFinetti closure* of the initial set of statements. Given a set of statements A the DeFinetti closure of A, $DC(A)$, may be formally defined as follows:

1. Every statement in A is also in $DC(A)$.
2. If the statements S and W are in $DC(A)$, so are the statements not S, (S or W) and (S & W).
3. If S and W are in $DC(A)$, so is the phrase S given W.
4. Nothing is in $DC(A)$ unless its being so follows from 1-3.

With the DeFinetti closure behind us let us return to the agent, you. You are expected to place bets on every statement in the DeFinetti closure of your initial set with a "bookie." But here the situation changes dramatically from the usual betting situation. For you must post the odds on *all* the statements and conditional bets in the DeFinetti closure, and that is all you are permitted to do. Once you set the odds, *the bookie determines all the other features of the bet*, including the amount at stake on the various bets and who bets for or against a given statement.

The situation with respect to a particular bet on a single statement p can be summarized by means of table 3-6. The entries under the statement p are

3-6	p	Payoff for p	Payoff against p
	T	$(1-a)S$	$-(1-a)S$
	F	$-aS$	aS

simply the truth values, true and false; the other entries tell how much you (or the bookie) win or lose for the various outcomes. Thus if you are betting for p and p is false, you "win" $-aS$ and the bookie wins aS. Notice that the entries in a row under "for" and "against" are the negatives of each other, so that the person "for" always wins (or loses) an amount equal to that lost (or won) by the person "against." S is the stake for the bets, which is always some positive amount of money, aS and $(1-a)S$ are portions of the stake, and a is a number, called *the betting quotient* for p, the ratio of a to $1-a$ constitutes the odds you set for the statement p. (Note that $aS + (1-a)S = S$.) When you set the odds for the statement p at a to $1-a$, you must be prepared to lose a portion a of the stake S if p turns out to be false. The higher you set the betting quotient a, the greater portion of the stake you risk losing; so, presuming you are rational and prudent, you will not set high odds for a statement unless you are quite confident it is true.

The only feature of table 3-6 you control is the odds a to $1 - a$. The bookie not only fixes the amount S at stake but also decides who is to be for p and who is to be against p. (However, he cannot bet for p and also against p, nor can he force you to do so.) To complicate matters, remember that you must post odds for many statements and take many other bets at the terms the bookie sets.

Before considering the rest of DeFinetti's argument, let us use an example to relate our concepts to conventional betting odds. Suppose the Golden Circle Race Track posts odds of 99 to 1 on Fancy Dancer to win. This means that if the horse wins, the track will pay us $100 for every $1 "to win" ticket for that horse that we have purchased. The total stake for a $1 ticket is $100. We risk $1/100$ of it, the track risks $99/100$ of it. In our terms the track's betting quotient is $99/100$, and the odds are $99/100$ to $1/100$. More generally, suppose that in a conventional betting situation someone offers odds of a to b on a given outcome. Then they are willing to risk losing a portion $a/(a + b)$ of a stake in case the outcome fails to obtain so long as we are willing to risk losing the portion $b/(a + b)$ in case the outcome does obtain. In our terms the odds are $a/(a + b)$ to $b/(a + b)$ and the betting quotient is $a/(a + b)$.

Returning to DeFinetti's work, suppose you were in the kind of situation with which DeFinetti is concerned. Then a clever bookie might be able to arrange the bets so that he was bound to have a net gain no matter what happened. For instance, suppose you posted odds of $9/10$ to $1/10$ on a statement p and odds of $1/2$ to $1/2$ on its negation not p. Although the bookie cannot force you to bet for p and also against p, he can force you to bet for p and for not p. Suppose that he does and fixes the stake at $1. Then if p is true, he loses $.10 on his bet against p and wins $.50 on his bet against not p. That is a net gain of $.40. (Check and you will see that you will have a net loss of $.40.) On the other hand, if p is false, the bookie wins $.90 on his bet against p and loses $.50 on his bet against not p — again a net gain of $.40. The bookie has made a *Dutch Book* against you. You could have prevented this by posting odds of $1/10$ to $9/10$ on not p or odds of $1/2$ to $1/2$ on p, or any other combination of odds under which your betting quotients for p and not p summed to 1. In short, so long as your betting quotients for p and not p sum to 1, you have protected yourself against this type of Dutch Book. DeFinetti generalized this to prove the following:

DUTCH BOOK THEOREM. *Suppose that no Dutch Book can be made against an agent using the odds he posts on the DeFinetti closure of set of statements. Then his betting quotients for the DeFinetti closure in question satisfy the probability calculus.*

This means that the agent's betting quotients form a satisfactory interpretation of the probability calculus.

To establish the Dutch Book theorem, we will set

$P(p) =$ the agent's (your) betting quotient for $p = a$

and verify that $P(p)$ (i.e., a) satisfies the axioms of the probability calculus provided that no Dutch Book can be made against you.

Turning to axiom 1a, we must show that if no Dutch Book can be made against you,

$$0 \leq a \leq 1.$$

We will use an indirect proof to do this, however. We will first assume that $a < 0$ and show how to make a Dutch Book against you, and then assume that $a > 1$ and again show how to make a Dutch Book against you. This will be our general strategy: In each case, we will show that if your betting quotients violate one of the axioms of the probability calculus, a Dutch Book can be made against you.

Suppose then that $a < 0$. Then $-a > 0$, $(1 - a) > 1$, and both are positive. Now reconsider table 3-6 for the bets involving p. Since both the payoffs $-aS$ and $(1 - a)S$ are positive, the bookie can guarantee himself a net gain by betting for p at any positive stake S. (For simplicity, we will assume that the stake is 1.) Whether p is true or false, his payoffs are positive. Yours are negative, since you must bet against p.

On the other hand, if $a > 1$, then $1 - a < 0$ and both $-(1 - a)$ and a are positive. So the bookie can make a Dutch Book against you by betting against p. His payoffs, being in the column under "Payoff against p," are bound to be positive.

Let us deal with axiom 2 next. Let us suppose that p is certain and show that if your betting quotient for p is less than 1, a Dutch Book can be made against you. (We have already established that it cannot be greater than 1.)

Since p is certain, we know that the bottom row of table 3-6 will never apply. So we need only consider table 3-7. If $a < 1$, then $(1 - a)$ is positive;

3-7	p	Payoff for p	Payoff against p
	T	$(1 - a)$	$-(1 - a)$

clearly the bookie can make a Dutch Book against you by betting for p.

Stepping up in difficulty, let us turn to axiom 3. Here we are concerned with the probabilities of p, q, and their disjunction "p or q." Let a be your betting quotient for p, b the one for q and c that for "p or q." We must now use the next betting table (table 3-8) with three bets—one for each betting quotient. The payoffs under p and q are determined by referring to the columns under "p" and "q" to determine whether they are true or false, and then applying our original table (3-6) for a single statement. The payoffs under "p or q" are determined in the same way, but since it is true in the first three rows, its payoffs are the same in those rows. I have set the stakes at 1 throughout table 3-8.

3-8		p		q		p or q	
p	q	For	Against	For	Against	For	Against
T	T	$1-a$	$-(1-a)$	$1-b$	$-(1-b)$	$1-c$	$-(1-c)$
T	F	$1-a$	$-(1-a)$	$-b$	b	$1-c$	$-(1-c)$
F	T	$-a$	a	$1-b$	$-(1-b)$	$1-c$	$-(1-c)$
F	F	$-a$	a	$-b$	b	$-c$	c

Axiom 3 states that if p and q are mutually exclusive, $P(p$ or $q) = P(p)$ + $P(q)$. Thus we must show that if p and q are mutually exclusive and $c \neq a + b$, a Dutch Book can be made against you. Let us assume then that p and q are mutually exclusive. This means that the first row of betting table 3-8 never applies and can be ignored. Also assume that $c \neq a + b$. Then either $c < a + b$ or $c > a + b$. I will show how to construct a Dutch Book against you for the first case and leave the second case to you.

Since $c < a + b$, $(a + b) - c$ is positive. If the bookie bets against p and against q but for "p or q" his total payoffs for the last three rows of the table all equal $(a + b) - c$. (In the second row he is paid $-(1 - a)$, b, $1 - c$; these sum to

$$-1 + a + b + 1 - c = (a + b) - c.$$

Check the other rows.) Thus by betting as indicated, the bookie can guarantee himself a positive net gain no matter what the truth values of p and q turn out to be.

Before we can handle axioms 1b and 4, we must interpret $P(p/q)$ in terms of betting quotients. This involves the use of *conditional bets*, such as a bet you might make that a horse will win *given* that the track is dry. The bet is off if the track is not dry and nobody wins or loses. Similarly, we will construe a bet on "q given p" as on only when p is true, and then as won according to whether q is true or false. Using odds of a to $1 - a$ for the conditional bet "q given p," this leads to table 3-9—(we use payoffs of 0 to handle cases in which the bet is off).

3-9	p	q	For "q given p"	Against "q given p"
	T	T	$1-a$	$-(1-a)$
	T	F	$-a$	a
	F	T	0	0
	F	F	0	0

It is easy to see that if $a < 0$, the bookie can make a Dutch Book against you by betting for "q given p." It is also easy to show that he can make a Dutch Book against you if $a > 1$. Thus we know that axiom 1b must hold if we interpret "$P(q/p)$" as your betting quotient for "q given p."

Axiom 4 states that $P(p \& q) = P(p) \times P(q/p)$. To establish it, assume your betting quotient for "$p \& q$" is c, that for p is a, and that for "q given p" is b. Here is the relevant betting table (3-10). (There are zeros under "q given p" because it is a conditional bet.)

3-10

p	q	p For	p Against	q given p For	q given p Against	$p \& q$ For	$p \& q$ Against
T	T	$1-a$	$-(1-a)$	$1-b$	$-(1-b)$	$1-c$	$-(1-c)$
T	F	$1-a$	$-(1-a)$	$-b$	b	$-c$	c
F	T	$-a$	a	0	0	$-c$	c
F	F	$-a$	a	0	0	$-c$	c

We want to prove that if $c \neq ab$, a Dutch Book can be made against you. But no payoff is the product of any of the other payoffs, so our previous strategy for making Dutch Books does not seem applicable. But remember that the bookie is free to choose the stake for each bet. Until now we have let this equal 1 for the sake of simplicity. But now let us have the bookie set the stake at b for the bets on p. That changes the payoffs under p to

$$
\begin{array}{ll}
(1-a)b & -(1-a)b \\
(1-a)b & -(1-a)b \\
-ab & ab \\
-ab & ab.
\end{array}
$$

Now suppose $c \neq ab$. Then as before $c < ab$ or $c > ab$. Suppose that the first case holds. Then $ab - c$ is positive. So if the bookie bets against p, against "q given p," and for "$p \& q$," he will be paid $ab - c$ no matter what. (Check this.) This means that he can make a Dutch Book against you. The case where $c > ab$ is handled similarly and is left to you as an exercise.

PROBLEMS

1. Return to the Dutch Book argument for axiom 3 and complete the case for $c > a + b$ that I left as an exercise.
2. Construct Dutch Book arguments to show that $0 \leq a \leq 1$, where a is your betting quotient for "q given p."
3. Carry out the check I asked you to make in the argument for axiom 4.

4. Complete the argument for axiom 4 for the case when $c > ab$.
5. Give a Dutch Book argument to establish directly each of the following:
   a. If p is impossible, $P(p) = 0$.
   b. $P(p) + P(\text{not } p) = 1$.
   c. If p logically implies q, $P(p) \leq P(q)$.

3-3d. Coherence and Conditionalization

DeFinetti called an agent's betting quotients *coherent* in case no Dutch Book can be made against him. We can summarize DeFinetti's theorem as showing that if an agent's subjective probabilities (betting quotients) are coherent, they obey the probability calculus. Now coherence is a very plausible condition of (idealized) rationality, since few of us think that it would make sense to place ourselves in a position where we were bound to suffer a net loss on our bets. If we accept coherence as a condition of rationality, DeFinetti's conclusion can be paraphrased as *the laws of probability are necessary conditions for rationality*.

Since DeFinetti first proved his theorem others have proved that having subjective probabilities that obey the probability calculus is also sufficient for coherence. In other words, if an agent picks his betting quotients so as to satisfy the laws of probability, no Dutch Book can be made against him. This is called the *converse Dutch Book theorem*. I will leave it as additional reading for those of you who are studying to be bookies. (Note: We proved that if the agent did *not* pick his betting quotients thus, a Dutch Book can be made against him.)

Rational people modify their degrees of belief (subjective probabilities) in the light of new data. Whereas it would be reasonable for me to be quite confident that my spanking new car will not break down before I get it home, I would be much less confident about this if someone told me my new car was actually a "lemon" that had just been returned to the dealer. In view of this we might ask whether there are any rules for modifying subjective probabilities in the light of new data. One very popular proposal is that we use the following *rule of conditionalization*: Suppose that D is the conjunction of the statements describing the new data. Then for each statement p, take $P_N(p) = P_O(p/D)$. In other words, let the new probabilities be the old probabilities conditional on the data. Notice that since $P(D/D) = 1$, this rule has the effect of assigning the probability of 1 to the data.

If we replace "$P(p)$" with "$P(p/D)$" and "$P(q/p)$" with "$P(q/p \text{ \& } D)$" in every axiom of the probability calculus, the formulas we obtain will be laws of probability too. This means that if we use the rule of conditionalization to modify our subjective probabilities, the new ones will obey the laws of probability too, and thus by the converse Dutch Book theorem will be coherent. A reason favoring using conditionalization to change our probabilities, then, is that it guarantees the coherence of our new probabilities.

There is also a Dutch Book argument supporting conditionalization, but it depends on our willingness to bridge our old and new probabilities with bets. To see how it runs, suppose you have revised the probability of D to 1, that of p to a, and that your old $P(p/D)$ was b. Now if $a \neq b$, and if the bookie knows this in advance, he can make a Dutch Book against you. Here is how. Before the truth of D is known, he places two bets that are not to take effect until D is verified: one for p—if $a < b$—or against p—if $a > b$; the other placed oppositely on "p given D." He sets the stakes at \$1. Then after D is verified, his payoffs on each bet will be determined according to whether p is true. Thus he will win one bet and lose the other, but because of his choices and your bad odds he will have a net gain. For example, if $a < b$, and p is true, he is paid $1 - a$ from the bet for p and $-(1 - b)$ from the bet against "p given D." His net is $b - a$, which is positive. He receives the same net if p is false, since the first bet pays $-a$ and the second b.

If D does not come true, the bookie neither gains nor loses since none of his bets are in effect. But he can assure himself of a gain even then by placing a side bet against D. Suppose that c is your betting quotient for D and d is $1/2$ the absolute difference between a and b. Then the bookie sets the stake for the bet on D at $d/(1 - c)$. If D is false, he is paid $c[d/(1 - c)]$, which is positive. If D is true, he is paid $-(1 - c)[d/(1 - c)]$ (i.e., $-d$) from the bet on D and the absolute difference between a and b (i.e., $2d$) from his other two bets. Although $-d$ is negative, his net winnings are d and that is positive.

Let me summarize what has been established so far. If an agent's subjective probability assignments are rational in the sense of being coherent, then it follows, by the Dutch Book theorem, that they obey the laws of the probability calculus. Furthermore, by the converse Dutch Book theorem, obeying the laws of probability is sufficient for having coherent subjective probabilities. What is more, using the rule of conditionalization will allow an agent to form new coherent probability assignments as he learns new data and will protect him against future Dutch Books. Finally, since subjective probabilities are defined in terms of publicly observable betting behavior, they can be measured and objectively known.

PROBLEMS

1. Show that we obtain a law of the probability calculus when $P(p/D)$ is substituted for $P(p)$ in axiom 1a.
2. Do the same for axiom 2.
3. Do the same for axiom 3.

Have we made much of a case for the subjective approach? Is not coherence such a loose requirement that probability assignments based on it are useless for scientists and decision makers? If I am coherent in my betting at a racetrack, even if I bet on all the horses, the track will not be assured of a profit—no matter what. But I might lose my shirt, all the same. If prior to a match race between a Kentucky Derby prospect and my old nag, I assign a 90% chance of winning to the old nag and a 10% chance to the racehorse, then I am coherent. Yet unless I know something very unusual about the race (such as that the racehorse has been given a horse-sized dosage of sleeping pills), I would be foolish to take bets at those odds.

This example suggests that coherence is not a strong enough requirement for rationally assigning probabilities. There is a sense in which it would be irrational for me to set those odds on the old nag. (Of course, I might belie my true beliefs because I did not want to let the old fellow down by showing my lack of confidence in him. But I am assuming that such considerations do not intrude here.) The subjectivist has a response to this objection, however. The irrationality we sense in this example will be a genuine case of incoherence when we consider the other information I possess about horses and horseraces and my probability assignments to other statements. Since I know a fair bit about horses, I know that healthy young racehorses such as this one, participating in a normal match race against an old tired horse, are (virtually) certain to win. Given that, I should assign a probability of (nearly) 1 to the racehorse winning. My current probability assignment would not cohere with the probabilities I assign to other statements about horses and horseraces.

But what about those who know nothing about horses? What should they do at the track? Says the subjectivist: First of all, they should bet coherently. Then they should try to learn more about the horses and about horses in general. As they acquire new information, they should modify their probability assignments. If they use conditionalization, they can be assured of preserving coherence. Furthermore, the convergence theorems we mentioned in connection with Bayes's theorem may apply. If so, in the long run their odds are likely to be as good as those of the experts.

More boldly put, the convergence theorems show that in a wide class of cases, a person can start with completely heretical probability assignments, modify them by conditionalizing, and be assured in the long run of converging to the probabilities used by the experts. Subjectivists appeal to this to argue that subjective probabilities are suitable for scientists and decision makers. Convergence implies that those who derive their probabilities from observed frequencies will tend to agree in the long run with those who initially use hunches— provided, of course, that the latter use the data furnished by their frequentist colleagues. Consequently, subjectivists can provide empirically based probabilities whenever anyone can. That should satisfy scientists. But, it can be argued, subjectivists can do more: They can assign probabilities where frequencies, propensities, or logically based measures are unavailable or in principle unattainable.

Decision makers ask for nothing more than probabilities furnished by the "experts," and, in the long run, subjectivists can give them that. Moreover, and this can be crucial, they can supply probabilities in cases where frequentists, logicists, or propensity theorists must stand by with their hands in their pockets.

The capstone of the subjectivist defense consists in noting that subjective elements intrude in the ascertainment of so-called objective probabilities too. Under the classical view, we must choose the "equiprobable" possibilities to assign to a statement. This choice is based on a personal and subjective judgment that we have the right set of possibilities and that they are *equiprobable*, since the classical view fails to supply any methods for associating a set of equiprobable possibilities with a given statement. Similarly, when we decide, after seeing a coin land heads on 511 of 1,000 tosses, that the long-run relative frequency of heads is 1/2, we are making a personal assessment of the *probable* future behavior of the coin. Also we must decide whether a theory is sufficiently *probable* given the evidence for it before we can accept the claims it makes about propensities. In short, the application of objective probabilities is dependent on subjective ones. Subjective probabilities are thus both fundamental and unavoidable.

This is a persuasive argument—one that should make us seriously consider the merits of the subjective approach—but it is not airtight. Subjectivists are right, I think, in claiming that in applying the objective theories of probability, we will often be faced with decisions that are not clear-cut. That in turn could lead different people to make different probability assignments. But it does not follow from this that it is never possible to objectively ground probability assignments, and that is what subjectivists must show for their point to stick.

Furthermore, the subjective approach faces some problems of its own that are not unlike those faced by the previous views. First, subjectivists' assurances about long-run convergence may fail to work out in practice. If the initial probabilities are widely divergent and the data either sparse or inconclusive, convergence may not come until long after a decision based on the probabilities in question is due.

Second, there is a plethora of statements for which we can set betting quotients at values that do not comply with the probability calculus without having to worry about being trapped in a Dutch Book. A bet on whether the heat death of the universe will ever occur is a case in point. If it does occur, no one will be around to be paid; if it is not going to occur, we might not know that with enough certainty to settle the bet. Another example would be a bet on whether there is life outside the observable portion of the universe. "Can't we settle those bets by appealing to science?" subjectivists might respond. Here we cannot. Science has no definite answers to these questions; it tells us only that each of the outcomes is possible.

A related problem is that the betting approach presumes that once we make a bet it will remain clear what winning means until the bet is settled. But that it not always so. Frequently, we find ourselves in situations where we initially wonder whether something is true and then find that our very question does not really make sense or fails to have a definite answer. Suppose, for example, that you bet that the fellow in the corner drinking gin knows how to play bridge and I bet that he does not. Next suppose we learn that no one in that corner is drinking gin, although one of the men is drinking vodka—and he does play bridge. Is our bet still on? You say it is and claim that it was clear that we meant *that fellow*—the one over there. I say that it is not and that I meant *the gin drinker*, since I would never bet on a vodka drinker's being able to play bridge. I do not think that you could hold me to the bet. If we turn to the history of science and mathematics, we can even find cases where our conception of what counts as an "answer" to a question changed in the course of finding one.

This and the previous point show that we can no more count on the subjective approach to be universally applicable than we could count on the previous approaches we considered. In addition, subjectivists face a difficult dilemma concerning the revision of probabilities. As we have seen, coherence is the sole condition that subjectivists impose on anyone's initial probability assignments. Now suppose I, who know nothing of abstract art, have become friendly with some art critics and start to visit museums of modern art with them. I know what I like, but I try to guess at what the critics like. At first, I use my best hunches to assign probabilities to their liking various paintings and other art objects, being sure, of course, to be coherent. Later, when I learn what the critics have to say, I see that my probabilities must be modified. How should I do this?

An obvious proposal is to use the rule of conditionalization. But, let us suppose, I find that that rule yields probabilities that are still far from those I am now inclined to hold. (One way this could occur is if the conditional probabilities I use are, themselves, "way off"; another is through my initial assignments being wildly at variance with the critics' judgments.) What should I do? Stick with the rule and hope that convergence will soon come? Or give up my initial priors and start with a new set? Some subjectivists would advise me to stick by the rule no matter what. That opens them to the charge of stubborn tenacity. Others would allow me to pick a new set of priors whenever I wish with coherence being the only requirement I must meet. And that seems flippant. The challenge for the subjectivist is to propose a middle course, that is, a rational method for the modification of probabilities that is wedded to neither unwarranted tenacity nor flippancy.

Solutions to this problem have been proposed, but I will not delve into them here. I will only remark that they have been tied to the abandonment of a unique prior probability assignment in favor of sets of assignments or intervals between upper and lower probabilities. This amounts to rejecting the original subjectivist view—at least in its full particulars.

Our discussion of decisions under ignorance left several important issues unsettled; that was to be expected since we had reached the philosophical frontiers of the subject. The same has now happened with our discussion of probability, and I am forced to conclude it with no decision as to which conception is best. However, at least you should have a clear idea of the difficulties a successful view must overcome and of the advantages and drawbacks to the major views that have been proposed so far.

3-4. References

Skyrms 1975 contains a good introduction to probability theory and the interpretations of probability. *Chernoff and Moses* expound somewhat more advanced material. *Raiffa* presents an excellent discussion of the use of Bayes's theorem in decision theory as well as an introduction to subjective probability. *Carnap* is a classic on the logical and philosophical foundations of probability. The papers by DeFinetti and Ramsey are reprinted in *Kyburg and Smokler*. Also see

Savage and *Eells* for defenses of the subjective approach. *Kyburg* presents an account of probability that fails to obey the entire probability calculus; it also contains a number of critical papers on the various interpretations of probability as well as further references. See *Levi* for another novel approach and further criticism of standard Bayesianism.

Chapter 4

DECISIONS UNDER RISK:
UTILITY

4-1. Interval Utility Scales

Utilities are just as critical to our account of decisions under risk as probabilities since the rule of maximizing expected utility operates on them. But what are utilities? And what do utility scales measure? In discussing decisions under ignorance I hinted at answers to these questions. But such allusions will not suffice for a full and proper understanding of decisions under risk. So let us begin with a more thorough and systematic examination of the concept of utility.

The first point we should observe is that ordinal utility scales do not suffice for making decisions under risk. Tables 4-1 and 4-2 illustrate why this is so. The

4-1

A_1	6 ¼	1 ¾
A_2	5 ¼	2 ¾

expected utilities of A_1 and A_2 are 9/4 and 11/4, respectively, and so A_2 would be picked. But if we transform table 4-1 ordinally to table 4-2 by simply raising

4-2

A_1	20 ¼	1 ¾
A_2	5 ¼	2 ¾

the utility number 6 to 20, the expected utilities are now 23/4 and 11/4, which results in A_1 being picked. Thus two scales that are ordinal transformations of each other might fail to be equivalent with respect to decisions under risk.

This stands to reason anyway. Ordinal scales represent only the relative standings of the outcomes; they tell us what is ranked first and second, above, and below, but no more. In a decision under risk it is often not enough to know that you prefer one outcome to another; you might also need to know whether

81

you prefer an outcome *enough* to take the risks involved in obtaining it. This is reflected in our disposition to require a much greater return on an investment of $1,000,000 than on one of $10 — even when the probabilities of losing the investment are the same.

Happily, interval scales are all we require for decisions under risk. In addition to recording an agent's ranking of outcomes, we need measure only the relative lengths of the "preference intervals" between them. To understand what is at stake, suppose I have represented my preferences for cola (C), ice cream (I), apples (A), and popcorn (P) on the following line.

least preferred   most preferred

```
___._____._____._____._____
    P        A                    C                        I
```

If I now form a scale by assigning numbers to the line, using an ordinal scale would require me only to use numbers in ascending order as I go from left to right. But if I use an interval scale, I must be sure that the *relative* lengths of the intervals on the line are reflected as well. Thus I could not assign 0 to P, 1 to A, 2 to C, and 3 to I, for this would falsely equate the interval between, say P and A with that between C and I. More generally, if items x, y, z, and w are assigned utility numbers $u(x)$, $u(y)$, $u(z)$, and $u(w)$ on an interval scale, these numbers must satisfy the following conditions:

    a. xPy if and only if $u(x) > u(y)$.

    b. xIy if and only if $u(x) = u(y)$.

        the preference interval between x and y is greater than or equal to that between z and w if and only if

$$|u(x) - u(y)| \geq |u(z) - u(w)|.$$

More than one assignment of numbers will satisfy these two conditions but every assignment that does is a positive linear transformation of every other one that does. To illustrate this point, suppose I assign numbers to my preferences as indicated here.

least preferred   most preferred

```
    1        2                    7                        10
___._____._____._____._____
    P        A                    C                        I
```

Then I have properly represented both the ordinal and interval information. But I could have used other numbers, such as the next set.

least preferred   most preferred

```
   15        25                   75                       105
___._____._____._____._____
    P        A                    C                        I
```

These are obtained from the first set by a positive linear transformation. (What is it?)

Two ordinal scales count as equivalent if and only if they can be obtained from each other by means of order-preserving (ordinal) transformations. Two interval scales will count as equivalent if and only if they can be obtained from each other by means of positive linear transformations.

Another type of scale with which you are familiar is ratio scales. We use these for measuring lengths (in yards, feet, meters) or weights (in pounds, grams, ounces). The scales all share two important features: First, they all have natural zero points (no length, no speed, no weight), and second, the scales are used to represent the ratio of a thing measured to some standard unit of measurement. (Something 10 yards long bears the ratio of 10 to 1 to a standard yardstick; the latter can be laid off ten times against the former.) In converting from one ratio scale to another we multiply by a positive constant. (Thus, to obtain inches from feet we multiply by 12.) This turns out to be the equivalence condition for ratio scales: Two ratio scales are equivalent to each other if and only if they may be obtained from each other by multiplying by positive constants. This is a special case of a positive linear transformation; thus ratio scales are a tighter kind of interval scale.

One way to appreciate the difference between ratio and interval scales is to think of changing scales in terms of changing the labels on our measuring instruments. If we had a measuring rod 9 feet long, labeled in feet, and relabeled it in yards, we would need fewer marks on the stick. If we labeled it in inches we would need more marks. But in either case the zero point would remain the same. This is not necessarily so with interval scales. If we had a thermometer marked in degrees Fahrenheit and changed it to degrees Celsius, we would use fewer marks (between the freezing and boiling points of water there are 100 Celsius units in contrast to 180 Fahrenheit units), and we would also shift the zero point upward. Because there is no fixed zero point on our temperature scales, we must be quite careful when we say that something is twice as hot as something else. Suppose that at noon yesterday, the outdoor temperature was at the freezing point of water and that today at noon it measured 64 degrees on the Fahrenheit scale. Was it twice as hot today at noon as it was yesterday? On the Fahrenheit scale, yes, but not on the Celsius scale. Suppose, for contrast, that I am driving at 60 miles per hour and you are driving at 30. Now convert our speeds to kilometers per hour. You will see that I would still be driving twice as fast as you.

Since we will use interval scales rather than ratio scales to represent preference intervals, we cannot assume that arithmetic operations that we perform freely on speeds, weights, or distances make sense for utilities. I will return to this point later.

We have already seen that decisions under risk require more than ordinal scales. Will interval scales suffice? Or must we move on to ratio scales? No, we need not, for *any two scales that are positive linear transformations of each other will produce the same ranking of acts in a decision table* and, thus, will yield the same decisions. In short, interval scales suffice for decisions under risk. Let us now prove this.

Let table 4-3 represent any decision table and any two acts in it. I will call the acts A_i and A_j, and for convenience I will write them next to each other, but in fact they might have many rows between them or above and below them.

4-3

A_i	u_1	u_2	$\cdots$	u_n
	p_1	p_2	$\cdots$	p_n
A_j	v_1	v_2	$\cdots$	v_n
	q_1	q_2	$\cdots$	q_n

The u's and v's are utility numbers and the p's and q's are probabilities. Since the states may be dependent on the acts, we cannot assume that the p's and q's are equal. However, we can assume that the probabilities across for each row sum to 1. The expected utilities for A_i and A_j are given by the formulas

$$EU(A_i) = u_1 p_1 + u_2 p_2 + \ldots + u_n p_n$$
$$EU(A_j) = v_1 q_1 + v_2 q_2 + \ldots + v_n q_n.$$

Now a positive linear transformation of the scale used in table 4-3 would cause each u and each v to be replaced, respectively, by $au + b$ and $av + b$ (with $a > 0$). Thus after the equation the formulas for the expected utilities would be

$$EU_{new}(A_i) = (au_1 + b)p_1 + (au_2 + b)p_2 + \ldots + (au_n + b)p_n$$
$$EU_{new}(A_j) = (av_1 + b)q_1 + (av_2 + b)q_2 + \ldots + (av_n + b)q_n.$$

If we multiply through by the p's and q's and then gather at the end all the terms that contain no u's or v's we obtain

$$EU_{new}(A_i) = [au_1 p_1 + au_2 p_2 + \ldots + au_n p_n] +$$
$$[bp_1 + bp_2 + \ldots + bp_n]$$
$$EU_{new}(A_j) = [av_1 q_1 + av_2 q_2 + \ldots + av_n q_n] +$$
$$[bq_1 + bq_2 + \ldots + bq_n].$$

If we now factor out the a's the expressions remaining in the left-hand brackets are the old expected utilities. On the other hand, if we factor out the b's the expressions remaining in the right-hand brackets are p's and q's that sum to 1. Thus our new utilities are given by this pair of equations:

$$EU_{new}(A_i) = aEU(A_i) + b$$
$$EU_{new}(A_j) = aEU(A_j) + b.$$

Now since $a > 0$, $aEU(A_i)$ is greater than (less than, or equal to) $aEU(A_j)$ just in case $EU(A_i)$ stands in the same relation to $EU(A_j)$. Furthermore, this relation is preserved if we add b to $aEU(A_i)$ and $aEU(A_j)$. In other words, $EU_{new}(A_i)$ and $EU_{new}(A_j)$ will stand in the same order as $EU(A_i)$ and $EU(A_j)$. This means that using expected utilities to rank the two acts A_i and A_j will yield the same results whether we use the original scale or the positive linear transformation of it. But our reasoning has been entirely general, so the same conclusion holds for all expected utility rankings of any acts using these two scales. In short, they are equivalent with respect to decision making under risk.

PROBLEMS

1. Suppose you can bet on one of two horses — Ace or Jack — in a match race. If Ace wins you are paid $5; if he loses you must pay $2 to the track. If you bet on Jack and he loses, you pay the track $10. You judge each horse to be as likely to win as the other. Assuming you make your decisions on the basis of expected monetary values, how much would a winning bet on Jack have to pay before you would be willing to risk $10?

2. Suppose the interval scale u may be transformed into u' by means of the transformation

   $$u' = au + b \qquad (a > 0).$$

   Give the transformation that converts u' back into u.

3. Suppose the u' of the last problem can be transformed into u'' by means of the transformation

   $$u'' = cu' + d \qquad (c > 0).$$

   Give the transformation for converting u into u''.

4. Suppose s and s' are equivalent ratio scales. Show that if $s(x) = 2s(y)$, then $s'(x) = 2s'(y)$.

5. Suppose you have a table for a decision under risk in which the probabilities are independent of the acts. Show that if you transform your utility numbers by adding the number b_i to each utility in column i (and assume that the numbers used in different columns are not necessarily the same), the new table will yield the same ordering of the acts.

4-2. Monetary Values vs. Utilities

A popular and often convenient method for determining how strongly a person prefers something is to find out how much money he or she will pay for it. As a general rule people pay more for what they want more; so a monetary scale can be expected to be at least an ordinal scale. But it often works as an interval scale too — at least over a limited range of items. A rough test of this is the agent's being indifferent between the same increase (or reduction) in prices over a range of prices, since the intervals remain the same though the prices change. Thus if I sense no difference between $5 increases (e.g., from $100 to $105) for prices between $100 and $200, it is likely that a monetary scale can adequately function as an interval scale for my preferences for items in that price range. Within this range it would make sense for me to make decisions under risk on the basis of expected monetary values (EMVs).

Since we are so used to valuing things in terms of money — we even price intangibles, such as our own labor and time or a beautiful sunset, as well as necessities, such as food and clothing — it is no surprise that EMVs are often used as a basis for decisions under risk. My earlier insurance and car purchase examples typify this approach. Perhaps this is the easiest and most appropriate method for making business decisions, for here the profit motive is paramount.

It is both surprising and disquieting that a large number of nonbusiness decisions are made on the basis of EMVs. For example, it is not unusual for government policy analysts to use monetary values to scale nonmonetary outcomes such as an increase or decrease in highway deaths or pollution-induced cancers. To make a hypothetical example of a historical case, consider the federal government's decision in 1975 to vaccinate the population against an expected epidemic of swine flu. The *actual relevant outcomes* might have been specified in terms of the number of people contracting the disease, the number of deaths and permanent disabilities, and the cost and inconvenience of giving or receiving the vaccine, but instead of assigning values to these outcomes, I will suppose (as is probably the case) that policy analysts turned to their economic consequences. This meant evaluating alternatives first in terms of lost working days and then in terms of a reduced gross national product (GNP), and so on until the cost of administering the vaccine could be compared to the expected benefit to be derived from it. To illustrate this in a simplified form using made-up figures, suppose a flu epidemic will remove five million people from the work force for a period of five days. (Some will be sick, others will care for the sick. I am also talking about absences over and above those expected in normal times.) Further, suppose the average worker contributes $200 per five days of work to the GNP. Finally, suppose the GNP cost of the vaccine program is $40,000,000, that without it there is a 90% chance of an epidemic and with it only a 10% chance. Then we can set up decision table 4-4, which values out-

4-4	Epidemic	No Epidemic
Have Vaccine Program	− $1,040 million .1	− $40 million .9
No Program	− $1,000 million .9	0 .1

comes in terms of dollar costs to the GNP. The EMV of having the program is − $140 million and that of not having it is − $900 million; thus, under this approach at least, the program should be initiated since it minimizes the cost to the GNP. (This example also illustrates an equivalent approach to decisions under risk: Instead of maximizing expected gains one minimizes expected losses. See exercises 1–3 in the next Problems section.)

Perhaps the EMV approach to large-scale decisions is the only practical alternative available to policy analysts. After all, they should make some attempt to factor risks into an analysis of costs and benefits, and that will require at least an approximation to an interval scale. Monetary values provide an accessible and publicly understandable basis for such a scale.

But few people would find EMVs a satisfactory basis for every decision; they will not even suffice for certain business decisions. Sometimes making greater (after-tax) profits is not worth the effort. Just as we are rapidly reaching the point where it is not worth bending over to pick up a single penny, it might not be worth a company's effort to make an extra $20,000. More money would actually have less utility; so money could not even function as an ordinal scale. Of course, this completely contravenes the way an EMVer sees things.

Furthermore, some apparently rational businesspeople gladly sacrifice profits for humanitarian, moral, or aesthetic considerations—even when those considerations cannot be justified in greater profits in the long run. Many companies sponsor scholarships for college students, knowing full well that the associated tax benefits, improvements in corporate image, and recruitment have but a small probability of producing profits in excess of the costs. These people cannot base their decisions solely on EMVs.

On a personal level, too, the "true value" of an alternative is often above or below its EMV. Thus I might pay more for a house in the mountains than its EMV (calculated, say, by real estate investment counselors) because the beauty and solitude of its setting make up the extra value *to me*, or I might continue to drive the old family car out of sentiment long after it has stopped being economical to do so. To see the divergence between EMVs and true values in simple decision problems, consider these examples.

Example 1. True value below EMV. After ten years of work you have saved $15,000 as a down payment on your dream house. You know the house you want and need only turn over your money to have it. Before you can do that your stockbroker calls with a "very hot tip." If you can invest your $15,000 for one month, he can assure you an 80% chance at a $50,000 return. Unfortunately, if the investment fails, you lose everything. Now the EMV of this investment is $37,000—well above the $15,000 you now have in hand. Your broker points out that you can still buy the house a month from now and urges you to make the investment. But you do not, because you feel you cannot afford to risk the $15,000. For you, making the investment is worth less than having $15,000 in hand, and thus it is worth less than its EMV.

Example 2. True value above EMV. Suppose you have been trying to purchase a ticket for a championship basketball game. Tickets are available at $20 but you have only $10 on you. A fellow comes along and offers to match your $10 on a single roll of the dice. If you roll snake eyes, you get the total pot; otherwise he takes it. This means that your chances are 1 in 12 of ending up with the $20 you need and 11 in 12 of losing all you have. The EMV of this is −$7.50—definitely below the $10 you have in hand. But you take the bet, since having the $20 is worth the risk to you. Thus the EMV of this bet is below its true value to you.

In addition to practical problems with EMVs there is an important philosophical difficulty. Even if you are guided solely by the profit motive, there is no logical connection between the EMV of a risk and its monetary value. Consider this example. You alone have been given a ticket for the one and only lottery your state will have. (Although the lottery is in its very first year, the legislature has already passed a bill repealing it.) The ticket gives you one chance in a million of winning $1,000,000. Since you lose nothing if you fail to win, the EMV of the ticket is $1. After the lottery is drawn you win nothing or

$1,000,000 — but never $1. Thus how can we connect this figure with a cash value for the bet? Why — assuming money is all that counts — would it be rational for you to sell your ticket for $2? One is tempted to answer in terms of averages or long runs: If there were many people in your situation, their winnings would average $1; if this happened to you year after year, your winnings would average $1. But this will not work for the case at hand, since, by hypothesis, you alone have a free ticket and there will be only one lottery. With a one-shot decision there is nothing to average; so we have still failed to connect EMVs with cash values.

PROBLEMS

1. Given a utility scale u, we can formulate a disutility scale, $d(u)$, by multiplying each entry on the u-scale by -1. The expected disutility of an act is calculated in the same way as its expected utility except that every utility is replaced by its corresponding disutility. Reformulate the rule for maximizing expected utilities as a rule involving expected disutilities.

2. Show that the expected disutility of an act is equal to -1 times its expected utility.

3. Show that using a disutility scale and the rule you formulated in problem 1 yields the same rankings of acts as maximizing expected utilities does.

4. The St. Petersburg game is played as follows. There is one player and a "bank." The bank tosses a fair coin once. If it comes up heads, the player is paid $2; otherwise the coin is tossed again with the player being paid $4 if it lands heads. The game continues in this way with the bank continuing to double the amount set. The game stops when the coin lands heads.

    Consider a modified version of this game. The coin will be tossed no more than two times. If heads comes up on neither toss, the player is paid nothing. What is the EMV of this game?

    Suppose the coin will be tossed no more than n times. What is the EMV of the game?

    Explain why an EMVer should be willing to pay any amount to play the unrestricted St. Petersburg game.

5. Consider the following answer to the one-shot lottery objection to EMVs: True, there is only one lottery and only one person has a free ticket. But in a hypothetical case in which there were many such persons or many lotteries, we would find that the average winnings would be $1. Let us identify the cash value of the ticket with the average winnings in such hypothetical cases. It follows immediately that the cash value equals the EMV.

    Do you think this approach is an adequate solution to the problem of relating EMVs to cash values?

4-3. Von Neumann-Morgenstern Utility Theory

John Von Neumann, a mathematician, and Oskar Morgenstern, an economist, developed an approach to utility that avoids the objections we raised to EMVs.

Although Ramsey's approach to utility antedates theirs, today theirs is better known and more entrenched among social scientists. I present it here because it separates utility from probability, whereas Ramsey's approach generates utility and subjective probability functions simultaneously.

Von Neumann and Morgenstern base their theory on the idea of measuring the strength of a person's preference for a thing by the risks he or she is willing to take to receive it. To illustrate that idea, suppose that we know that you prefer a trip to Washington to one to New York to one to Los Angeles. We still do not know how *much more* you prefer going to Washington to going to New York, but we can measure that by asking you the following question: Suppose you were offered a choice between a trip to New York and a lottery that will give you a trip to Washington if you "win" and one to Los Angeles if you "lose." How great a chance of winning would you need to have in order to be indifferent between these two choices? Presumably, if you prefer New York quite a bit more than Los Angeles, you will demand a high chance at Washington before giving up a guaranteed trip to New York. On the other hand, if you only slightly prefer New York to Los Angeles, a small chance will suffice. Let us suppose that you reply that you would need a 75% chance at Washington—no more and no less. Then, according to Von Neumann and Morgenstern, we should conclude that the New York trip occurs 3/4 of the way between Washington and Los Angeles on your scale.

Another way of representing this is to think of you as supplying a ranking not only of the three trips but also of a lottery (or gamble) involving the best and worst trips. You must be indifferent between this lottery and the middle-ranked trip. Suppose we let the expression

$$L(a, x, y)$$

stand for the lottery that gives you a chance equal to a at the prize x and a chance equal to $1 - a$ at the prize y. Then your ranking can be represented as

Washington
New York, L(3/4, Washington, Los Angeles)
Los Angeles.

We can use this to construct a utility scale for these alternatives by assigning one number to Los Angeles, a greater one to Washington, and the number 3/4 of the way between them to New York. Using a 0 to 1 scale, we would assign 3/4 to New York—but any other scale obtained from this by a positive linear transformation will do as well.

Notice that since the New York trip and the lottery are indifferent they are ranked together on your scale. Thus the utility of the lottery itself is 3/4 on a 0 to 1 scale. But since on that scale the utilities of its two "prizes" (the trips) are 0 and 1, the expected utility of the lottery is also 3/4. We seem to have forged a link between utilities and expected utilities. Indeed, Von Neumann and Morgenstern showed that if an agent ranks lotteries in the manner of our example, their utilities will equal their expected utilities. Let us also note that the Von

Neumann-Morgenstern approach can be applied to any kind of item—whether or not we can sensibly set a price for it—and that it yields an agent's personal utilities rather than monetary values generated by the marketplace. This permits us to avoid our previous problems with monetary values and EMVs.

(You might have noticed the resemblance between the Von Neumann-Morgenstern approach and our earlier approach to subjective probability, where we measured degrees of belief by the amount of a valued quantity the agent was willing to stake. Ramsey's trick consisted in using these two insights together without generating the obvious circle of defining probability in terms of utility and utility in turn in terms of probability.)

The Von Neumann-Morgenstern approach to utility places much stronger demands on agents' abilities to fix their preferences than do our previous conditions of rationality. Not only must agents be able to order the outcomes relevant to their decision problems, they must also be able to order all lotteries involving these outcomes, all compound lotteries involving those initial lotteries, all lotteries compounded from those lotteries, and so on. Furthermore, this ordering of lotteries and outcomes (I will start calling these *prizes*) is subject to constraints in addition to the ordering condition. Put in brief and rough form, these are: (1) Agents must evaluate compound lotteries in agreement with the probability calculus (reduction-of-compound-lotteries condition); (2) given three alternatives A, B, C with B ranked between A and C, agents must be indifferent between B and some lottery yielding A and C as prizes (continuity condition); (3) given two other lotteries agents will prefer the one giving the better "first" prize—if everything else is equal (better-prizes condition); (4) given two otherwise identical lotteries, agents will prefer the one that gives them the best chance at the "first" prize (better-chances condition). If agents can satisfy these four conditions plus the ordering condition of chapter 2, we can construct an interval utility function u with the following properties:

(1) $u(x) > u(y)$ if and only if xPy
(2) $u(x) = u(y)$ if and only if xIy
(3) $u[L(a, x, y)] = au(x) + (1 - a)u(y)$
(4) Any u' also satisfying (1)–(3) is a positive linear transformation of u.

You should recognize (1) and (2) from our discussion of decisions under ignorance (chapter 2). They imply that u is at least an ordinal utility function. But (3) is new. It states that the utility of a lottery is equal to its expected utility. We can also express this by saying that u has the *expected utility property*. The entire result given by (1)–(4) is known as the *expected utility theorem*. Let us now turn to a rigorous proof of it.

First we must specify lotteries more precisely than we have. The agent is concerned with determining the utilities for some set of outcomes, alternatives, or prizes. Let us call these *basic prizes*. Let us also assume that the number of basic prizes is a finite number greater than 1 and that the agent is not indifferent between all of them. Since we can assume that the agent has ranked the prizes, some will be ranked at the top and others at the bottom. For future reference, let us select a top-ranked prize and label it "*B*" (for best). Let us also select a bottom-ranked prize and label it "*W*" (for worst).

I will now introduce compound lotteries by the following rule of construction. (In mathematical logic this is called an inductive definition.)

Rule for Constructing Lotteries:
1. Every basic prize is a lottery.
2. If L_1 and L_2 are lotteries, so is $L(a, L_1, L_2)$, where $0 \leq a \leq 1$.
3. Something is a lottery if and only if it can be constructed according to conditions 1 and 2.

Thus lotteries consist of basic prizes, simple lotteries involving basic prizes, further lotteries involving basic prizes or simple lotteries, ad infinitum. This means that *B* and *W* are lotteries, $L(1/2, B, W)$ and $L(3/4, W, B)$ are, and so are $L(2/3, B, L(1/2, B, W))$ and $L(1, L(0, B, W), W)$

PROBLEMS

1. Why can we not assume that there is a single best prize?
2. Why have I assumed that there is more than one basic prize? That the agent is not indifferent between all the prizes? If these assumptions were not true, would the expected utility theorem be false?
3. What chance at *B* does each of the following lotteries give?
   a. $L(1, B, W)$
   b. $L(1/2, L(1, W, B), L(1/2, B, W))$
   c. $L(a, B, B)$
4. Why should an agent be indifferent between $L(a, B, W)$ and $L(1 - a, W, B)$?
5. Show how to construct one of our lotteries that is equivalent to the lottery with *three* prizes, *A*, *B*, and *C*, that offers a 50% chance of yielding *A* and 25% chances of yielding *B* and *C*.

Now that we have a precise characterization of lotteries, let us turn to precise formulations of the "rationality" conditions the agent must satisfy. The first of these is the familiar *ordering condition*, applied this time not just to basic prizes but also to all lotteries. This means that conditions O1–O8 (discussed in chapter 2) apply to all lotteries. An immediate consequence of this is that we can partition the lotteries into ranks so as to rank together lotteries between which the agent is indifferent while placing each lottery below those the agent prefers to it.

The next condition is called the *continuity condition* because one of its consequences is that the ordering of the lotteries is continuous. It is formulated as follows:

For any lotteries *x*, *y*, and *z*, if *xPy* and *yPz*, then there is some real number *a* such that $0 \leq a \leq 1$ and *y I L(a, x, z)*.

In less formal terms this says that if the agent ranks *y* between *x* and *z*, there is some lottery with *x* and *z* as prizes that the agent ranks along with *y*.

The *better-prizes condition* is next. Intuitively, it says that other things being equal, the agent prefers one lottery to another just in case the former involves better prizes. Put formally:

For any lotteries x, y, and z and any number a ($0 \leq a \leq 1$), xPy if and only if $L(a, z, x) \; P \; L(a, z, y)$ and $L(a, x, z) \; P \; L(a, y, z)$.

There is also the *better-chances condition*, which says roughly that, other things being equal, the agent prefers one lottery to another just in case the former gives a better chance at the better prize. Put in precise terms:

For any lotteries x and y and any numbers a and b (both between 0 and 1, inclusively), if xPy, then $a > b$ just in case $L(a, x, y) \; P \; L(b, x, y)$.

The final condition is called the *reduction-of-compound-lotteries condition* and requires the agent to evaluate compound lotteries in accordance with the probability calculus. To be exact, it goes:

For any lotteries x and y and any numbers a, b, c, d (again between 0 and 1 inclusively), if $d = ab + (1 - a)c$, then $L(a, L(b, x,y), L(c, x, y)) \; I \; L(d, x, y)$.

To get a better grip on this condition, let us introduce the *lottery tree* notation (figure 4-1), which is similar to the decision tree notation.

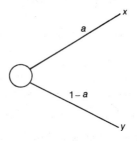

Figure 4-1

This diagram represents the simple lottery that yields the prize x with a chance of a and the prize y with a chance of $1 - a$. Compound lotteries can be represented by iterating this sort of construction, as figure 4-2 illustrates. This is a two-stage lottery whose final prizes are x and y. What are the chances of getting x in this lottery? There is a chance of a at getting into lottery 2 from lottery 1 and a chance of b of getting x. In other words, there is an ab chance of getting x through lottery 2. Similarly, there is a $(1 - a)c$ chance of getting x through lottery 3. Since these are the only routes to x and they are mutually exclusive, the chances for x are $ab + (1 - a)c$. The same type of reasoning shows that the chances for y are $a(1 - b) + (1 - a)(1 - c)$. If we set $d = ab + (1 - a)c$, a little algebra will show that $1 - d = a(1 - b) + (1 - a)c$. The reduction-of-compound-lotteries condition simply tells us that the agent must be indifferent between the compound lottery given earlier and the next simple one (figure 4-3). Notice, by the way, that the condition is improperly named, since the agent is indifferent

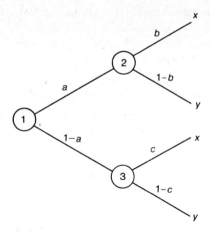

Figure 4-2

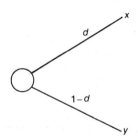

Figure 4-3

to both reductions and *expansions* of lotteries so long as they accord with the probability calculus.

Let us turn now to the proof of the expected utility theorem. I will divide the proof into two parts. The first part will establish that, given that the agent satisfies the ordering, continuity, better-prizes, better-chances, and reduction-of-compound-lotteries conditions, there is a utility function, u, satisfying the expected utility property that represents his preferences. This is called the *existence* part of the proof, since it proves that there exists a utility function having the characteristics given in the theorem. The second part of the proof is called the *uniqueness* part, because it establishes that the utility function constructed in the first part is unique up to positive linear transformations; that is, it is an interval utility function.

Directing ourselves now to the proof of the existence of u, recall that we have already established that there are at least two basic prizes B and W, where the agent prefers B to W and regards B as at least as good as any basic prize and every basic prize as at least as good as W. Since all lotteries ultimately pay in basic prizes and are evaluated by the agent in terms of the probability calculus, there is no lottery ranked above B or below W. (See exercises 4-8 in the next problems section.) Accordingly, fixing the top of our utility scale at 1 and the bottom at 0, we stipulate that

$u(B) = 1$ and $u(x) = 1$ for all lotteries x indifferent to B,
$u(W) = 0$ and $u(x) = 0$ for all lotteries x indifferent to W.

Having taken care of the lotteries at the extremes we must now define u for those in between. So let x be any lottery for which

BPx and xPW

holds. Applying the continuity axiom to this case, we can conclude that there is a number a, where $0 \leq a \leq 1$, such that

$x \, I \, L(a, B, W)$.

If there is just one such a, we will be justified in stipulating that $u(x) = a$. So let us assume that $a' \neq a$ and $x \, I \, L(a', x, y)$ and derive a contradiction. Since a and a' are assumed to be distinct, one is less than the other. Suppose $a < a'$. Then by the better-chances condition,

$L(a', B, W) \, P \, L(a, B, W)$,

but this contradicts the ordering condition since both lotteries are indifferent to x. A similiar contradiction follows from the alternative that $a' < a$. Having derived a contradiction from either alternative, we may conclude that $a = a'$.

We are now justified in stipulating that

$u(x) = a$,

where a is the number for which $x \, I \, L(a, B, W)$. Note that by substituting equals for equals we obtain

$(*) \; x \, I \, L(u(x), B, W)$;

that is, the agent is indifferent between x and the lottery that gives a $u(x)$ chance at B and a $1 - u(x)$ chance at W.

So far we have simply established the existence of a function u that assigns a number to each lottery. We must also show that this is an (interval) utility function that satisfies the expected utility property.

Let us first show that, for all lotteries x and y,

(1) xPy if and only if $u(x) > u(y)$.

By the better chances condition we have

(a) $L(u(x), B, W) \, P \, L(u(y), B, W)$ if and only if $u(x) > u(y)$.

By $(*)$, above, we have

(b) $x \, I \, L(u(x), B, W)$ and $y \, I \, L(u(y), B, W)$.

Using the ordering condition, we can easily prove

(c) for all lotteries x, y, z, and w, if xIy and zIw, then xPz if and only if yPw.

This together with (a) and (b) immediately yields (1).

It is now easy to prove

(2) xIy if and only if $u(x) = u(y)$, for all lotteries x and y.

For if xIy and $u(x) > u(y)$, then, by (1) xPy — a contradiction; so if xIy, then not $u(x) > u(y)$. Similarly, if xIy, then it is false that $u(y) > u(x)$. Thus if xIy, $u(x) = u(y)$. On the other hand, if $u(x) = u(y)$, we can have neither xPy nor yPx without contradicting (1) and the ordering condition. This means that if $u(x) = u(y)$, then xIy, since the ordering condition implies that either xIy, xPy, or yPx.

The rest of this part of our proof will be concerned with showing that for all lotteries x and y,

(3) $u(L(a, x, y)) = au(x) + (1 - a)u(y)$.

To prove this, however, it will be convenient for us to first prove that the following condition follows from the others.

Substitution-of-Lotteries Condition: If $x I L(a, y, z)$, then both
(a) $L(c, x, v) I L(c, L(a, y, z), v)$
(b) $L(c, v, x) I L(c, v, L(a, y, z))$.

This condition states that if the agent is indifferent between a prize (lottery) x and some lottery $L(a, y, z)$, the agent is also indifferent to substituting the lottery $L(a, y, z)$ for x as a prize in another lottery.

Turning to the derivation of the substitution condition, let us abbreviate "$L(a, y, z)$" by "L". Now assume that xIL. We want to show that (a) and (b) hold. I will derive (a) and leave (b) as an exercise. By the ordering condition, $L(c, x, v)$ is indifferent to $L(c, L, v)$ or one is preferred to the other. If $L(c, x, v)$ is preferred to $L(c, L, v)$, then by the better-prizes condition, xPL. But that contradicts xIL. Similarly, if $L(b, L, w)$ is preferred to $L(b, x, w)$, then LPx — again contradicting xIL. So the only alternative left is that the two lotteries are indifferent. This establishes (a).

With the substitution condition in hand we can now turn to the proof of (3). Let us use "L" this time to abbreviate "$L(a, x, y)$." By (*) we have

i) $L I L(u(L), B, W)$
ii) $x I L(u(x), B, W)$
iii) $y I L(u(y), B, W)$.

Thus by substituting $L(u(x), B, W)$ for x and $L(u(y), B, W)$ for y in the lottery L and applying the substitution condition, we obtain

$L I L(a, L(u(x), B, W), L(u(y), B, W))$.

We can reduce the compound lottery on the right to a simple lottery, thus obtaining

$L(a, L(u(x), B, W), L(u(y), B, W))\ I\ L(d, B, W),$

where $d = au(x) + (1 - a)u(y)$. But then by the ordering condition we must have

$L\ I\ L(d, B, W),$

which together with (i) yields

$L(u(L), B, W)\ I\ L(d, B, W).$

If $u(L) > d$ or $d > u(L)$, we would contradict the better-chances condition. So $u(L) = d$. But this is just an abbreviated form of (3).

This completes the existence part of the expected utility theorem.

PROBLEMS

1. Using the existence part of the expected utility theorem show
   a. $L(1, x, y)\ I\ x$
   b. $L(0, x, y)\ I\ y$
   c. $L(a, x, y)\ I\ L(1 - a, y, x)$
   d. $L(a, x, x)\ I\ x$

2. Derive part (b) of the substitution-of-lotteries condition.
3. Using just the ordering condition, prove:

   If xIy and zIw, then xPz if and only if yPw.

4. In this and the following exercises *do not* appeal to the expected utility theorem. Instead reason directly from the rationality conditions of the theorem.
   a. There is no number a or basic prize x distinct from B for which $L(a, x, B)\ P\ L(a, B, B)$ or $L(a, B, x)\ P\ L(a, B, B)$.
   b. There is no number a or basic prizes x and y distinct from B for which $L(a, x, y)\ P\ L(a, B, B)$.

5. Define the degree of a lottery as follows:
   All basic prizes are of degree zero.
   Let n be the maximum of the degrees of L_1 and L_2, then the degree of $L(a, L_1, L_2)$ is equal to $n + 1$.
   Suppose no lottery of degree less than n is preferred to B. Show that
   There is no number a and lottery L of degree less than n for which $L(a, B, L)\ P\ L(a, B, B)$ or $L(a, L, B)\ P\ L(a, B, B)$.
   There is no number a and no lotteries L_1 and L_2 of degree less than n for which $L(a, L_1, L_2)\ P\ L(a, B, B)$.
   It follows from this and the previous exercise that no lottery of degree greater than 0 is preferred to $L(a, B, B)$ for any number a.

6. Show that for no number a, $L(a, B, B)\ P\ B$. Hint: Apply the conclusion of exercise 5 to $L(a, L(a, B, B), L(a, B, B))$.
7. Show that for no number a, $B\ P\ L(a, B, B)$.
   Exercises 5–7 establish that no lottery is preferred to B. We can similarly show that no lottery is less preferred than W.

8. Show that if BPx and xPW, then $L(a, x, x)\ I\ x$ for any number a.

Let us turn now to the uniqueness part of the proof. Now our task is to show that if u' is a utility function defined for the same preferences as u that satisfies

(1) $u'(x) > u'(y)$ if and only if xPy,
(2) $u'(x) = u'(y)$ if and only if xIy,
(3) $u'[L(a, x, y)] = au'(x) + (1-a)u'(y)$,

then there are numbers c and d with $c > 0$ such that

$u'(x) = cu(x) + d.$

Since the two functions u and u' give rise to utility scales for the same preference ordering, we can picture the situation as follows (figure 4-4). (We

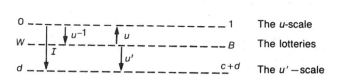

Figure 4-4

know that the end points of the u'-scale will be d and $c + d$ if our proof is correct, since

$cu(W) + d = c0 + d = d,$
$cu(B) + d = c1 + d = c + d.)$

The function u assigns utilities on the u-scale, the function u' assigns them on the u'-scale, and the function I converts assignments on the u-scale into assignments on the u'-scale. Given a number e on the u-scale, the function I first selects a lottery L for which $u(L) = e$ [this is $u^{-1}(e)$], then I applies the function u' to L to find the number $f[=u'(L)]$. In short, we have

(a) $I(e) = u'[u^{-1}(e)] = f.$

Now let k and m be any numbers on the u-scale. Note that for any number a, such that $0 \le a \le 1$, the number $ak + (1-a)m$ is between k and m or one of them. So the number $ak + (1-a)m$ is also on the u-scale. Substituting this number in (a), we obtain

(b) $I[ak + (1-a)]m = u'\{u^{-1}[ak + (1-a)m]\}.$

But $u^{-1}[ak + (1-a)m]$ is a lottery whose utility on the u-scale is $ak + (1-a)m$. Since k and m are also on the u-scale, they are utilities of some lotteries x and y; that is, $u(x) = k$ and $u(y) = m$. But then by (3), the expected utility condition, we have

(c) $u[L(a, x, y)] = au(x) + (1-a)u(y) = ak + (1-a)m.$

From which it follows that

(d) $I[ak + (1-a)m] = u'[L(a, x, y)].$

Since u' also satisfies the expected utility condition we have

(e) $u'[L(a, x, y)] = au'(x) + (1 - a)u'(y)$,

and since $u(\dot{x}) = k$ and $u(y) = m$ we must have

(f) $I(k) = u'(x)$ and $I(m) = u'(y)$.

Putting these in (e) and (d) we obtain

(g) $I[ak + (1 - a)m] = aI(k) + (1 - a)I(m)$.

With (g) in hand (which tells us that I mimicks the expected utility property) we can complete the proof. Since each number k on the u-scale is $u(x)$ for some lottery x, we have

(h) $I[u(x)] = u'(x)$.

But by simple algebra

(i) $u(x) = u(x)1 + [1 - u(x)]0$

Thus by (g), (h), and (j)

(j) $u'(x) = I[u(x)] = I\{u(x)1 + [1 - u(x)]0\}$
$= u(x)I(1) + [1 - u(x)]I(0)$
$= u(x)[I(1) - I(0)] + I(0)$.

Thus by setting

(k) $c = I(1) - I(0)$ and $d = I(0)$

and substituting in (j), we have

$u'(x) = cu(x) + d$.

To finish our proof we need only show that $c > 0$. That is left as an exercise.

PROBLEMS

1. Prove that c as defined in (k) above is greater than zero.
2. Prove that given any number k on the u-scale, there is some lottery x for which $u(x) = k$.
3. Show how to transform a 0 to 1 scale into a 1 to 100 scale using a positive linear transformation. Similarly, show how to transform a -5 to $+5$ scale into a 0 to 1 scale.
4. If we measure an agent's preferences on a Von Neumann-Morgenstern utility scale, does it make sense to say that the agent prefers a given prize twice as much as another?

4-3a. Some Comments and Qualifications on the Expected Utility Theorem

Now that we have concluded the proof of the expected utility theorem, let us reflect on what it has accomplished for us. The theorem is a *representation theorem*; that is, it shows that a certain nonnumerical structure can be represented numerically. Specifically, it tells us that if an agent's preferences have a sufficiently rich structure, that structure can be represented numerically by means of an interval utility function having the expected utility property. We proved the theorem by assigning numbers to each prize and lottery and then verifying that the resulting numerical scale had the desired properties. However, if the agent's preferences had failed to satisfy any one of the conditions of the theorem, then our construction would have failed to have the desired properties. For example, without the continuity condition we could not be assured of a numerical assignment for each lottery or prize, and without the reduction-of-compound-lotteries condition we could not have established the expected utility property. In a sense, then, the theorem merely takes information already present in facts about the agent's preferences and reformulates it in more convenient numerical terms. It is essential to keep this in mind when applying the theorem and discussing its philosophical ramifications.

How might we apply the theorem? Recall that we needed an interval utility scale for use with the rule of maximizing expected utility. Monetary scales proved unsatisfactory, because monetary values sometimes part company with our true preferences and because EMVs cannot ground our one-time decisions.

By contrast, utility scales do assign "true values" in the sense that utilities march along with an agent's preferences. Furthermore, each act in a decision under risk is itself a lottery involving one or more of the outcomes of the decision. Thus we can expect our agent to rank all the acts open to him along with all the prizes and lotteries. When he applies the rule of maximizing expected utility, he chooses an act whose expected utility is maximal among his options. But the utility of that act, since it is a lottery, is equal to its expected utility. Thus the agent chooses an act whose utility is highest. If there were an act he preferred to that one, it would have a higher utility. Hence in picking this act, the agent is simply taking his most preferred option. This is true even in the case of a one-shot decision. So we now know what justifies the use of expected utilities in making decisions under risk—in particular one-time decisions. It is this: In choosing an act whose expected utility is maximal an agent is simply doing what he wants to do!

Closer reflection on these facts about the theorem may cause you to wonder how it can have any use at all. For the theorem can be applied only to those agents with a sufficiently rich preference structure; and if they have such a structure, they will not need utility theory—because they will already prefer what it would advise them to prefer.

Still, decision theory can be useful to us mortals. Although the agents of the theorem are ideal and hypothetical beings, we can use them as guides for our own decision making. For example, although we may find that (unlike the ideal agents) we must calculate the expected utility of an act before we can rank it, this still does not prevent us from ranking one act above another if its expected utility is higher. We also can try to bring our preferences into conformity with the conditions of the expected utility theorem. In practice we might construct our personal utility functions by setting utilities for some reasonably small number of alternatives and then obtain a tentative utility function from these points by extrapolation and curve fitting. This tentative function can be modified by checking its fit with additional alternatives and a new function can be projected from the results, and so on, until we obtain a function satisfactory for our current purposes.

Furthermore, utility functions are useful even for ideally rational agents — for the same reason that arabic numerals are preferable to roman numerals. Utility functions facilitate the manipulation of information concerning preferences — even if the manipulator is an ideally rational being.

But, whether they are our own or those of ideally rational beings, we must approach such manipulations with caution. Suppose an agent assigns a utility of 2 to having a dish of ice cream. Can we conclude that the agent will assign a utility of 4 to having two dishes? No, utility is not an additive quantity; that is, there is no general way of combining prizes with the result that the utility of the combination equals the sum of the utilities of the components. As a result, it does not make sense to add, subtract, multiply, or divide utilities. In particular, we have no license to conclude that two dishes of ice cream will be worth twice the utility of one to our agent. If eating the second dish would violate his diet, then having two dishes might even be worth less to him than having one.

It would also be fallacious to conclude, for example, that something assigned a utility of 2 on a given scale is twice as preferable to something assigned a 1 on the same scale. For suppose that the original scale is a 1 to 10 scale. If we transform it to a 1 to 91 scale by the permissible transformation of multiplying every number by 10 and then subtracting 9, the item originally assigned 1 will continue to be assigned 1 but the one assigned 2 will be assigned 11. Thus its being assigned twice the utility on the first scale is simply an artifice of the scale and not a scale-invariant property of the agent's preferences.

As a general rule, we must be cautious about projecting properties of utility numbers onto agents preferences. A utility scale is only a numerical representation of the latter. Consequently, agents have no preferences *because* of the properties of their utility scales; rather their utility scales have some of their properties because the agents have the preferences they have.

PROBLEMS

1. Suppose that yesterday the highest temperature in New York was 40 degrees Fahrenheit whereas in Miami it was 80 degrees Fahrenheit. Would it be correct to say that Miami was twice as hot as New York?

2. To graph utility against money, we represent amounts of money on the x-axis and utilities for amounts of money on the y-axis and draw utility graphs in the usual way. One utility graph for an EMVer is the straight line given by the equation $y = x$. This graphs the function $u(x) = x$. All the other utility functions of the EMVer are positive linear transformations of this one. Describe their graphs.

3. Suppose you have an aversion to monetary risks; that is, you prefer having an amount of money for certain to having a lottery whose EMV is that amount. What does your utility graph for money look like in comparison to the graph $y = x$?

4. Suppose you welcome monetary risks in the sense that you would rather take a gamble whose EMV was a certain amount than have that amount for certain. Now what does your utility graph look like?

5. What could we conclude about the preferences of someone whose utility function for money was given by

$$u(x) = x^2$$

in the $0 to $100,000 range and by

$$u(x) = (100,000)^2$$

for amounts greater than or equal to $100,000?

4-4. Criticisms of Utility Theory

A number of thinkers have criticized utility theory and the expected utility theorem. I will begin by discussing some criticisms of the better-chances condition, the reduction-of-compound-lotteries condition, and the continuity condition. Then I will turn to three paradoxes that have been used to criticize the theory as a whole.

Some have objected to the better-chances condition as a requirement of rationality on the grounds that if you prefer life to death, the condition requires you to prefer any act that does not increase your risk of death to one that does — no matter how small the increase might be. But such preferences could lead to total and irrational paralysis. You would not even get out of bed in the morning for fear of dying. The answer to this criticism is that the better-chances condition has no such implications. When, for instance, I compare an afternoon in front of the TV with one hang gliding, I am not comparing one pure life-and-death lottery with another. I am comparing a safe but *dull* afternoon with a dangerous but *thrilling* one. For the better-chances condition to apply the two lotteries must involve the same outcomes, and here they plainly do not. I might die during the afternoon while I watch TV just as I might die while hang gliding. But dying while watching TV is surely a different and less noble outcome than dying while hang gliding. (You might think it is irrational to go hang gliding, or, if you prefer, to play Russian roulette, because the chances of dying are so great. Remember that decision theory concerns itself only with the form of an agent's preferences and not with their specifics. Decision theory will not tell you not to prefer Russian roulette to ordinary roulette, but it will tell you that if you prefer one to the other, you cannot also be indifferent between them.)

The standard objection to the reduction-of-compound-lotteries condition is not so easily dismissed. Since utility theory forces an agent to regard compound lotteries as indifferent to certain simple ones, it (or so the objection goes) abstracts from the pleasures and anxieties associated with gambling. The avid gambler will not be indifferent between a single-stage lottery and a multistage one, whereas someone who regards gambling as wrong, will want to do it as little as possible. Utility theory, with its reduction-of-lotteries condition, has no place for these preferences and aversions.

To respond to this criticism we must distinguish between those multistage lotteries that are simply theoretical idealizations introduced for calibrating utility scales and real-life multistage lotteries that may take weeks or months to be completed. We can think of theoretical lotteries as being run and paid off in an instant. Given this it would not make sense for an agent to distinguish between having, say, a $100 ticket to an instantaneous simple lottery ticket paying $100 unconditionally and an instantaneous multistage lottery with the same outcome. In this case we need not take the objection seriously.

On the other hand, if a multistage lottery takes place over time, we cannot use this reply. Suppose, for example, that in situation A an agent is faced with the prospect of a 25% chance of selling her house today and a 75% chance of never selling it. In situation B, the same agent is faced with a 50% chance of agreeing today on an option to sell the house within the week and a 50% chance of never selling it. However, if the option is taken, the agent faces a 50% chance that the prospective buyer will obtain a loan and buy the house within the week and a 50% chance that the deal will collapse and the house will never be sold. Using lottery trees we might represent the two situations as follows (figure 4-5).

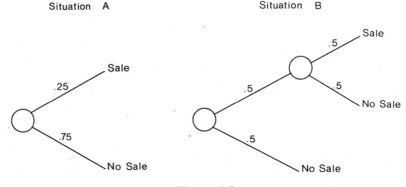

Figure 4-5

If the outcomes are as these trees represent them, the compound lottery in B reduces to the simple lottery in A in accordance with the reduction-of-compound-lotteries condition. That would constitute a genuine objection to a theory since an agent who sorely needs to sell her house today would rightly prefer A to B. But are the outcomes really as the trees represent them? I think not, for in situation B the sale is not made today but within the week. Someone who needs his money now or dislikes the suspense of waiting as much as one week will not view the outcomes in A and B as the same. Thus the compound lottery in B and the simple one in A do not satisfy the antecedent of the reduction condition and, accordingly, do not qualify as counterexamples. I would expect that other "over time" counterexamples could be dissolved similarly.

The objection to the continuity condition is similar to that to the better-chances condition. Suppose I prefer living another ten years to receiving a gift of one cent right now to dying immediately. Then the continuity condition requires me to be indifferent between receiving the penny right now and accepting a lottery that gives me some positive chance of dying on the spot. One might object that it is irrational for me to risk an additional chance of dying for a mere penny. But note that the continuity condition requires only that the chance be positive — not that it constitute a significant increase in my chances of dying. So all I am required to do is to be indifferent between receiving the penny and positively increasing my chances of dying by *as little as I want*. There need be nothing irrational in that at all.

Although most decision theorists do not take the objection to the continuity axiom seriously, some have developed utility theories that do not use the continuity condition. These are multidimensional or multiattribute utility theories in which outcomes are evaluated along several dimensions (or with respect to several attributes). For example, in choosing between having and not having an operation to relieve chronic back pain, a person could consider several attributes of each of the outcomes, such as the risk of death, the attendant pain, the length of the recovery period, the costs, and so on. It may well be that this person can order the outcomes in terms of priorities — for example, minimizing disability might have the highest priority, minimizing long-term pain the next, minimizing the risk of death the next, and so on. Yet this person might be unable or unwilling to make "trade-offs," for example, to trade more disability for less pain, and thus unable or unwilling to combine the many dimensions into one. This would violate the continuity condition since that condition requires all the outcomes to be ranked on the same numerical scale. But this does not seem irrational in itself. A properly constructed multidimensional utility theory should be able to deal with this question. But I will not be able to explore this matter further here.

4-4a. Allais's Paradox

I will now turn to three "paradoxes" directed at utility theory as a whole. The first, proposed by the contemporary French economist Maurice Allais, presents us with two situations. In situation A we offer an agent a choice between receiving $1,000,000 for certain and a lottery that furnishes him a .1 chance of winning $5,000,000, a .89 chance of winning $1,000,000 and a .01 chance of receiving nothing at all. In situation B the choice is between two lotteries. One offers a .1 chance at $5,000,000 and a .9 chance at nothing, the other offers a .11 chance of $1,000,000 and a .89 chance of nothing. Figure 4-6 presents the decision trees for these two situations. The paradox is this. Many presumably rational and reflective people find that they would prefer *a* (the bird in the hand) to *b* if they were in situation A and would prefer *c* to *d* in situation B. But no matter what your utility for money is, the choices of *a* in A and *c* in B, or *b*

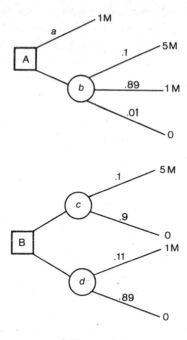

Figure 4-6

in A and *d* in B contradict utility theory. To see how, let us compute the utilities for *a*, *b*, *c*, and *d*. They are:

$$u(a) = u(1M)$$
$$u(b) = .1u(5M) + .89u(1M) + .01u(0)$$
$$u(c) = .1u(5M) + .9u(0)$$
$$u(d) = .11u(1M) + .89u(0).$$

But it then follows by simple arithmetic that

$$u(a) - u(b) = .11u(1M) - [.1u(5M) + .01u(0)]$$
$$u(d) - u(c) = .11u(1M) - [.1u(5M) + .01u(0)].$$

Now if you prefer *a* to *b*, then $u(a) > u(b)$, so $u(a) - u(b) > 0$. But then $u(d) > u(c)$, so you must prefer *d* to *c* to conform to utility theory. A similar argument shows that if you prefer *b* to *a*, you ought to prefer *c* to *d*. But, of course, many people balk at these recommendations.

Several resolutions of this paradox have been advanced and each has been criticized. Two deserve examination here. The first follows the line I used in responding to the counterexamples to the better-chances and reduction conditions. It consists in arguing that the formal representation of situations A and B is incorrect and that, consequently, nobody who chooses *a* in A and *c* in B contravenes utility theory. The argument turns on the claim that anyone who chooses *b* in situation A and ends up with nothing has done so *when he could have had $1,000,000 for certain*. No one would be passing up a certain $1,000,000 in situation B. Thus we have misrepresented the two situations by using 0 in both to stand for the outcome in which the agent receives nothing. The outcome designated as 0 in situation A presumably has a lower utility than its correspondent in B. Once this is acknowledged the rest of the argument breaks down, since we can no longer count on the truth of $u(a) - u(b) = u(d) - u(c)$.

Another resolution, proposed by the statistician Leonard Savage, tries to persuade us that the reasoning that leads people to choose a in A and c in B is fallacious. Savage asks us to represent the two situations as involving choices between lotteries with 100 tickets where the payoffs are given according to table 4-5. (Here is how row b is obtained: the .01 chance of 0 is con-

4-5

		Ticket Number		
		1	2-11	12-100
A	a	1M	1M	1M
	b	0	5M	1M
B	c	0	5M	0
	d	1M	1M	0

verted to a payoff of 0 for 1 ticket out of 100 [ticket number 1]; the chance of .1 at $5,000,000 is converted to a payoff of $5,000,000 for 10 tickets out of 100 [tickets 2-11], and the .89 chance at $1,000,000 is converted to a payoff of $1,000,000 for 89 tickets of the 100. The rest of table 4-5 is obtained similarly.)

Now in choosing lotteries in either situation tickets 12–100 can be ignored, because they give the same prizes in their respective situations. Thus the decisions between a and b and between c and d should be based on the first two columns of the table. However, the first two columns of a and d are identical and so are those of b and c. Accordingly, it is obviously mistaken to choose a in A and not d in B or b in A and not c in B.

In short, Savage claims that those who succumb to the Allais paradox have simply made a mistake in reasoning. This is no different, he urges, than the mistakes otherwise intelligent people often make in estimating probabilities or in carrying out complicated mathematical arguments. In each case all we need do to correct them is to point out their errors clearly and perspicuously. I will let you decide whether you find this or the previous resolution of the Allais paradox convincing.

4-4b. Ellsberg's Paradox

The Allais paradox derives its force from our tendency to prefer having a good for certain to having a chance at a greater good. The next paradox, developed by Daniel Ellsberg, appeals to our preference for known risks over unknown ones.

Here is a version of the Ellsberg paradox that is quite similar to Allais's paradox. An urn contains ninety uniformly sized balls, which are randomly distributed. Thirty of the balls are yellow, the remaining sixty are red or blue. We are not told how many red (blue) balls are in the urn—except that they number anywhere from zero to sixty. Now consider the following pair of situations. In each situation a ball will be drawn and we will be offered a bet on its color. In situation A we will choose between betting that it is yellow or that it is red. In situation B we will choose between betting that it is red or blue or that it is yellow or blue. The payoffs are given in table 4-6.

4-6		Yellow 30	Red	Blue 60
A	a	100	0	0
	b	0	100	0
B	c	0	100	100
	d	100	0	100

When confronted with this decision people frequently reason as follows. In situation A, I will pick bet a (yellow), since the chance of the ball's being red might be quite small. But in situation B, I will pick bet c (red or blue). That gives me sixty chances out of ninety at winning, whereas if I took bet d (yellow or red), I might have only thirty out of ninety chances.

Now suppose that we reasoned this way. Then our choices could not consistently reflect the expected utilities of the bets. For let p be the probability of getting a blue ball given that the ball is red or blue and let A be the utility of 100 and B the utility of 0. Then the expected utilities are:

$$EU(a) = (1/3)A + (2/3)pB + (2/3)(1-p)B = (1/3)A + (2/3)B$$
$$EU(b) = (1/3)B + (2/3)pA + (2/3)(1-p)B = B + (2/3)p(A-B)$$
$$EU(c) = (1/3)B + (2/3)pA + (2/3)(1-p)A = (1/3)B + (2/3)A$$
$$EU(d) = (1/3)A + (2/3)pB + (2/3)(1-p)A = A + (2/3)p(B-A).$$

Now subtract $EU(b)$ from $EU(a)$ and $EU(d)$ from $EU(c)$. You will find that

$$EU(a) - EU(b) = -[EU(c) - EU(d)].$$

This means that our preferences will accord with expected utilities if and only if our preferences for a and b are the reverse of those for c and d. So we cannot pick a in situation A and c in situation B without contravening utility theory.

I will present two responses to the Ellsberg paradox, although, as with the paradox by Allais, there have been numerous discussions of it. The first response mimics Savage's resolution of the Allais paradox. Notice that the figures in the third column for *a* and *b* in table 4-6 are identical and so are those for *c* and *d*. Hence, or so Savage would claim, the third column can be ignored in making our decisions. If we do that, *a* and *d* are equivalent and *b* and *c* are equivalent. It follows immediately that we should prefer *a* to *b* just in case we prefer *d* to *c*.

Furthermore, there is a mistake in the reasoning that leads people to choose *a* and *c*. They say that they will pick *a* over *b* because the probability of getting a red ball might be quite small. In fact, it has to be less than 1/3 for the choice of *a* to be better than that of *b*. This would mean that the probability of getting a blue ball would be 1/3 or greater. This is inconsistent with the reasoning they give for choosing *c* over *d*. For that choice makes sense only if the probability of getting a blue ball is less than 1/3.

The other resolution consists in noting that we do not know the probability *p* used in comparing the expected utilities of the four bets. Thus these are decisions under ignorance rather than under risk, so the rule of maximizing expected utilities does not apply.

If you accept the subjective theory of probability, however, this alternative is not open to you. For the mere fact that nobody has told us the ratio of red to blue balls will not prevent us from assigning a subjective probability to the color of the ball that is drawn. This being so, choosing bets *a* and *c* would contradict the combined theories of utility and subjective probability. Perhaps this speaks against the combined theories, but those who believe the combined approach is the correct one could make a virtue out of this vice. They could argue that the combined theories present simultaneous constraints on our assignments of probabilities and our preference orderings. Obeying them is a difficult and complex task, so we should expect that from time to time our initial hunches will need to be corrected by the theory. To take a well-known example from probability theory, since one spin of a roulette wheel is independent of any other, it would be wrong for you to conclude after a long losing streak at the roulette table that you were almost certain to win on the next spin. Drawing such a conclusion is called the gambler's fallacy. Having been educated in the ways of probability, we can appreciate why it is a fallacy, but I am sure that each of us either has committed it or has been sorely tempted to do so. Someone like Savage would urge that the Allais and Ellsberg paradoxes play a similar role in our intellectual life. Those of us uneducated in decision theory react as Allais and Ellsberg tempt us to react. But once we have learned the theory and have correctly reflected on its morals, the paradoxes join the ranks of old mistakes along with the gambler's fallacy.

4-4c. The St. Petersburg Paradox

The next paradox, known as the St. Petersburg paradox, does not apply to the version of utility theory presented earlier, because it depends on the assumption that there is no upper bound to the agent's utility scale. This happens when for any basic prize there is always a better one. The purpose of the paradox is to show that under this assumption the agent will assign something an infinite utility—even if he assigns only finite utilities to the basic prizes.

Before passing to the derivation of the paradox let me note that unbounded utility scales can be constructed along the same lines as we used in constructing bounded utility scales. Although the construction is mathematically more complicated, it requires no further conditions on the rationality of the agent's preferences.

The St. Petersburg paradox is based on the St. Petersburg game, which is played as follows. A fair coin is tossed until it lands heads up. If the first toss is heads, then the player is given a prize worth 2 on his utility scale (2 utiles, for short). If it lands heads on the second toss, he is given a prize worth 4 utiles, and so on, with heads on the nth toss paying 2^n utiles. The paradox is simply that playing the St. Petersburg game has an infinite utility to the agent. Thus he should be willing to surrender any basic prize as the price of admission to the game.

To see why, note that the probability of heads on the first toss is 1/2, that of heads on the second but not the first is 1/4, . . . , that on the nth but not on the first $n-1$ tosses is $1/2^n$. Thus the expected utility of the game is

$$(1/2)2 + (1/4)4 + \ . \ . \ . \ (1/2^n)(2^n) + \ . \ . \ . \ = 1 + 1 + 1 + \ . \ . \ .$$

which is larger than any finite number. And utility theory tells us that the expected utility of the game is its utility.

One might object that we have not made sense of infinite lotteries in our development of utility theory and that the St. Petersburg game is essentially an infinite lottery. True, but many decision theorists would not be moved by this. For utility theory is easily extended to cover infinite lotteries, and it must be in order to handle more advanced problems in statistical decision theory. From the mathematical and logical point of view, the derivation of the St. Peterburg paradox is impeccable.

The only alternative then, short of modifying utility theory, is to question the assumption on which it is built—that is, that the agent's utility scale is unbounded. Now it must be admitted that this assumption simplifies the mathematical treatment of many advanced applications of utility theory. Also there is nothing irrational on the face of it in having an unbounded utility scale. So responding to the paradox by prohibiting such scales is not an attractive option. My inclination is to see the paradox as simply showing us the music agents must face if they do not bound their preferences. Although I see nothing irrational in unbounded preferences per se, the St. Petersburg paradox favors avoiding them.

On the other hand, I see no reason for the St. Petersburg paradox to arise in practice. No one is insatiable; there can be too much of anything—even life, money, and power. When the saturation point with respect to a "commodity" is reached there is a disutility to having more of it. (What would you do with all the money in the world? What value would it have if you had it all?) If this is correct, the paradox is based on a theoretically possible but unrealistic assumption. On the other hand, in a theory of ideal rational beings theoretical possibilities cannot be treated lightly. Some decision theorists have taken the paradox quite seriously and have proposed modifications of utility theory to avoid it.

PROBLEMS

1. Ellsberg presented another paradox. If we offer people a bet on a fair coin, most are indifferent between betting on heads and betting on tails. They are similarly indifferent when offered a bet on biased coins when they are not told the bias. However, when offered the choice

    bet heads on the fair coin vs. bet tails on the biased one

   they prefer to bet on the fair coin. Suppose that whichever coin is involved in a winning bet pays \$1, whereas a losing one pays nothing. Show that the choices most people make contradict the combined theories of utility and subjective probability.

2. Of course, if you are a fan of utility theory and have reservations about subjective probabilities, the Ellsberg paradox confirms your suspicions. Explain why.

3. In both the Allais and Ellsberg paradoxes we have appealed to what "most people" think or to what "many apparently rational and thoughtful people" think. What bearing, if any, does this have on decision theory, construed as a theory of ideally rational beings?

4. Utility theory originated in attempts to deal with a version of the St. Petersburg game played with monetary prizes. In 1730, Daniel Bernoulli proposed that monetary values be replaced with their logarithms. If we use logarithms to the base 10, then the expected value of this version of the St. Petersburg game is

    $$(1/2)\log_{10}(2) + (1/4)\log_{10}(4) + (1/8)\log_{10}(8) + \ldots ,$$

    which converges to a finite sum. Notice, however, that $\log_{10}(10) = 1$, $\log_{10}(100) = 2$, $\log_{10}(1{,}000) = 3$, etc., so that we can reinstate the St. Petersburg paradox by increasing the payoffs. Give a detailed explanation of how this can be done.

4-5. The Predictor Paradox

Here is a paradox, introduced by a physicist named Newcomb, which has generated more controversy than all the others combined.

Suppose a being with miraculous powers of foresight, called *the Predictor*, offers you the following choice. There are two shoe boxes on the table between the two of you. One is red, the other blue. The tops are off the boxes and you can see that the red box has \$1,000 in it and that the blue box is empty. The Predictor tells you that you are to leave the room and return in five minutes. When you return you will be offered the choice of having the contents of the blue box or that of both boxes. The Predictor also tells you that while you are out of the room he will place \$1,000,000 in the blue box if he predicts that you will take just the blue box, and he will leave it empty if he predicts that you will take both boxes. You leave the room and return after five minutes. The top is still off the red box and the $1,000 is still in it. The blue box is now closed. You have heard about the Predictor before. You know that almost everyone who has taken both boxes has received just $1,000 while almost everyone who has taken just the blue box has received $1,000,000. What is your choice?

Suppose you use decision theory to help with your choice and your utility for money is equal to its EMV. Then you will have decision table 4-7. The

4-7	Blue Box Empty	Not Empty
Take Blue Box	0 .1	1M .9
Take Both Boxes	$1,000 .9	1M + $1,000 .1

probabilities are determined as follows: You reckon that if you take just the blue box there is a 90% chance that the Predictor will have predicted that you would and will have put $1,000,000 in that box. You also think that there is only a 10% chance that he will have predicted incorrectly and left the box empty. Similarly you reckon that if you take both boxes, there is a 90% chance that he will have predicted that and left the blue box empty. It is easy to see that, given this problem specification, you will maximize expected utility by taking just the blue box. Recalling all your rich friends who took just the blue box, you are about to reach for it.

But doubt strikes. You notice that the dominant choice is to take both boxes. What then should you do? Decision theory's two most venerable rules offer you conflicting prescriptions!

Then you remember that the dominance principle is supposed to yield to the principle of maximizing expected utility when the probabilities of one or more states are dependent on the choices made. This made good sense in the nuclear disarmament example because disarming made an attack by the other side highly likely. But does it make good sense in this case? You argue to yourself: The $1,000,000 is already in the blue box or it is not. My choice cannot change things now. If there is $1,000,000 in the blue box, then taking both will yield $1,001,000 which is better than taking just the blue box. If the $1,000,000 is not there, I can get $1,000 by taking both boxes, and that's better than taking just the blue box and getting nothing. So in either case I am better off taking both boxes.

Yet next you remember that your friends who reasoned in this way are still poor whereas those who took the blue box are rich. But that does not seem to make sense either. Can the Predictor exercise mind control and influence your choice, thereby making his prediction come true? But how? He has not even told you what his prediction is. Or can your choice somehow influence his prediction? But again how? You choose *after* he predicts.

The dilemma is this. If we use the dominance principle to decide, we must ignore all the empirical data pointing to the folly of choosing both boxes; but if we follow the data and maximize expected utility, we are at a loss to explain why the data are relevant. So what is your choice?

If you do not know what to do, take comfort: You are not alone. Many decision theorists think you should take both boxes but many others think you should take just the blue one. Moreover, this paradox has shaken decision theory to its foundations.

Before we consider some of the growing number of responses to the Predictor paradox, let us bring it down to Earth. (Not that this fanciful example is not useful, for, even if it might not arise in practice, it points to a conceptual weakness in decision theory.) Here are two real-life problems closely related to the Predictor paradox.

The first is derived from the religious views of the sixteenth-century Protestant theologian John Calvin. According to one interpretation of Calvin's views, God has already determined who will go to Heaven and nothing we do during our lifetimes—whether we be saints or sinners—will change this. On the other hand, although no mortal can know whom God has chosen, Calvinists believe that there is a high correlation between being chosen and being devout. Now suppose you are a dyed-in-the-wool Calvinist and are sorely tempted to commit some sin. You consider two arguments. According to the first you should pick the dominant act. Go ahead and sin, since that is not going to affect your going to Heaven anyway, and an earthly life with pleasure is better than one of Calvinist abstinence. But the other argument tells you that you should restrain yourself. As a devout Calvinist, you are certain that your sinning would be a clear sign that you are not among the elect.

Now for a contemporary example. Smoking cigarettes is highly correlated with heart disease. Smokers are much more likely to have heart troubles than nonsmokers and heavy smokers are at greater risk than light ones. Heart disease also seems to run in families and to be associated with ambitious, serious, and competitive individuals, known as type A personalities. Today most people researching the causes of heart disease regard smoking, genetic predisposition, and the type A personality as independent contributing causes of heart disease. However, suppose the causal story went as follows instead: Type A personality is inherited (just as breeding has made race-horses high strung and draft horses calm), and people with type A personalities have a greater need to smoke than do other people. However, smoking does not cause heart disease, rather the cause is the same genetic defect that produces the type A personality. Thus the cause of smoking and heart disease is at bottom one and the same—a genetic defect. Let us suppose that the same story held for the other diseases—for example, cancer, emphysema—in which smoking has been implicated. If you believed this story and were trying to decide whether to smoke, you might be in a dilemma similar to the Predictor paradox. For the high correlation between smoking and various diseases bestows a higher expected utility on not smoking. But you would either have a disease-causing genetic defect or not. If you had it, smoking would not increase your risk of disease, and it would (or so I will suppose) lead to a more pleasurable life than would abstaining from smoking. So dominance considerations would argue for smoking. Once again the rule of maximizing expected utility and the dominance principle would conflict.

PROBLEMS

1. I formulated the Predictor paradox using .9 as the probability of the correct predictions, but it need not be that high. Assuming, as indicated in table 4-7, that $P(S_1/A_1) = P(S_2/A_2)$, how low can it get subject to the condition that taking the blue box remains the act with greatest expected utility?

2. Set up a decision table for the Calvinist example that will establish it as a variant of the Predictor paradox.

3. Do the same for the smoking example.

4-6. Causal Decision Theory

The Predictor paradox, the Calvinist example, and our fanciful speculations on the causes of smoking-related diseases remind us that from time to time there can be a high correlation between two sorts of phenomena without any causal relation between them. Almost every time the thermometers go up in my house it is hot. The same thing happens in every other house I know. So the probability that it is hot given that the thermometer readings are high is close to 1. Does that mean that the high thermometer readings cause it to get hot? Obviously not. Everything we know about temperatures and thermometers tells us that the causal relation goes oppositely. Because of this it would be silly to try to heat a room by holding a match under the thermometer on the wall. But would it not be just as silly for someone who really believed my fantasy about the causes of heart disease to try to erase its genetic cause by not smoking? Or for my Calvinist to try to get into Heaven by being devout? Of course, the Calvinist does not know whether he is among the elect and the potential victim of heart disease might not know whether she has unlucky genes. But that does not matter since, under the terms of the stories, the woman considering smoking knows that her doing so will not alter her chances of getting heart disease and the Calvinist knows that his sin will not consign him to Hell.

These examples show that even though a state is highly probable given an act, the act itself need not be an effective method for bringing about the state. Given everything we know about causal relationships, taking just the blue box is not an effective method for ensuring that there will be $1,000,000 in it. Perhaps we were mistaken then in using conditional probabilities in setting up the decision table for the Predictor paradox. Let us try again using the unconditional probabilities of the states. Since we do not what they are, I will denote them by "p" and "$1-p$." This yields table 4-8. Then whatever the value of p, taking both boxes has the higher expected utility, which agrees with the recommendation of the dominance principle. Applying the same strategy to the smoking and Calvinist cases yields similar results. This is how *causal decision theory* solves the Predictor paradox.

112

4-8	Blue Box Empty	Not Empty
Take Blue Box	0 p	1M $1-p$
Take Both Boxes	$1,000 p	1M + $1,000 $1-p$

However, there is more to causal decision theory than I have indicated so far. It does not advocate an unqualified return to unconditional probabilities. If you believe, as most of us do, that smoking does cause disease, then, despite smoking's dominating, causal decision theory recommends that you not smoke. Given our current beliefs about the *causal* relationship between smoking and disease, causal decision theory tells us to calculate expected utilities in the old way, that is, by using probabilities conditional on the acts of smoking and not smoking.

To have a more general formulation of causal decision theory, let us define the *conditional causal probability* of a state given an act as *the propensity for the act to produce or prevent the state*. Notice that if an act has a propensity to bring about a state, the conditional causal probability of that act will be greater than the unconditional probability of the state. If, on the other hand, the act has a propensity to prevent the state, the latter probability will be higher than the former. Finally, if an act has no propensity to affect the state, the probabilities will be the same.

Causal decision theory uses causal conditional probabilities in place of unqualified conditional probabilities. Warmer rooms do have a propensity to bring about higher thermometer readings, but the converse is not so. Thus, in applying causal decision theory, we can use the probability that a thermometer will rise given that it is located in a room that is becoming hotter. However, we must replace the converse conditional probability by the absolute probability, because the thermometer's rising has no propensity to bring about a rise in the room's temperature.

We can now see the rationale for causal decision theory's solution to the Predictor paradox. In making decisions we select acts in virtue of their power to produce the outcomes we desire (and hence the states that foster those outcomes). In view of this, it would be wrong for us to endow our decision theoretic framework with indicators of the efficacy of our acts that we know to be misleading. In the Predictor, Calvinist, and smoking examples, there is, as far as we can tell, no propensity for the acts to bring about the states. Thus standard decision theory used the wrong indicators in treating them. No wonder, then, that it produced an apparently inexplicable contradiction between the principle of maximizing expected utility and the dominance principle.

Sometimes a decision maker will be quite certain that an act will affect a state, but be uncertain about its ultimate outcomes because of other states she is unable to affect by her choices. A physician, for example, might be certain that giving an injection of penicillin is an effective way to cure a patient's infected toenail, but be uncertain whether it will cause a dangerous penicillin reaction—something over which she has no control. She should use conditional probabilities for evaluating the consequences of giving penicillin as far as the infection is concerned and unconditional probabilities for the allergic reaction. We could put this in the form of decision table 4-9 as follows. (For the sake of generating probability numbers, I will assume that the patient has a 50% chance of being allergic, that penicillin is an effective cure 75% of the time, and that the patient has a 30% of "curing himself" if no penicillin is given. Being cured of the infection is independent of having a reaction, so I will multiply the probabilities in calculating the probabilities of the various conjunctive states. I will also omit utilities.)

4-9	Patient Allergic Infection		Not Allergic Infection	
	Cured	Not Cured	Cured	Not Cured
Give Penicillin	Cure & Reaction .375	No Cure & Reaction .125	Cure & No Reaction .375	No Cure & No Reaction .125
Do not	Cure & No Reaction .15	No Cure & No Reaction .35	Cure & No Reaction .15	No Cure & No Reaction .35

Another sort of case is one in which the decision maker is unsure of the propensity of a given act to bring about a given state. Consider our physician again. Let us suppose she knows that her patient is not allergic to penicillin, but this time the patient has a staph infection. Here the physician might vacillate between thinking that penicillin has only a 50% chance of curing the patient and thinking that it has a 75% chance, while assigning a probability of 50% to each hypothesis. Suppose her other choice is to use antibiotic X in place of penicillin and that she is certain this is 60% effective. Then her decision could be represented as follows in table 4-10. (Again, I will omit utilities.)

4-10	Pen. 50% Effective Infection		Pen. 75% Effective Infection	
	Cured	Not Cured	Cured	Not Cured
Give Penicillin	Cure .25	No Cure .25	Cure .375	No Cure .125
Give X	Cure .30	No Cure .20	Cure .30	No Cure .20

The general form of these two examples is this. We first set out a mutually exclusive and exhaustive list of states that represent those factors relevant to the decision that will not be affected by the acts. This may include possibilities concerning the propensity of one or more of our acts to affect other states. Then under each of these states we set up a mutually exclusive and exhaustive list of relevant states that will be affected by the act, repeating this division under each state from the first group. Using absolute probabilities for states in the first group and causal conditional probabilities for those in the second group, we calculate the probabilities for each square of decision table 4-10 by multiplying the probabilities of the two states that determine it. Expected utilities are then calculated in the usual way: Multiply each utility in a square by the corresponding probability and sum across the rows.

PROBLEMS

1. Suppose in the first penicillin example the physician's utilities are as follows: u(cure & no reaction) = 1, u(cure & reaction) = .5, u(no cure & no reaction) = .25, u(no cure & reaction) = 0. Should the physician use penicillin?
2. Suppose in the second penicillin example the physician is also uncertain about the effectiveness of antibiotic X. She thinks there is a 50% chance that it is 70% effective and a 50% chance that it is 40% effective. Set up a decision table for this example, supplying probabilities for each square.

4-6a. Objections and Alternatives

Causal decision theory is certainly a reasonable and attractive alternative to the standard theory of expected utility maximization. But I would be remiss if I did not point out that it too must deal with philosophical difficulties of its own. The most prominent of these is its appeal to causal necessities (as opposed to mere statistical regularities), which have been philosophically suspect ever since Hume's critique of causality. Hume's thesis was a simple one: What pass for causal necessities are in fact nothing but statistical regularities; for, try as we may, we will never find evidence for causal necessities but only for statistical regularities. Since Hume's claim might seem very implausible to you, let us consider an example where causal necessity seems to be plainly at work. You grab a handful of snow, pack it into a ball, and throw it at one of your friends. The snowball hits his back and splatters. On the face of it causes abound here: Your exerting force on the snow causes it to form a hard ball, your hurling it causes it to fly through the air, its impacting your friend's back causes it to splatter, and so on. Let us focus on your packing the snow, since here you seem to able to even *feel* causal powers at work. Now Hume would not deny that whenever you or anyone you know has packed snow into a ball, shortly thereafter there has been a snowball in your or his hand. He would simply deny that this gives us any evidence that you *caused* the snow to form a ball, in the sense that your action *necessitated* the observed effect. If the cause must necessarily produce the effect it is inconceivable for the cause to occur without the effect's occurring.

But we can easily conceive of cases in which we apply the "cause" to the snow and no snowball results. For example, as we pack the ball, someone might shine a heat lamp on the snow, "causing" it to melt. Now you might think that all this shows is that we can cause the snow to form a ball so long as no *interfering causes* prevent it. But given any putative list of interfering causes, it is still easy to conceive of our packing the snow and the snow's still failing to form a ball despite the absence of each of the interfering causes in our list. Besides, we have helped ourselves freely to the notion of causality in describing the example. If we take a neutral stance, we should describe ourselves as having observed that whenever we have had "snowball-packing" sensations we have found a snowball in our hands. But once we look at the example in this way, Hume's point becomes almost obvious. For we can have snowball-packing sensations without even having anything in our hands!

If Hume is correct, there are no causal powers or laws—just highly confirmed regularities—and causal decision theory is without foundation. Viewing the heart disease example from the Humean point of view, we will find no basis for distinguishing the high correlation between smoking and heart disease and between the genetic defect and heart disease. Given that you smoke, it is highly probable that you will get heart disease. Given that you have the defect, it is highly probable that you will smoke and have heart disease. But without appealing to the concept of causality (or something similar) we have no grounds for claiming that your smoking will *affect* your chances of having heart disease. Similarly, we cannot, strictly speaking, say that your taking both boxes will have no effect on whether there is $1,000,000 in the blue box; for the language of cause and effects is not available to us. We are left then with nothing but correlations. And given the correlations, we are best advised not to smoke and to take just the blue box.

There is a practical and epistemological aspect to Hume's problem too. For even those who believe in causality have been hard pressed to specify methods for distinguishing genuine causal relations from mere statistical regularities. This problem bears on the applicability of causal decision theory, since it requires us to segregate states over which we have causal control from those that are connected to our acts by mere statistical regularities.

Although these difficulties favor a more Humean approach to decision theory, causal theorists have a biting response. The point of decision theory, they argue, is to develop methods for choosing acts that yield desirable consequences. If our acts have no effect on the outcomes, what is the point of choosing? We might as well just watch whatever happens, happen. Indeed, if there are no causes, we act, if we can call it that, by being passive observers. How, then, can we continue to speak of choosing between such *acts* as, say, *replacing the window myself* or *hiring someone to do it*?

Some Humean theorists, or as they are now called, *evidential decision theorists*, although acknowledging this point, respond that the true role for decision theory is to help us determine our preferences for *news items*. Pushed to the limit, this would mean that when we decide between, say, marrying at eighteen or jilting our sweetheart and joining the Foreign Legion, we are determining whether we would prefer to learn the news that we had married at eighteen or instead that we had jilted our sweetheart and joined the Foreign Legion. Making a choice is to pick from among such news items.

As long as one is consistent about this, decision theory retains its point. Suppose that, in casual terms, I buy a brand-new Mercedes to ensure that people will think I am rich. The evidential theorist can recast this as my choosing to learn that I own a new Mercedes on the grounds that (1) I know there is a high correlation between owning a Mercedes and being thought rich and (2) I desire to learn that people think I am rich.

In the Predictor case causal decision theory advises us to take both boxes because doing so cannot affect their contents. Evidential decision theory advises us to pay attention to the evidence: There can be no evidence of causality since there is no causality; but there is plenty of evidence that after we pick just the blue box we are almost certain to learn that we are rich. So we ought to take just the blue box. And so the debate goes.

Recently, Ellery Eells has indicated a way in which one can arrive at the same recommendations as causal decision theory without having to base decision theory on the distinction between those states that are under our causal control and those that are not. However, unlike the dyed-in-the-wool Humean, Eells does assume that it makes sense to speak of causes. Consider the smoking example again. Eells describes it in causal terms as we did before: A birth defect is the common cause of both smoking and heart disease, and that is why there is a high correlation between smoking and heart disease. However, Eells parts company with the causal decision theorist at this point, for he does not simply dismiss the high correlation between smoking and heart disease on the grounds that we have no control over whether we have the genetic cause of both smoking and heart disease. Instead he argues that if you are sufficiently rational and intelligent, you will see that the high correlation in no way entails that the probability that you, in particular, will get heart disease given that you smoke is greater than the probability that you will get it given that you do not smoke. Eells bases his reasoning on the assumption that you do not know whether you have the birth defect and that you believe it is the common cause of both smoking and heart disease. Given this, you might think that you should assign a high probability to getting heart disease given that you smoke, since smoking is an indication that you have the birth defect. But Eells parries this move by introducing another assumption, namely, that you believe the common cause can cause you to decide to smoke only by causing you to have desires and beliefs that entail that smoking is an optimal act for you. Given this, you will believe that the variables determining your choice to smoke or not are fully captured in the particular beliefs and desires you have when you make the decision. Eells assumes that you know what your beliefs and desires are, although you do not know whether you have the defect leading to smoking. But this means that you would believe that any rational agent who had your beliefs and desires would, regardless of having or not having the defect, arrive at the same decision. Thus *you* should assign the same probability to your deciding to smoke (and doing so) given that you have the defect as you would assign to your deciding to smoke (and doing so) given that you do not have the defect. Once you do that, however, the dominant act is the rational one for you to choose.

Eells then argues that the same idea applies to the Predictor. Assuming that as a rational agent you do not believe in backward causation, mind control, or miracles, Eells concludes that you must believe that some common cause is responsible for both your choice and the Predictor's prediction. Perhaps there is something about our appearance that distinguishes those who will take just the blue box from those who will take both. Perhaps the Predictor is not even conscious of this. But no matter; you do not need to know what the common cause is or whether you have it. You simply need to believe that the Predictor case follows the same model as the smoking decision. Then the same reasoning shows that you should assign the same probability to there being $1,000,000 in the blue box given that you chose it alone as you would to there being $1,000,000 in it given that you took both.

Although the Eells solution to the Predictor paradox avoids importing causality directly into the formal scaffolding of decision theory, it still depends heavily on causal reasoning in analyzing the problematic decisions. If you do not believe in causality, then you could hardly accept Eells's assumptions to the effect that rational agents in the Predictor situation will believe that there must be a common cause that links their choice and the Predictor's prediction. A full reconciliation between causal and evidential decision theory is thus still not in the offing.

(A final note: There are variants of causal decision theory that reduce causal necessities to something else, for example, to natural laws. But Humean objections apply to these views too. Also I have only stated a response to Hume that happens to be particularly suited to our concern with decision theory. Philosophers have propounded several subtle and profound responses to Hume. Yet the debate over the reality of causality rages on, with the advent of causal decision theory adding fuel to the fire.)

4-6b. Concluding Remarks on the Paradoxes

We have just reviewed a potpourri of paradoxes and have found definitive resolutions to none of them. Does this mean that utility theory is doomed? That its foundations are rotten and crumbling? How should we respond to the paradoxes?

First, we must determine the type of evidence that is to count as relevant to utility theory. The fact that most people have an aversion to betting on coins of unknown bias or prefer the bird in the hand, facts on which the Ellsberg and Allais paradoxes depend, need not be relevant to abstract decision theory. For the theory claims to describe the behavior of ideally rational beings rather than that of ordinary people. On the other hand, we cannot determine what an ideally rational agent would do by asking one or observing one in a psychological laboratory. Such beings are, after all, merely hypothetical extrapolations based on what we think we would do if we had better memories, longer attention spans, quicker brains, sharper mathematical powers, and so forth. Thus our judgment that a given act is irrational could be entirely relevant to a theory of an ideally rational agent. In confronting the Ellsberg and Allais paradoxes, then, one of the chief issues will be whether we should take our aversion to the choices recommended by utility theory as failures on our part to be less than fully rational or as evidence that utility theory has incorrectly characterized rational choice under risk.

Decision theorists have taken both approaches to those paradoxes. Savage, you will recall, tried to show us that the Allais paradox is simply a trick that is easily explained away when seen in a clear light. But others have complicated and revised decision theory to discount the utility of acts involving systems whose biases are unknown and to mark up those involving certainties. If we decide to reject Savage's or similar resolutions, we should take such theories seriously and see whether they harbor their own paradoxes or anomalies. Since these theories are even more complicated than standard utility theory, I must forgo that task here.

The St. Petersburg and Predictor paradoxes, by contrast, are intended to show not that utility theory conflicts with our untutored views of rationality but rather that it is internally incoherent: that it offers, as in the Predictor paradox, conflicting recommendations, or that it commits us to something of infinite utility so long as there is no upper bound to our preferences. Again, there are those who have taken these paradoxes to heart and have offered revised versions of utility theory. Causal decision theory is an example. And again, there are experts who believe that these paradoxes dissolve when carefully analyzed. Eells is a case in point.

There has been an additional and most interesting reaction to the Predictor paradox, however. Some people believe that it reveals that there are *two types of rationality*. One type is captured by decision theories that apply the dominance rule to the Predictor problem; the other is captured by theories that follow the rule of expected utility maximization. Thus, just as we have had alternative geometries for over a hundred years and alternative logics and set theories for the last fifty years, we might now have alternative decision theories.

In sum, reactions to the paradoxes range from dismissing them as intellectual illusions to proposing revisions of utility theory to entertaining the possibility of alternative conceptions of rational choice. Plainly, it will be a while before a consensus on the paradoxes is obtained.

4-7. References

The classic presentation of the version of utility theory expounded in this chapter is contained in *Von Neumann and Morgenstern*. *Raiffa* is a clear introductory account, which focuses more on the relation between monetary values and utility than I have here. *Savage* contains a brief history of the concept of utility. For the Ellsberg and Allais paradoxes see *Ellsberg* and *Allais*, respectively. Replies may be found in *Savage*, *Raiffa*, and *Eells*. *Jeffrey* has a discussion of and response to the St. Petersburg paradox. *Eells* is also a good general review of utility theory and causal decision theory. See also Skyrm's *Causal Necessity*, *Gibbard and Harper*, and *Lewis*. *Nozick* announced the Predictor paradox to the philosophical world. *Eells* lists much of the extensive literature on that paradox.

Chapter 5
GAME THEORY

5-1. The Basic Concepts of Game Theory

Individual decision theory focuses on decisions involving the choices of one agent and outcomes determined by the agent's choices and the background environment. Its paradigms are those of a single person deciding whether to wear a raincoat, place a bet, invest in a stock, or attend a law school. Some of its examples, such as the choice between taking a course under Professor Smith rather than under Professor Jones, involve other individuals, but in analyzing such examples it treats the additional individuals as part of the environment. Now we will expand our analytic framework to include cases in which the decisions of other individuals are represented as playing an *active* role in determining the outcomes; these situations are called *games*. Games include ordinary parlor games, such as chess, bridge, Monopoly, or Scrabble; they also include serious decision-making situations as well, such as competitive bidding on oil leases, choosing weapons systems, pricing perfume, selling or holding stocks of grain, or proposing terms of peace.

To get a firmer grip on the game concept let us look closely at two games, a diverting one—chess—and a deadly serious one—negotiating a peace treaty. In chess there are two *players*; at a peace conference each nation is a player and there are often more than two. Each chess player aims to win; each nation negotiating peace seeks terms most favorable to it. Chess is played by one player making a move, the other responding, and so forth, until one wins or there is a draw. At the negotiating table players make proposals and counterproposals, but the outcomes are nowhere as clearly defined as in chess. Peace talks may drag on for years, with the attendant delays costing one or both sides dearly in human or economic tolls; or they may quickly conclude in a settlement because one nation has gained clear military superiority; or they may be broken off and the war continued. Furthermore, in real peace talks the rules are minimal and quite vague; there is no limited set of choices open to each negotiator nor are the outcomes limited to a definite set. In treating peace talks by means of game theory, however, we must assume that definite sets of choices are open to the negotiators, that the outcomes are limited, and that the "rules" determine which outcomes are associated with each series of choices by the players. Unlike chess, the environment determines outcomes of peace talks too. If the rainy season is especially severe, the more mobile army can get the upper hand; if there are storms at sea, supply lines can be cut. In this respect, peace talks are best treated like gin rummy, bridge, poker, and other *games of chance*. This is done in game theory by introducing an additional player, called *Chance*, who makes choices using a randomizing device of one kind or another. Rolling dice in Monopoly, dealing hands of cards in bridge, dealing and drawing cards in gin are treated as moves by Chance.

Some of the elements of a game are beginning to emerge from our discussion. First, each game has two or more *players*. If the game is one of chance, there are at least three players with Chance being one of them. Second, each game has one or more *moves* with one or more players being allowed a choice at each move. Third, the rules of the game determine for each sequence of moves whether it results in an *outcome*, and if it does, what the outcome is. A sequence of moves terminating in an outcome of a game is called a *play*. Some games have short plays. The children's game scissors, paper, and stone is usually played with both players revealing their choices at the same time. The outcome is immediate: Scissors beats paper, paper beats stone, stone beats scissors, anything else is a draw. Chess, by contrast, has plays of every finite length, provided players are allowed to repeat sequences of moves.

Game theory uses two means for representing games formally. The *game-tree method* uses structures similar to decision trees to represent games. Each move is represented by a labeled node of the tree — a circle with a numeral within it — indicating which player is given a choice at that node. The choices open to the player are represented by branches emanating from the node. Outcomes are assigned to the end of each branch and are usually represented by means of one or more numbers that indicate the utility received by each player for the outcome.

A game tree for scissors, paper, and stone cannot represent the players as choosing simultaneously, because only one player is assigned to each node. Game theory handles this problem by representing the second player as making a choice without knowing what choice the first player made. (Similarly, the effect of simultaneous bidding on a contract is often achieved by having potential contractors submit sealed bids prior to an announced time at which all bids are to be opened.) Thus after the first player has made a choice, the second player will not know whether he or she is at the node following the first's choice of scissors or at the one following the choice of paper or the one following the choice of stone. These nodes are said to belong to the same *information set*, and the second player is said to have *imperfect information* because he or she is unable to distinguish between the various nodes within the information set. In the game tree depicted in figure 5-1, there is a dotted line surrounding all the second player's nodes to indicate that they all belong to the same information set. The outcomes are given as wins, losses, or draws for player 1.

122

Scissors, paper, and stone, as represented here, and bridge and Monopoly, in actual practice, are games of imperfect information: Even players with perfect

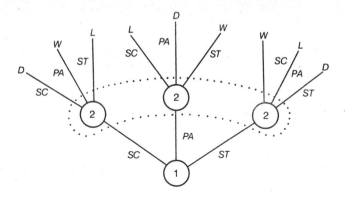

Figure 5-1

memories cannot know the entire history of the play preceding their moves. Thus, although in principle Monopoly players can know the assets and liabilities of the other players, and where they have landed, they cannot know, at least not until quite late in the game, what move Chance made initially when arranging the "chance" and "community chest" cards. Chess and checkers, on the other hand, are games of perfect information. Games of chance are not necessarily games of imperfect information; Monopoly without "chance" and "community chest" cards would be a game of perfect information despite Chance's making every other move. Nor are Chance moves required for a game of imperfect information; the tree version of scissors, paper, and stone has no place for Chance.

Game theory abstracts from most of the psychological and practical features of a game; it counts any two games having the same game tree as the same game. Chess played with carved ivory pieces is the same game as chess played with plastic pieces. That is not remarkable. On the other hand, it is interesting that chess played with a one-second time limit is still regular chess as far as game theory is concerned. The next example is even more notable. The game of fifteen has two players who use nine cards, an ace through a nine. These cards are laid face up on a table in front of the players, who take turns picking up cards. The object of the game is to achieve a total of 15 with exactly three cards before the other player does. (An ace counts as a 1.) The game ends in a draw if all the cards are drawn with no player achieving a 15 with exactly three cards. Now consider any tick-tack-toe board and think of the squares as numbered according to the scheme in table 5-1.

The diagonals, the middle column, and the middle row sum to 15; thus, the game of fifteen has the same game tree as that restricted version of tick-tack-toe that counts "three in a row" only if they fall on a diagonal or middle row

123

or column. If you draw game trees for restricted tick-tack-toe and the game of fifteen you will see that they are the same. (Do not try unless you have a big

5-1	1	2	3
	4	5	6
	7	8	9

sheet of paper, time, and patience; the first move has nine branches.)

Just as decision trees can be reduced to decision tables, so too can game trees be reduced to game matrices or tables by using strategies. Two-person games can be represented by m-by-n tables, with the m rows and n columns corresponding to strategies and the entries in the squares representing the *payoffs* or outcomes for each player for the pair of strategies (row, column) determining the square in question. Here is game table 5-2 for scissors, paper, and stone.

5-2   Col's Strategies

		SC	PA	ST
		SC	PA	ST
Row's Strategies	SC	D, D	W, L	L, W
	PA	L, W	D, D	W, L
	ST	W, L	L, W	D, D

The first payoff given in each square is for the player using the strategies assigned to the rows; the second payoff is for the player using those heading the columns. For convenience we will call the first player "Row" and the second "Col." Thus when Row plays SC (scissors) and Col plays ST (stone), the payoff to Row is an L (loss) and that to Col is a W (win). Any game involving a series of moves will have a large number of strategies and, thus, a huge table or matrix. Despite this, many of the theoretical and philosophical features of game theory can be best understood in terms of games in matrix form. Consequently we will henceforth restrict ourselves to games in this form.

Chance is no longer represented in the matrix form of a game. Her role is absorbed in the payoffs. The example of gin will be used to explain how this happens. Gin is put into matrix form by having both players make just one move each—they pick a strategy. Their individual strategies will consist in a complete list of instructions for reacting to any hand they may be dealt, any cards they may draw, any cards their opponent may discard, and so on. Because gin is a game of chance, a selection of strategies by players alone does not determine a unique outcome; different distributions of the cards will generally result in different winners for the same selection of strategies. Yet each selection of strategies does determine a lottery among the possible outcomes, with the possible distributions of cards yielding the probabilities in the lottery. Suppose, for example, the game is being played by just Row and Col, who have selected two strategies R_1 and C_1. Let us further suppose that for a third of the arrangements of the cards the pair (R_1, C_1) yields a win for Row, for another third it yields a win for Col, and for the balance it yields a draw. Then we can associate with the pair (R_1, C_1) the lottery that yields an equal chance of a draw, Row's winning, and Col's winning. This takes Chance's role as a player and adsorbs it into the outcomes.

Game theory takes this a step further. Each player is assumed to have a utility function for outcomes that abides by the expected utility theorem. Thus the utility of an outcome that happens to be a lottery is equal to its expected utility, and outcomes, whether lotteries or certainties, can be represented by utility numbers. The net effect is that a game of chance and a game of certainty could be represented by the same game matrix and would thus be counted as the same game by the theory. Here is an artificial example to illustrate this. In the game of even and odd two players choose between two strategies, E and O. E beats O; otherwise there is a draw. If we use 1 to represent a win, -1 a loss, and 0 a draw, the table for the game is given on the left (5-3). (Payoffs are given

5-3	E	O
E	0	1
O	-1	0

5-4	E	O
E	0	0
O	0	0

for Row.) Consider now a chancy version of even and odd. Players again choose between the two strategies, but then a coin is flipped. On heads, the result is the same as in even and odd; on tails, the result is calculated as if each player had the opposite strategies. Thus the pairs (E, E) and (O, O) yield the same results in either game, since each ends in a draw. Yet in the chancy version the payoff to Row for (E, O) is a coin toss, which yields a win on heads and a loss on tails. Thus its expected utility is $(1/2)1 + (1/2) - 1$, namely, 0. Finally, consider a two-player game of certainty with two strategies that always ends in a draw. This will have the same game table as the chancy version of odd and even; namely, table 5-4.

As we have already seen, game theory assumes that the players have utility functions producing interval scales for outcomes and lotteries involving outcomes. The theory also assumes that given a choice of strategies by his opponents, each player will choose those strategies that maximize his expected utility. On the other hand, the theory does not require the players to prefer winning; if a parent prefers to throw a game of checkers to boost her child's spirits, the parent's utility function will assign higher utility to losing. However, game theory will represent this version of checkers by a different table or tree than the standard version, since high utilities for winning outcomes will be replaced with low ones. Despite this, whichever game the parent plays, the theory will assume that she seeks to maximize her utility.

Game theory also assumes that all players know both the entire game tree or table, whichever is relevant, and their own and all other players' utilities for outcomes. Furthermore, each player is taken to know that every player knows all this. This means that in thinking about a game all players can assume that they are playing with perfect opponents, who will always make optimal responses to every move or strategy choice. *The object of game theory is to determine the outcome or possible outcomes of each game, given these assumptions about the players.* To do this for a game is to *solve* it.

Before proceeding further let us see how game theory solves a simple game. The game is given in table 5-5. The best strategy for Col is C_2; he re-

5-5	C_1	C_2	C_3
R_1	0, 0	1, 2	0, 2
R_2	1, 3	1, 4	0, 0

ceives 2 or 4, which is at least as good as his payoffs for C_1 and C_3. The same reasoning shows that the best choice for Row is R_2. Thus the game will be played via the strategy pair (R_2, C_2); Row will get a payoff of 1, Col one of 4. (Note: Row's utilities are taken to be fully specified; it would be fallacious to reason that Row would prefer to see Col get 2, and thus, knowing that C_2 will be chosen in any case, will choose R_1.)

There are several branches of game theory. The most important division is between the theory of two-person games and that of games involving more than two persons. (In this classification Chance does not count as a person.) The latter is usually called "n-person game theory." It is much more complicated than the two-person branch, because players can form coalitions and overwhelm another player, which makes it useful in analyzing political and economic situations. Unfortunately, the n-person theory is also in a less satisfactory mathematical state than the two-person theory. Accordingly, we will restrict our discussion, in the main, to the two-person theory.

Games are also classified according to whether the players' interests are entirely opposed (strictly competitive games) or in partial agreement. Monopoly and chess count as strictly competitive, but two drivers trying to avoid a head-on collision are involved in a game that is not strictly competitive. Nonstrictly competitive games are further divided according to whether the players are permitted to communicate with each other to coordinate stategies. If they can, the game is called a *cooperative game*. These games may allow the players to form binding agreements and even to redistribute the payoffs. Labor negotiators play cooperative games that end in binding agreements. When a play is sold to a movie company, the playwright's agent and a movie producer play a cooperative game which ends with a contract for distributing the profits of the sale. On the other hand, two friends who have been separated at a crowded rock concert play a simple nonstrictly competitive game as they try to find each other.

Parlor games and sports may be the only games that are strictly competitive in reality. Even in war no nation seeks the total destruction of its opponent; thus the players have some common interests, and at peace conferences nations not only communicate but also agree to share certain payoffs. Despite this, game theorists often find it useful to analyze wars as strictly competitive games, since in the choice of strategies for battle the noncompetitive aspects of war are usually negligible.

In a strictly competitive game communication and contracts play no role, even if the rules permit them. For there is no reason to trust one's opponents; they can be expected to lie or cheat if doing so promotes their interests. Every player knows this and thus puts no stock in what the others say, threaten, or gesture. Game theory reflects this by letting lapse the distinction between games with and without communication when analyzing strictly competitive games.

PROBLEMS

1. Which of the following are games of perfect information?
    a. checkers
    b. poker
    c. tick-tack-toe
    d. bridge
    e. Chinese checkers
2. Discuss basketball from the point of view of game theory. How many players are there? Is an actual basketball game a single big game or a series of games? Are the games strictly competitive or cooperative? Does communication play any role?
3. Discuss the process of nominating a candidate for the U.S. presidency in game theoretic terms. Who are the players? Is the game strictly competitive? Can the players make agreements to distribute payoffs?
4. Why does prohibiting communication make no difference in the outcome of a strictly competitive game among perfectly rational players?

5-2. Two-Person Strictly Competitive Games

The most fully developed part of game theory is the theory of two-person strictly competitive games. Since in many ways it is also the easiest portion of game theory to grasp, we will start our study with it.

In a strictly competitive game the preferences of the two players are in exact opposition. To the extent one gains from an outcome of the game, the other loses. If we think of the gains and losses in terms of monetary payoffs, the winner receives the winnings in terms of a payoff from the loser. But the very reasons that led us to replace monetary values with utilities in individual decision theory will again lead us to make the same substitution in game theory. First, monetary or other concrete payoffs might not reflect the true values of the players. In a game between two unmitigated altruists, winning in the ordinary sense is actually the worst outcome for each. Yet their preferences are in com-

GAME THEORY

plete opposition: For them the game is strictly competitive—each does his damnedest to lose—but their preferences are just the opposite of those of ordinary players. For that reason they are playing a different game, and thus representing it requires us to replace concrete payoffs with the utilities each player assigns them. A second reason for using utilities is that outcomes frequently are best represented as lotteries. When this is done, explaining why maximizing expected utilities is the rational approach to these games—even when played only once or just a few times—drives us to identify the utility of a gamble with its expected utility. The need for doing this will be even more pressing later when we introduce mixed strategies.

In any two-person strictly competitive game the utility function of Col is the negative of that for Row, since Row and Col have strictly opposing preferences. Let $u(A)$ be Row's utility for the outcome A. Then Col's utility for A is $-u(A)$, and their utilities sum to zero. For this reason two-person strictly competitive games are often known as *zero sum games*. In a zero sum game table or tree we need not present the utilities for both players, since one's can be deduced from the other's. From now on payoffs will be given in the form of Row's utilities only.

Table 5-6 presents a simple zero sum game. Let us see how the theory solves it. Remember, Row seeks to maximize the outcome numbers and Col

5-6	C_1	C_2	C_3	C_4
R_1	0	1	7	7
R_2	4	1	2	10
R_3	3	1	0	25
R_4	0	0	7	10

tries to keep them down. A quick check will show that none of Row's strategies are dominated by the others, and that Col's C_4 is dominated by all his other strategies. So Col will not play C_4 and Row knows this. Knowing this, he also knows he can now ignore all the entries in the fourth column when picking his strategy. The game, in effect, reduces from a four-by-four game to a four-by-three game. But then R_3 can be deleted; it is dominated by R_2 once the 25 at the end of the row is ignored. Our game now amounts to this one (table 5-7).

5-7	C_1	C_2	C_3
R_1	0	1	7
R_2	4	1	2
R_3	0	0	7

In this game, however, C_3 is dominated by both C_1 and C_2; so Col will not play it. Knowing this, Row will play R_2, and knowing that in turn, Col will play C_2. So the solution to the games is this: Row and Col play the strategy pair (R_2, C_2), and the payoff to Row is 1. The payoff received by Row according to the game's solution is called *the value of the game*.

PROBLEMS

Use dominance reasoning to solve the following games (tables 5-8, 5-9, 5-10).

5-8

7	6	4
3	2	1
5	6	4

5-9

10	1	3
4	2	4

5-10

2	2	4	5
7	1	5	3
4	2	3	1

5-3. Equilibrium Strategy Pairs

One might think that all zero sum games can be solved by simple considerations of dominance—if they have a solution at all. But table 5-11 shows that this plainly is not so. Neither Row nor Col has a dominated strategy; so the process of elimination used to solve the last game cannot get started. Despite that, the

5-11

	C_1	C_2	C_3
R_1	8	8	7
R_2	0	10	4
R_3	9	0	1

solution of the game is readily at hand. Consider the strategy pair (R_1, C_3). If Row knew that Col would play C_3, then he, Row, would play R_1 because that is the best he can do against C_3. On the other hand, if Col knew that Row would play R_1, then he, Col, would play C_3 since that would bring Row's payoff down to the lowest point possible. The strategies (R_1, C_3) are in *equilibrium* in the sense that once this pair is chosen neither player will prefer to change unilaterally to another strategy. He *cannot* do better by changing. In general we will say that a pair of strategies is an *equilibrium pair* or is in equilibrium just in case

129

neither player can do better by unilaterally changing his strategy. The payoff associated with an equilibrium pair is called an *equilibrium value.*

Once the players hit on an equilibrium pair, neither has any reason for changing his strategy choice unless the other player does too. But what reason is there to expect that they will hit on one? In a zero sum game communication and bargaining are excluded; the only way they could both decide upon an equilibrium pair is for each to decide on his own that his half of the pair is the best strategy for him. How can that happen?

Return to the game presented in table 5-11. Other things being equal, the best strategy for Row is R_2; it gives him a chance at the highest payoff. But other things are not equal; Row must contend with Col's strategy choice, and Col would pick C_1 if he thought Row would pick R_2. Row knows this, and he knows that Col knows that he knows, and so on. On the other hand, Col would most prefer the payoffs of 0 afforded by C_1 and C_2 — if Row would only cooperate and pick R_2 and R_3, respectively. But Col knows that he cannot count on that. Moreover, Row can see that if he picks R_1, he can depend on a payoff of at least 7, whereas any other strategy might yield a 0, a 1, or a 4. Col also sees that he can depend on holding Row down to a 7 if he, Col, chooses C_3, but any other choice might allow Row a gain of 8, 9, or 10. Each sees then that by playing his half of the equilibrium pair he can guarantee a certain value, *his security level* for the game; playing another strategy might lead to a less favorable outcome. Given that each knows he is playing against a perfect player, neither will risk taking a strategy that does not yield his security level for the game. By independent reasoning, then, each picks his half of the equilibirium pair.

The definition of equilibrium pairs is fit for other branches of game theory. There is, however, a simpler criterion for equilibrium pairs in zero sum games. Let us call it *the minimax equilibrium test for zero sum games.* It reads: *In a zero sum game a necessary and sufficient condition for a pair of strategies to be in equilibrium is that the payoff determined by them equal the minimal value of its row and the maximal value of its column.* In the game in table 5-12, for example, the equilibrium test picks out (R_2, C_2) as the equilibrium pair. Notice that al-

5-12	C_1	C_2	C_3
R_1	1	3	6
R_2	7	5	5
R_3	3	4	10

though the 5 at the intersection of row 2 and column 3 is the minimal value for row 2, it is not the maximal value for column 3; so the pair (R_2, C_3) is not in equilibrium.

Some games have several equilibrium pairs. The game in table 5-13 has two, that in table 5-14 has four. This raises a serious question: If a game has more than one equilibrium pair, need the players worry about coordinating their choices to guarantee that the strategy pair they pick will in fact be in equilibrium? Since communication, and thus coordination, is pointless in a zero sum game, the use of equilibrium solutions for zero sum games appears to be jeopardized. Fortunately there is no need to worry. The answer to our question is negative. Examine the two games in tables 5-13 and 5-14. In the first, Row

5-13	C_1	C_2	C_3
R_1	0	8	3
R_2	0	1	10
R_3	-2	6	5

5-14	C_1	C_2	C_3	C_4
R_1	1	2	3	1
R_2	0	5	0	0
R_3	1	6	4	1

has to worry about coordination; his equilibrium strategies are R_1 and R_2. But this is no problem for Row; for both (R_1, C_1) and (R_2, C_1) are in equilibrium. Either choice he makes will be fine. The second example is more complicated. Row has two choices, R_1 and R_3, and Col has two also, C_1 and C_4. Yet no matter which choice either makes they will achieve equilibrium; (R_1, C_1), (R_1, C_4), (R_3, C_1), and (R_3, C_4) are all equilibrium pairs and each has the same value.

These examples are instances of a general theorem, which I will call the *coordination theorem for zero sum games*. It reads:

If, in a zero sum game, the pairs (R_i, C_j) and (R_l, C_m) are in equilibrium, so are the pairs (R_i, C_m) and (R_l, C_j); furthermore, the values for each of the pairs are the same.

PROOF. Let v_{ij}, v_{lm}, v_{im}, and v_{lj} be the values for the pairs (R_i, C_j), (R_l, C_m), (R_i, C_m), and (R_l, C_j), respectively. Since the game is assumed to be zero sum, the equilibrium test applies to it. Thus v_{ij} and v_{lm} are minimal values for their rows and maximal values for their columns. Since v_{ij} and v_{im} occur in the same row and v_{ij} is an equilibrium value, we know that

(1) $v_{ij} \leq v_{im}$.

But since v_{lm} and v_{im} are in the same column and the latter is an equilibrium value, we have

(2) $v_{im} \leq v_{lm}$.

Since v_{lj} and v_{lm} are in the same row, we have

(3) $v_{lm} \leq v_{lj}$.

Finally, since v_{lj} and v_{ij} are in the same column,

(4) $v_{lm} \leq v_{ij}$.

Putting (1)–(4) together we find that

(5) $v_{ij} \leq v_{im} \leq v_{lm} \leq v_{lj} \leq v_{ij}$,

and this happens only if these values are all equal. But if the values are all equal, the pairs (R_1, C_j) and (R_i, C_m) must be in equilibrium too for, occurring as they do in the same rows and columns as other equilibrium pairs having their value, they must be the minimal values for their rows and maximal values for their columns.

PROBLEMS

1. Prove that if a game has a dominant row and column, that row and column determine an equilibrium pair for the game.
2. Prove that every strategy pair that passes the equilibrium test is in equilibrium in the originally defined sense, and conversely.
3. Give an example of a game with an equilibrium pair whose row is dominated.
4. Suppose in game G row R is strictly dominated by some row S, that is, every entry in S is greater than its correspondent in R. Can R be half of an equilibrium pair for G?

5-3a. Mixed Strategies

If every zero sum game had at least one pair of strategies in equilibrium, the theory of zero sum games would now be complete. Given any game of that kind, we could apply the maximin test and mechanically solve the game. The bad news is that some zero sum games fail to succumb to this method; the good news is that there still is a complete and mathematically rich account of zero sum games.

Consider the following situation. You are playing scissors, paper, and stone against a perfect player who is also a perfect mind reader. Thus whenever you decide on a strategy she picks one that beats it. If you pick paper, she picks scissors; if you pick stone, she picks paper; if you pick scissors, she picks stone. Look at game table 5-15. No pair of strategies is in equilibrium; so you cannot

5-15	SC	PA	ST
SC	0	1	−1
PA	−1	0	1
ST	1	−1	0

even guarantee yourself a draw.

There is a way out of this trap and it leads to a general solution for games of this type. Suppose that instead of picking your strategy directly you choose it by means of a chance mechanism that can yield any of the three possible strategies. For example, you could roll a die and then play play scissors on 1 or 2, paper on 3 or 4, and stone on 5 or 6. In effect you have adopted a strategy that is a mixture of your original strategies and that, when played against any strategy of your opponent's, yields an equal chance of the outcomes determined by your original strategies. In particular, when played against stone your strategy has a probability of 1/3 of yielding -1, the same probability of yielding 0 and the same probability of yielding 1. Thus its expected utility is 0, which is an improvement over your previous situation with its expected utility of -1. It is also easy to see that this mixed strategy has the same expected utility when played against your opponent's strategy of paper or scissors.

By picking a mixed strategy you also defuse your opponent's power to read your mind. For once you have decided on a mixed strategy, you can turn the rest of the game over to a suitably constructed machine. For example, the machine could consist of a drum spinning inside a box with a window that exposes only a third of the drum's surface at any one time—like the slot machines in Las Vegas. Turning the machine on would give the drum an initial spin. The drum would eventually stop and, with a probability determined by the fraction of the drum allocated to each word, display one of the words "scissors," "paper," or "stone." The word displayed would then be used to compute the outcome of the game against your opponent's choice. Since you would have chosen no specific strategy prior to turning the machine on, and since once the machine is on you have no further choices to make, it would be impossible for your opponent to choose a winning counterstrategy by reading your mind.

By the way, this is not a farfetched idea. In war, where the element of surprise can make all the difference, the threat of espionage is ever present. One way to protect oneself is to develop several strategies and choose to act on one only at the last possible minute. Letting a chance mechanism make the choice for you is a refinement of this idea.

So far we appear to have improved your situation, but can we not expect your opponent to counter with a mixed strategy of her own? Yes, but it makes no difference in this game. Your mixed strategy has the expected utility of 0 against any strategy she plays, mixed or not. Before trying to show this we must introduce some terminology and additional symbolism. Let us call the original strategies *pure strategies* to distinguish them from mixed ones. Both you and your opponent have the same pure strategies in this game, namely, SC, PA, ST. So far we have considered one mixed strategy for you, namely, one that involves an equal chance of playing SC, PA, or ST. We can write this as

(1/3 SC, 1/3 PA, 1/3 ST).

There are other mixed strategies available to you; for instance, you could play SC with probability of 1/2 and PA and ST each with a probability of 1/4. We can represent this by

(1/2 SC, 1/4 PA, 1/4 ST).

More generally, we can represent any of your mixed strategies by

(x SC, y PA, z ST),

where x, y, and z are real numbers between 0 and 1, inclusively, which sum to 1. These numbers give the probability with which one of the pure strategies will be played. In the game at hand both players happen to have three strategies, but in other games they might have a different number of strategies. Suppose the pure strategies available to Row in a game are $R_1, R_2, \ldots, R_n$. Then his mixed strategies take the form

$$(x_1 R_1, x_2 R_2, \ldots, x_n R_n);$$

where each x_i is a real number between 0 and 1 inclusively, and the sum of the x_i's equals 1. Col's mixed strategies are given a similar representation.

Notice that pure strategies are special cases of mixed ones. The pure strategy ST is equivalent to the mixed strategy

$$(0\ SC,\ 0\ PA,\ 1\ ST),$$

in which the probability of playing ST is 1.

Now let us return to our example. You are playing the mixed strategy ($1/3$ SC, $1/3$ PA, $1/3$ ST); your opponent is going to play some unknown mixed strategy ($x\ SC$, $y\ PA$, $z\ ST$). (Given what has just been said, this also allows for her playing any of her pure strategies as well.) Let us calculate your expected utility for this pair of strategies. Think of your situation as involving a compound gamble. The larger gamble gives you an equal chance of playing SC, PA or ST. Having played these you engage in one of three smaller gambles determined by the mixed strategy used by your opponent. You have a $1/3$ chance of playing SC, and if you play it you have an x chance of having that met by SC, a y chance of having it met by PA, and a z chance of having it met by ST. Your payoffs are 0, 1, and -1, respectively, for those combinations of strategies. Thus the expected utility of this smaller gamble is $0x + 1y + -1z$. You also have a $1/3$ chance of playing PA and ST and your expected utilities for the smaller gambles resulting from those strategies are $-1x + 0y + 1z$ and $1x + -1y + 0z$, respectively. Thus your expected utility from the strategy as a whole is

$$1/3\ (0x + 1y + -1z) +$$
$$1/3\ (-1x + 0y + 1z) +$$
$$1/3\ (1x + -1y + 0z).$$

Since each component has the same factor of $1/3$, we can add up all the x components, all the y components, and all the z components without explicitly distributing $1/3$ through the entire sum. I have arranged these components in columns so that you can see at a glance that each sums to 0. Thus your expected utility for this strategy must be 0 too. This is exactly the same value we observed when we calculated your expected utility for ($1/3$ SC, $1/3$ PA, $1/3$ ST) against your opponent's use of the pure strategy ST. (This equals ($0\ SC$, $0\ PA$, $1\ ST$); so our first calculation is but a special case of the general one given just now.)

So long as you play ($1/3$ SC, $1/3$ PA, $1/3$ ST) you are guaranteed an expected utility of 0, and since we are assuming that you have a utility function satisfying the expected utility condition, this means that the utility of this strategy to you is 0. We have also found your security level for the game. But we have not found an equilibrium pair yet. If your opponent plays the pure strategy of SC, then although you can guarantee yourself a utility of 0 by playing the mixed ($1/3$ SC, $1/3$ PA, $1/3$ ST), you can do better against her SC — you can play ST and win. She cannot do better, of course, but since you can, the strategies are not in equilibrium. On the other hand, suppose your opponent plays the same mixed strategy you have been playing. Then she can hold your winnings to 0. So the pair of mixed strategies are in equilibrium, and for this particular game they are the only such pair. The game is thus fully solved; we have found its equilibrium pairs and its value.

Before proceeding further you should try to verify that the pair of mixed strategies that are in equilibrium in tables 5-16 and 5-17 are $(1/2\ R_1, 1/2\ R_2)$ and $(1/2\ C_1, 1/2\ C_2)$. What are the values of the games?

5-16	C_1	C_2
R_1	1	-1
R_2	-1	1

5-17	C_1	C_2
R_1	22	-18
R_2	-18	22

All the games we have considered so far have been symmetrical games and it has been easy to guess their equilibrium pairs. Finding the equilibrium pairs for the next game (table 5-18) is much harder. If we try the mixed strategy $(1/2\ R_1, 1/2\ R_2)$ against C_1, we find that its expected utility is 4 whereas its expected utility against C_2 is 7/2. Furthermore, the mixed strategy $(1/2\ C_1, 1/2\ C_2)$ for Col has an expected utility of 9/2 against R_1 and 3 against R_2.

5-18	C_1	C_2
R_1	6	3
R_2	2	4

The joint expected utility of the two mixed strategies is

$$(1/2)(1/2)6 + (1/2)(1/2)3 + (1/2)(1/2)2 + (1/2)(1/2)4 = 3\ 3/4.$$

Thus they cannot be an equilibrium pair, since Row is better off playing R_1 when Col plays his half. We can keep testing pairs of strategies to see if they are in equilibrium, but there are infinitely many to test and no guarantee that our best guesses will find one that works. Plainly, a systematic approach is required.

To this end, let p be the probability of playing R_1 for any given mixed strategy of Row's and let q be the probability of playing C_1 for any given mixed strategy of Col's. Then the expected utility for Row of these strategies being played jointly is given by

$$EU(p,\ q) = 6pq + 3p(1-q) + 2(1-p)q + 4(1-p)(1-q),$$

since there is a pq chance of ending with a 6, a $(1-p)q$ chance of ending with 3, and so on. Applying some algebra we can convert this equation to

$$EU(p,\ q) = 5pq - p - 2q + 4.$$

Now Row's object is to choose p so as to maximize this number while Col's is to choose q so as to minimize it. So let us do some fancy factoring to isolate Row's and Col's contributions to this number. We proceed as follows:

$$EU(p, q) = 5(pq - p/5 - 2q/5 + 4/5)$$
$$= 5(pq - p/5 - 2q/5 + 2/25 + 18/25)$$
$$= 5(pq - p/5 - 2q/5 + 2/25) + 18/5$$
$$= 5[(p - 2/5)(q - 1/5)] + 18/5.$$

If Row picks p as 2/5, his factor equals 0 and the value of $EU(p, q)$ is 18/5 no matter what q is; that is, $EU(2/5, q) = 18/5$ for all q. Similarly, $EU(p, 1/5) = 18/5$ for all p. Thus although each player might do better with a different p or q provided the other player played a bad strategy, we have found the security strategies for both players and they are in equilibrium. Thus we have obtained at least one equilibrium pair for this game.

Might there be more than one equilibrium pair? Suppose p_1 and q_1 also determine an equilibrium pair; that is, $(p_1 R_1, (1 - p_1) R_2)$ and $(q_1 C_1, (1 - q_1) C_2)$ are also in equilibrium. Then $EU(p_1, q_1) \leq EU(p_1, q)$ for all choices of q; otherwise Col would want to change when Row played the strategy determined by p_1. Similarly, $EU(p, q_1) \leq EU(p_1, q_1)$ for all choices of p. But we already know that

$$EU(p_1, 1/5) = 18/5 = EU(2/5, q_1),$$

and since $EU(p_1, q_1)$ is bounded above and below by those two identical quantities, it must equal them. In other words, if there are two equilibrium pairs, they give rise to the same security levels. It is also easily shown that if p_1 and q_1 determine an equilibrium pair, so do 2/5 and q_1 and p_1 and 1/5. We thus get a mixed-strategy version of the coordination theorem for this game.

Every two-person zero sum game has a solution. This follows immediately from the next theorem.

THE MAXIMIN THEOREM FOR TWO-PERSON ZERO SUM GAMES: *For every two-person zero sum game there is at least one strategy (mixed or pure) for Row and at least one strategy for Col that form an equilibrium pair. If there is more than one such pair, their expected utilities are equal.*

The expected utility for the equilibrium pair is called *the value v* of the game. It is the security level for the game for both Row and Col. In other words, by playing his half of the equilibrium pair Row can be sure of winning at least v, and by playing his half Col can be sure of holding Row's winnings to no more than v. Row's equilibrium strategy is called a *maximin strategy* because it maximizes his minimal outcomes; Col's is called a *minimax* strategy because it holds Row's maximums to a minimum. The maximin theorem is commonly approached from Col's more defensive viewpoint and called "the minimax theorem" instead. I am using the other name because my exposition has emphasized Row's point of view.

There are a number of proofs of the maximin theorem in the literature, but they all involve mathematical techniques far beyond those presupposed by this book. However, the method used in the last example can be generalized to

GAME THEORY

yield a simple proof of the maximin theorem for two-by-two games. So that will be our next topic.

PROBLEMS

1. Suppose Col has k pure strategies. What is the general form of his mixed strategies?
2. Show that in any game with the form shown in table 5-19 the strategies

5-19	a	$-b$
	$-b$	a

(1/2 R_1, 1/2 R_2) and (1/2 C_1, 1/2 C_2) are in equilibrium.
3. State precisely and prove the mixed-strategy coordination theorem for two-by-two zero sum games.

5-3b. Proof of the Maximin Theorem for Two-by-Two Games

In order to simplify our proof we will consider only games in a restricted form. It will be called the standard form (SF) and is represented by table 5-20. Here

		C_1	C_2
5-20	R_1	a	b
(SF)	R_2	c	d

a, b, c, and d must all be positive numbers and

$$a > c, \ d > b, \text{ and } d > c.$$

Restricting ourselves to games in standard form will not limit the scope of our theorem, because, as the exercises in the next Problems section show, any two-by-two game that is not in SF is either solvable by our previous methods or is equivalent to a game in SF from which its solution is easily obtained.

We can assume, then, that all the games under consideration are in SF. As we have already observed in dealing with preceding examples, the expected utility for any pair of strategies

$$(p \ R_1, \ (1-p) \ R_2); \ (q \ C_1, \ (1-q) \ C_2)$$

is given by the formula

$$EU(p, q) = apq + bp(1-q) + c(1-p)q + d(1-p)(1-q).$$

Applying some algebra to this, we obtain

$$EU(p, q) = apq + bp - bpq + cq - cpq + d - dp - dq + dpq$$
$$= (a - c + d - b)pq + (b - d)p + (c - d)q + d.$$

Given that $a > c$ and $d > b$, the sum $(a - c + d - b)$ must be positive while

137

$(b-d)$ and $(c-d)$ must both be negative. That means that our original equation now has the form

$$EU(p, \cdot q) = Apq - Bp - Cq + D,$$

where A, B, C, and D are all positive. Let us now apply some fancy factoring to it.

$$\begin{aligned} EU(p, q) &= Apq - Bp - Cq + D \\ &= A[pq - (B/A)p - (C/A)q + D/A] \\ &= A[pq - (B/A)p - (C/A)q + (BC)/(AA) + (DA - BC)/(AA)] \\ &= A[(p - C/A)(q - B/A) + (DA - BC)/(AA)] \\ &= A[(p - C/A)(q - B/A)] + (DA - BC)/A. \end{aligned}$$

It then follows that Col can prevent the outcome of the game from exceeding $(DA - BC)/A$ by playing the strategy in which $q = B/A$, and Row can guarantee himself the same value by playing the strategy in which $p = C/A$. We have thus found the value and an equilibrium strategy pair for the game.

To conclude the proof of the two-by-two case of the maximin theorem we must show that we can dispense with our restriction to games in SF. We will do this by showing that once we can solve games in SF we can solve all other two-by-two games. Most of this task will be left to you as exercises.

First let us note that the restriction to game tables with only positive entries is no impediment, since any table with zero or negative entries can be transformed into an equivalent game by adding a sufficiently large constant to each entry. The equilibrium strategies for the two games will involve the same probabilities for playing pure strategies and the values of the games can be obtained from each other by adding or subtracting the same constant. (See exercises 2 and 3 in the next Problems section.)

Restricting ourselves to games with $a > c$, $d > b$, and $d > c$ is no impediment to the generality of the proof either, since a game in which $c > a$ and $b > d$ can be converted into our restricted form by switching its rows. The two games will have the same values but the probabilities for their equilibrium strategies will be reversed. For example, if Row uses $(1/3\ R_1, 2/3\ R_2)$ in one, he will use $(2/3\ R_2, 1/3\ R_1)$ in the other. Furthermore, if a game cannot be put into the restricted form SF by switching rows, the game must already have one or more *pure* equilibrium pairs and is solvable by our previous methods. (See exercises 4 and 5 in the next Problems section.)

PROBLEMS

1. Transform the game in table 5-21 into one whose entries are all positive. Then solve the two games.

5-21	C_1	C_2
R_1	-1	-2
R_2	-2	-1

2. Let the expected utility for a pair of mixed strategies for a game be given by the formula

$$EU(p, q) = apq + bp(1-q) + c(1-p)q + d(1-p)(1-q),$$

where a, b, c, and d are the four entries in the game. Suppose the game is transformed by adding the same constant k to a, b, c, and d. Then let the new expected utility be $EU'(p, q)$. Show that $EU'(p, q) = EU(p, q) + k$.

3. Use exercise 2 to show that if game G_1 has zero or negative entries and G_2 is an SF game obtained from G_1 by adding the constant k to each of G_1's entries, then the probability mixtures for the equilibrium strategies for the two games are the same and the value of G_2 is $v + k$ where v is the value of G_1.

4. Prove that if a game cannot be put into SF, it must have at least one pair of pure equilibrium strategies.

5. Prove that if G_1 and G_2 can be transformed into each other by means of a positive linear transformation, then
   a. both use the same probabilities in their equilibrium strategies, and
   b. The values of the games can be transformed into each other by means of the same transformation used to transform the two games.

6. The game in table 5-22 is not in SF. Find its equivalent in SF. Use the method of the proof of the maximin theorem to solve that game. Then use its solution to solve the original game.

5-22	C_1	C_2
R_1	-2	-1
R_2	6	-3

5-3c. A Shortcut

Now that we know that each two-by-two game has a solution we can use a shortcut for solving them. This method avoids both the restriction to SF and the fancy factoring that make solutions by the method of our proof so tedious.

To use the method, first determine whether the game has any pure equilibrium pairs by using the maximin equilibrium test. If the test proves positive, the game is solved. So let us assume that our game has no pure equilibrium pairs. The game has the form given in table 5-23. But here there is no restriction

5-23	C_1	C_2
R_1	a	b
R_2	c	d

on a, b, c, and d. Our aim is to find values of p and q for which

$$(p\ R_1, (1-p)\ R_2);\ (q\ C_1, (1-q)\ C_2)$$

GAME THEORY

are an equilibrium pair. Examine the factored formula for Row's expected utility
when he plays his half of a mixed-strategy pair. You will see that when he plays
his half of an equilibrium strategy, he fixes the value of the game no matter what
strategy Col plays. The same is true for Col. Thus the expected utility for Row's
equilibrium strategy against Col's C_1 must be the same as it is against Col's C_2.
Similarly, the expected utility to Col for his half of the pair must be the same
whether Row plays R_1 or R_2. The expected utility for Row against C_1 is

$$ap + (1-p)c$$

and that against C_2 is

$$bp + (1-p)d.$$

Since they are equal we have the equation

$$ap + (1-p)c = bp + (1-p)d.$$

Solving this for p, we obtain

$$p = (d-c)/[(a+d) - (b+c)].$$

Using the same method, we can show that

$$q = (d-b)/[(a+d) - (b+c)].$$

Once we have obtained p and q, we can determine the value of the game
by evaluating *any one* of the formulas

$$ap + c(1-p); \quad bp + d(1-p); \quad aq + b(1-q); \quad cq + d(1-q),$$

since they have the same values.

Example. We will apply the shortcut method to solve the game in table 5-
24. We note first that there are no equilibrium points. So we must calculate the

5-24	3	4
	7	1 ·

p and q for Row's and Col's mixed strategies by applying the formulas derived
earlier. This yields

$$p = (1-7)/[(3+1) - (4+7)] \ = \ -6/-7 = 6/7$$
$$q = (1-4)/[(3+1) - (4+7)] \ = \ -3/-7 = 3/7$$

Thus Row's equilibrium strategy is $(6/7\ R_1, 1/7\ R_2)$ and Col's is $(3/7\ C_1, 4/7\ C_2)$. The value for the game is $3(6/7) + 7(1/7)$ or 3 4/7.

PROBLEMS

1. Solve these games (tables 5-25, 5-26).

5-25	C_1	C_2
R_1	3	1
R_2	-7	4

5-26	C_1	C_2
R_1	4	20
R_2	5	-3

140

2. Show that

$$q = (d - b)/[(a + d) - (b + c)].$$

5-3d. On Taking Chances

The use of mixed maximin strategies raises serious questions about the rationality of turning one's fate over to chance. The following story will serve to illustrate these questions.

Commander Smith, of the Brave Forces, has just landed his troops on the beach of the island of Evo. To his immediate right is Mt. Evo, a rugged but passable series of hills and valleys, which runs along the sea for a 20-mile stretch. Straight ahead and running around the inland edge of Mt. Evo is a grassy plain. The Forces of Exactness and the Brave Forces are engaged in a fierce battle at the far end of Mt. Evo. Smith's mission is to bring a battalion of reinforcements to the battle scene. Two routes to the battle are open to him—one around Mt. Evo via the plain, the other over Mt. Evo. Ordinarily, the plain route would be preferable since it puts less stress on the troops. However, the Forces of Exactness have dispatched Captain Jones to intercept and delay Commander Smith and his soldiers. If they meet on the plain Smith will suffer serious losses, since Jones has heavy armored vehicles and Smith and his men are mainly on foot; but Smith's losses will be light if they clash on Mt. Evo, since his forces are more mobile in rough terrain than Jones's. Commander Smith consults the game theorist under his command. After extensive assessments of the utilities involved, the game theorist represents his commander's dilemma as the following two-person zero sum game (table 5-27).

5-27

		Jones's Strategies	
		Mountain Route	Plain Route
Smith's Strategies	Mountain Route	− 50	100
	Plain Route	200	− 100

The solution to this game is:

Equilibrium pair: (2/3 mountain, 1/3 plain); (4/9 mountain, 5/9 plain).
Value: 33 1/3.

Exercise: Verify this solution.

Having calculated this himself, Major V. Major, Commander Smith's game theorist, recommends that Commander Smith roll a fair die and take the mountain route on 1, 2, 3, or 4 and the plain route on 5 or 6.

But our story does not end here. Commander Smith proceeds to discuss his problem with his intelligence officer, who challenges Major V. Major's recommendation. He says, "I am firmly convinced that Jones will simply flip a coin and take the mountain route on heads. He knows some game theory too. And he knows that no matter what he does, the expected utilities remain constant if you play your maximin strategy. So he won't bother with building a random device for giving himself a 4/9 chance of taking the mountain route. Now, you should take advantage of his folly. If he flips a coin, using the pure strategy of the plain route against him has an expected utility of 50, a considerable improvement over 33 1/3. So forget the die, head for the plain."

Commander Smith finds himself truly torn by the advice he has received. He decides that he will roll the die and see which strategy it "picks." The die comes up 5, picking the plain. Satisfied that he has followed not only his game theorist's advice but also that of his intelligence officer, Smith orders the army onto the plain. But as luck would have it, he is intercepted by Captain Jones and his forces.

Due to the failure of Smith's reinforcements to arrive, the Brave Forces are badly defeated at Mt. Evo. Smith's superiors order an investigation, and Smith is called home to defend his actions. This is what he tells the investigating panel: "Look, any way you look at it, I was taking chances. I only followed my game theorist's advice in making the theoretically best use of a risky situation. And in the end that coincided with my intelligence officer's recommendation too." Unfortunately for Smith, the panel knows nothing of game theory. Reasoning that no one should have decided a serious matter on the roll of a die, they recommend that Smith be relieved of his command.

This story raises several interesting issues about using mixed strategies. First, note that using a mixed strategy surrenders to chance the choice of the pure strategy one actually implements. That is what bothered the investigating committee. Second, although Smith implemented the pure strategy his intelligence officer recommended, he did so only as the result of following his maximin strategy. Thus we may ask, Was Smith irrational (or irresponsible) in not following his intelligence officer's advice to bypass the maximin strategy? And was he irrational (or irresponsible) in deciding on the basis of the roll of a die?

Turning to the first question, let us remember that the maximin theorem says only that your maximin strategy will guarantee that you receive the value of the game — it is your security level, but the theorem does not say that it is impossible to do better when playing against someone who is not playing his equilibrium strategy. It can be rational to play a strategy other than the maximin. If Commander Smith's intelligence officer had an accurate report, his advice would have been excellent, and Smith would have been irresponsible to not follow it.

On the other hand, Smith would not have been justified in departing from the maximin strategy if he had no idea at all about the strategy Jones would use. In this case he can have no assurance of raising his expected utility. Instead of taking a "calculated risk," he would be trusting his luck.

This brings us to the next question. The outcome of any actual play will be the same as that achieved by picking a pure strategy at the outset and, in most cases, will have a utility that is either above or below that of one's maximin strategy. How, then, can we rationalize the use of a chance mechanism to pick such a pure strategy? One way to allay these doubts is to remember that the numerical values used in game theory are not direct measures of dollars lost or gained or soldiers killed or saved. They are rather utilities of such outcomes. Furthermore, utility functions have the expected utility property. So given that Smith's maximin strategy has an expected utility of 33 1/3, he prefers to accept the gamble it involves—even though it is a one-shot gamble—rather than proceed to a direct engagement with the enemy. (Of course, he prefers avoiding such an engagement altogether.) Introducing a chance mechanism is simply a way of furnishing a gamble to Smith as an extra option.

Sometimes it is clearly rational to opt for a gamble rather than a certainty. If you are faced with a dreaded certainty and then offered a gamble that has some chance of resulting in a better outcome, your lot has improved. For instance, if an insane murderer offers to execute you on the spot by slowly mutilating your body or to let you jump off a nearby cliff into the sea, you would be irrational, or else a consummate masochist, not to take the gamble of jumping off the cliff.

Unfortunately, this way of defending the use of chance devices does not really address the issue. The murderer gives you a new option with a chance at a *new outcome*. Mixed strategies might qualify as new options, but they do not lead to new outcomes. None of our talk about the expected utility of a gamble equaling its utility can erase the fact that we are still faced with the same outcomes.

In the end, the strongest argument for using a mixed strategy is the secrecy argument: It makes it impossible for your opponent to know which pure stategy you are going to use until you actually use it. You can even announce your mixed strategy to the world.

When there is no question of your opponent discerning your intentions, the secrecy argument has no bite. Still, we might reconcile ourselves to mixed strategies by reminding ourselves that we use them only when a game has no solution via pure strategies. If you are involved in such a game, there is no reasonable pure strategy for you to pick. Given that you must pick one, it is not totally irrational to use a chance device to make the selection. The beauty of the maximin theorem is that once you have made the step to mixed strategies, it can point you to a rational choice.

Now Smith was in a bad situation. There was no way for him to avoid taking some risks. He could not fly his troops over the mountain; he could not obtain fully reliable information concerning Jones's route; he could not start on one route and then backtrack if he saw Jones advancing toward him. In short, whether he liked it or not, Smith had to play the game we described. Yet he could not justify taking any of the pure strategies open to him. Under the circumstances he might as well have rolled a die, and given that, abiding by the counsel of the maximin theorem was the most rational thing for him to do.

PROBLEMS

1. Statisticians often recommend using chance mechanisms to choose the members of a sample in order to avoid biases. Do you think that one can support the use of mixed strategies on the grounds that they protect one against irrational biases?

2. If an army commander would be justified in using a mixed strategy (in a

game without a pure equilibrium pair) to protect against spies, would it not also follow that he would be justified in using it even when there is no threat of spies?

3. In real life the people with whom one usually plays "games" are far from ideally rational agents. Do you think one should always follow the dictates of game theory when playing these games?

5-4. Two-Person Nonzero Sum Games: Failures of the Equilibrium Concept

In a zero sum game both parties can arrive at a rational, stable, and, in a sense, optimal resolution without the benefit of communication. For by simply pursuing their own interests in the most rational manner possible the players will arrive at an equilibrium strategy pair for the game. The resulting outcome is optimal in the sense that both players do as well as they can expect given their own opportunities and the wiles of their opponent. Oddly enough, the strictly competitive nature of these games is responsible for their theoretically satisfying solutions. For if we drop the assumption of strict competition while retaining our assumption that the players can neither communicate nor form binding agreements, we can find games for which the concepts of individual self-interested rationality and equilibrium strategies fail to produce satisfactory solutions and, worse, even produce plainly unsatisfactory ones. This not only raises serious questions about the nature of rationality in gaming situations but also suggests interesting connections between rationality and morality.

Because the traditional approach to games fails to solve many nonzero sum games, mathematical approaches to them are far more tentative than the mathematics of zero sum games. Accordingly, my account will focus on two specific games and the failures of the equilibrium approach to solve them.

5-4a. The Clash of Wills

This game traditionally has been known as "the battle of the sexes," but in the spirit of the times I am renaming it and altering the story that goes with it. Mathematically, of course, it is the same game as the one that goes with the older name and story.

Here is the story. Able and Baker, two fast friends who dwell in different cities, are planning a weekend together over the telephone. They have heard radio reports that the telephone service between their locations will be interrupted for several days and are trying to settle their plans while they can still communicate. Able wants to go a ski resort in the mountains; Baker wants to go to a music festival in a distant city. Although both prefer being together to being alone, Able prefers the ski resort to the festival and Baker has the opposite preference. However, both prefer going to either location to staying at home alone. At the beginning of their conversation they share this information, and it quickly becomes clear to both that neither will cheerfully yield to the other's wishes. Yet before they can start to work out a compromise the phones go out. What should they do?

Let us represent this situation by means of game table 5-28. Since staying at home is a dominated strategy for both players, we can use a two-by-two table instead of a three-by-three one. The first number in each square is Able's pay-

5-28

		Baker's Strategies	
		Go Skiing	Go to the Festival
Able's Strategies	Go Skiing	(2, 1)	(0, 0)
	Go to the Festival	(−1, −1)	(1, 2)

off, the second is Baker's. A purely ordinal utility scale will suffice for raising the difficulties with this game. So let us think of numbers being assigned to preferences according to the scheme in table 5-29. Notice that because Able and

5-29

Utility Numbers	Able's Preferences	Baker's Preferences
2	Ski with Baker	Festival with Able
1	Festival with Baker	Ski with Able
0	Ski alone	Festival alone
−1	Festival alone	Ski alone

Baker do not have completely opposite preferences, we cannot use the zero sum representation in this game. It is also important that an ordinal scale be sufficient for studying this game; otherwise we would have to deal with the very difficult question of how to compare Able's and Baker's scales. In fact, as you can verify for yourself a few paragraphs hence, exactly the same problems arise when each player is assigned a different ordinal scale. Thus the question of the interpersonal comparison of utility scales can be bypassed for the time being. (But we will deal with it in chapter 6.)

Let us turn now to the analysis of the abstract game itself. Neither player has a dominant strategy. Although the maximin equilibrium test applies only to zero sum games, it is easy to spot two equilibrium pairs. The pairs (R_1, C_1) and (R_2, C_2) are both in equilibrium: Given that one player will be at a given location, the other player would rather be there too. However, the two equilibrium pairs have different values for each player; Able does better with (R_1, C_1), Baker does better with (R_2, C_2). The coordination theorem, which held for zero sum games, fails here.

This means that we are still far from solving this game. If Able and Baker had been able to continue to talk to each other, we might have seen a *strong clash of wills*. Ideally they would try to find a method for picking one of the equilibrium pairs. But in pursuing their own interests they could fail to reach an ideal solution. Able, for instance, might threaten to go skiing regardless of whether Baker joined him. Baker might become so angered by this that he would rather not spend the weekend with Able. Given that Baker still prefers the festival to skiing, the game would change to this one (table 5-30). This does not

5-30	C_1	C_2
R_1	(2, −1)	(0, 2)
R_2	(−1, 1)	(1, 0)

even have equilibrium pairs! (As you might expect, in games in which communication is possible, threats can play a major role in determining an outcome.)

From the outside we can see a plausible solution to Able and Baker's problem. They could flip a coin and go skiing on heads, to the festival on tails. This *does* raise questions about their utility scales, however. First, since we would be confronting them with an even-chance gamble between the pairs of values (2, 1) and (1, 2), we would need to compare the utility of this gamble with the utility of the two outcomes. The pair of values (3/2, 3/2), for instance, would not make sense unless we assume that Able and Baker both have utility scales satisfying the expected utility condition. Second, to the extent that we view the suggested solution as equitable or fair or just, we are implicitly making an interpersonal comparison of the two utility scales. Suppose we replace Baker's 2 with 200 and his 1 with 100. Then the issue is between the pairs of values (2, 100) and (1, 200). Using a flip of a coin would result in the pair (3/2, 150), but who is to say that this is an equitable solution? If Baker already gets so much utility from skiing, by what right can he demand even more?

All this makes no difference to our two players anyway, because choosing the weekend meeting place by flipping a coin would be possible only if they could communicate with each other. By hypothesis they cannot. In the coin-flipping resolution we are, in effect, invoking a *jointly coordinated mixed strategy*, whereas the game only allows the players to pick mixed strategies separately. As a matter of fact the mixed strategies

$(1/2\ R_1,\ 1/2\ R_2);\ (1/2\ C_1,\ 1/2\ C_2)$

guarantee each player the security level of 1/2. Yet they are not in equilibrium. By playing his half of this pair, Baker can be sure of getting at least 1/2 but he cannot hold Able to 1/2; for Able the pure strategy R_1 has an expected utility of 1 against Baker's maximin strategy.

The upshot of this is that considerations of individual rationality, which we have considered so far, fail to produce a stable or optimal solution for this game. Both players can easily calculate the various equilibrium pairs and security levels available in the game; but, unlike the zero sum case, neither has any reason to choose one of these strategies as long as he cannot count on his "opponent" to cooperate. Ironically, the rational thing for them to do was not to play the game in the first place. In the case of our particular story this means that the rational thing for them to have done was to have made certain that their plans were firm before the phones went out.

One might suggest another solution to this game. Each player knows that he cannot count on his opponent to play the strategy yielding the equilibrium value he, the first player, prefers; thus each should assume that the other player will not play that strategy and then pick his best strategy under *that* assumption. In our example this means that Able will go skiing and Baker will go to the festival.

Accepting this proposal, however, forces us to conclude that the pair (R_1, C_2) with the value $(-1, -1)$ is the solution to the game, which is scarcely the best possible outcome. Can we endorse canons of rationality that drive individuals to outcomes that are clearly not optimal? Before examining this question let us consider another game in which the issue arises even more dramatically.

PROBLEMS

1. Show that the clash of wills can be fully represented without using utility numbers.
2. Explain why, if the two players coordinated their weekend by flipping a fair coin, it would make sense to assign the value 3/2 to each of them.
3. Show that if Able plays $(1/2\,R_1, 1/2\,R_2)$, Baker can do better than 3/2 by playing C_2.
4. In the rural community where I live, falling trees and lightning cause a fair number of electrical power failures. When these occur someone phones the electric company to report the outage and it is fixed within a few hours. Every time I have called the electric company I have been told that someone has already reported the outage and it will be repaired. Since the call is a long-distance one, I have felt that I wasted my money. The other night we had another power failure, and as I lay on my bed staring into the darkness, it occurred to me that in deciding whether to phone the company, I was playing a version of the clash of wills. Assuming that only one other person has been affected by the power failure, and thus that he is my opponent, represent my situation as a clash of wills.

5-4b. The Prisoner's Dilemma

The next game has a single equilibrium point and dominant strategies for each player. Thus, unlike the clash of wills, its outcome is fully predictable. The paradox is that although from the point of view of the individual players their chosen strategies are the only rational alternatives, the resulting outcome is patently nonoptimal. This suggests that there may be a fundamental conflict between the notions of individual and group rationality.

The game is named after a story about two prisoners. They have been arrested for vandalism and have been isolated from each other. There is sufficient evidence to convict them on the charge for which they have been arrested, but the prosecutor is after bigger game. He thinks that they robbed a bank together and that he can get them to confess to it. He summons each separately to an interrogation room and speaks to each as follows: "I am going to offer the same deal to your partner, and I will give you each an hour to think it over before I call you back. This is it: If one of you confesses to the bank robbery and the other does not, I will see to it that the confessor gets a one-year term and that the other guy gets a twenty-five year term. If you both confess, then it's ten years apiece. If neither of you confesses, then I can only get two years apiece on the vandalism charge; but that's not going to happen—at least one of you will confess." Sure enough, an hour later both confess, and both end up serving ten years. Let us see why they were forced to that outcome.

The game can be represented by table 5-31. Here I have used the length of the prisoners' sentences to assign numerical outcomes. It is easy to see that

5-31	Confess	Do Not
Confess	$(-10, -10)$	$(-1, -25)$
Do Not	$(-25, -1)$	$(-2, -2)$

confessing dominates for both players, and thus the $(-10, -10)$ outcome will be the one that our theory predicts "rational" players will achieve. But clearly *both* would be better off if they could achieve the outcome $(-2, -2)$. But $(-10, -10)$ and *not* $(-2, -2)$ is the equilibrium value, and the strategies producing it are recommended by one of our first and most fundamental principles of individual rationality—the dominance principle. The paradox is that following the dictates of individual rationality has put everyone in a worse position than they would have been if they had been less "rational."

Let us look at the prisoner's dilemma from an informal point of view. The prisoner, either one, knows that if neither confesses, both will be better off than if both confess. So he might consider not confessing. But he also knows that if he does not confess, he has placed himself in an extremely vulnerable position; a "double-crossing" partner could cost him twenty-five years of his life. Each prisoner suspects that his partner is thinking in the same way about the matter, and each sees that each has a strong reason to try for the double-cross. Both conclude that the only thing to do is to play it safe, but playing it safe means confessing.

As the informal version of the dilemma shows, no numerical reasoning is necessary to see how the game will go. Thus, we require only purely ordinal utility functions to represent this game, and need not concern ourselves with interpersonal comparisons of utility.

5-4c. Other Prisoner's Dilemmas

The situation arising in the prisoner's dilemma is not restricted to two-person games. Suppose the members of a cartel, OPEC, for instance, try to limit the total sales of their product in the hope, of course, of driving up prices and benefiting individually and as a group. Once prices start to rise, each member of the cartel will be sorely tempted to accept contracts at the higher prices and violate the production quotas assigned by the cartel. For, so long as he is the only one to do this, prices will not drop and nobody will try to repudiate their contracts with him. On the other hand, if enough members of the cartel try the same double-crossing strategy, there will be a glut on the market, contracts will be broken, and prices will tumble. Since this is known to all cartel members, they will find it nearly impossible to limit production in the first place. This multiperson prisoner's dilemma in which multiple double-crosses are possible is not far from real life.

One might be tempted to argue that criminals will *not* confess because each knows that double-crossers are killed by their fellow criminals. No doubt this is a factor in many real-life confrontations between criminals and prosecutors. But when this happens we do not have a true prisoner's dilemma game. For the outcome of confessing when one's partner does not is not just a one-year sentence; it is one year plus a good chance of being killed. Presumably, this is less preferable than a simple ten-year sentence. Thus the dominance argument no longer works.

Similarly, the members of a cartel know that they must deal with each other again and again. Some mutual trust is of the essence; thus there is a premium on not double-crossing. This can prevent the game from being a true prisoner's dilemma.

Ironically, one of these games based on an element of trust can develop into a prisoner's dilemma if the players know that mutual trust is no longer important to them as individuals. Suppose, for example, that over the years two competing stores located on the same block have, through mutual trust, avoided all-out price wars. Now suppose the entire block is to be demolished for an urban renewal project, and they will move to different locations never to compete again. Then trust is no longer a factor in their dealings. Each has a strong reason to cut prices just enough to draw away the competitor's customers. We have a prisoner's dilemma. It would be no wonder, then, if both began liquidation sales.

Moreover, if both competitors know the exact date on which they must close their doors, then no matter how cooperative they have been until now, they can reason themselves backward to a prisoner's dilemma right now. For suppose all occupants of the block must vacate in forty-five days. Then each knows that on the forty-fifth day it can no longer trust its competitor to maintain its prices. Trust being out of the question on day forty-five, each figures it might as well cut its prices on day forty-four to get the jump on the competitor. But since each knows that, trust is out of the question on day forty-four. Thus each reckons it must cut its prices by day forty-three. But then trust on day forty-three is out of the question; so we are back to day forty-two. This reasoning continues until each store concludes that it should cut prices today!

Such reasoning can even force competing stores to lower their prices to the point where both operate at a near loss. Suppose that two stores, X and Y, currently sell a given commodity for $2 and make a $.50 profit. Store X decides to cut its prices to $1.90 to attract some of Y's customers, figuring with the added volume to exceed its previous profits based on a lower volume and a higher per sale profit. Store X responds by cutting its prices to $1.80; Y responds by going to $1.70, and if X then sets its prices at $1.60, they will both end up making the same number of sales but at only one fifth the profit.

PROBLEMS

1. Show that the prisoner's dilemma arises when Col's sentences are as before

but Row is sentenced to fifteen years if both confess, five years if he does but Col does not, sixteen years if he does not but Col does, and six years if neither does.

2. Show that games of the prisoner's dilemma can be stated in entirely nonnumerical terms by referring to the players' preferences for outcomes.

3. Set up the final store example as a five-by-five two-person game. Assume that both stores combined sell 100 items (per day), that the one with the lowest prices gets all the sales, and that they split the sales evenly when both have the same prices. Use the five possible prices ($2.00, $1.90, $1.80, $1.70, $1.60) as strategies and the total profits as outcome values. Show that repeated dominance reasoning leads them to split the lowest total profit.

4. In the game of chicken two players race their automobiles straight at each other. If neither veers, they will crash and die heroes in the eyes of their friends. If one veers and the other holds fast, the one who holds fast will be regarded as a hero and the other will be branded a "chicken." If both veer, their reputations will remain unchanged. Assume that each player ranks the outcomes in this descending order: live hero, no change, dead hero, chicken. Show that the chicken game is a variant of the prisoner's dilemma.

5-4d. The Prisoner's Dilemma and the Predictor

As a number of people have noticed, there is a connection between the prisoner's dilemma and the Predictor paradox. Suppose you are one of the prisoners and you think that the other prisoner thinks very much like you do. By dominance reasoning you have tentatively decided not to confess. Thus in all probability so has the other fellow. Does this mean that you should go ahead and confess to take advantage of the double-cross? No, because the same thought will occur to the other fellow too. But you can use the information that he is likely to make the same choice as yours to calculate the expected utility of each choice.

Here is how. First, turn your half of the prisoner's dilemma into your own decision under risk. Use table 5-32. The utilities are, as before, just the lengths

	He Confesses	He Does Not
5-32		
Confess	-10 .9	-1 .1
Do Not	-25 .1	-2 .9

of the various prison sentences and the probabilities are those of the states conditional on your acts. Given that you think the other prisoner thinks like you do, you assign a high probability to his making a choice that matches yours and a low one to his not doing so. Now calculate the expected utilities. They are -9.1 for confessing and -4.3 for not confessing. So you maximize expected utility by not confessing.

So here is our old dilemma again. The dominance principle recommends that you confess, and the principle of maximizing expected utility tells you not to confess. Moreover, your choice cannot causally affect his choice; it is merely evidence of what his choice will be. So once again how you decide will depend on how you decide the conflict between causal and evidential decision theory.

PROBLEM FOR DISCUSSION

The preceding argument for not confessing is based on an analogy between your way of thinking and that of the other prisoner. Could one argue that the dispute between causal and evidential decision theorists shows that analogical reasoning is illegitimate in this instance?

5-4e. Morals for Rationality and Morality

In both the clash of wills and the prisoner's dilemma, the principles that game theory recommends for self-interested rational agents fail to produce the best outcome for either party. There is a term, named after the Italian economist Vilfredo Pareto, to characterize this situation—the outcomes are not *Pareto optimal*. Intuitively this means that there are outcomes in which at least one of the players does better while the other does no worse. Each outcome of a two-person game has a pair of values, (u_1, u_2), associated with it. This allows us to define Pareto optimality more formally as follows: An outcome associated with (u_1, u_2) is *Pareto optimal* just in case for no pair of values (v_1, v_2) associated with outcomes of the game, do we have either $v_1 > u_1$ and $v_2 \geq u_2$ or $v_2 > u_2$ and $v_1 \geq u_1$. Game theory fails to guarantee Pareto optimal outcomes for either the clash of wills or the prisoner's dilemma. The clash of wills is likely to end in $(0, 0)$, which is worse for both players than $(2, 1)$ and $(1, 2)$, whereas the prisoner's dilemma will result in $(-10, -10)$, which is worse for both players than $(-2, -2)$.

Recall that envy, goodwill, and other attitudes toward the other players' payoffs are already reflected in the utility one assigns to outcomes. Thus if under outcome A one player receives the same utility as he does under B while the other player receives a greater utility under B, the move from A to B costs the first player nothing—not even psychologically. Thus no player could have grounds for preferring an outcome that is not Pareto optimal to one that is. It thus seems eminently reasonable to require that the solution to a game be among its Pareto optimal outcomes if there are any.

The failure of game theory to yield Pareto optimal solutions for games such as the prisoner's dilemma has led some philosophers to search for other means to optimal solutions. Some have suggested that in situations such as the prisoner's dilemma another kind of rationality will become operative. Each prisoner will realize that the only way to achieve a decent outcome is to temper his self-interest by considerations of what is achievable for the group as a whole. Each will see that he must regard his preferences as linked to those of his fellows; he must, as it were, look at pairs of values instead of just his component of each pair.

This would solve the prisoner's dilemma since there is only one Pareto optimal outcome. Taking the point of view of "group rationality," each would see that it is only rational for both not to confess and achieve the outcome of (-2, -2). However, the concept of group rationality based on Pareto optimality will not solve the clash of wills. There are two Pareto optimal outcomes worth (2, 1) and (1, 2), respectively. Unless each player forfeits his individuality entirely, each will continue to prefer one outcome to the other. Unless the players can communicate, we have made no advance at all; neither the problem of determining whose preferences should be given greater weight nor the problem of coordinating their strategies has been resolved.

The best thing to do is to avoid games like the clash of wills and the prisoner's dilemma in the first place. People who are confronted with such situations quickly learn to take steps to avoid them. We have already mentioned the criminals' code of silence in connection with the prisoner's dilemma. Families often adopt rules for taking turns at tasks (dish washing) or pleasures (using the family car) to avoid repeated plays of the clash of wills. Since such rules represent a limited form of morality, we can see the breakdowns in game theory as paving the way for an argument that it is rational to be moral.

The argument runs like this. We can all see that there are certain games for which self-interested individual rationality provides no reasonable solution. If you are trapped in such a game you are lucky if you come out of it without the worst outcome. Furthermore, such games could easily occur in real life if we did not adopt ways of behaving to avoid them. Many of our moral principles are such ways of behaving, and thus even self-interested agents should see that they should abide by them.

This argument is by no means decisive. People have often replied that at best it shows that truly self-interested agents would go along with morality so long as they felt it was in their interests to do so. However, whenever they felt they could get away with being immoral, it would only be rational for them to take advantage of the system. In short, morality only provides an environment for a large-scale prisoner's dilemma.

A similar quandary for politicians and political philosophy is the free rider problem. To illustrate it, suppose the citizens of Smallville have a bus system supported by riders depositing 50 cents in the fare box each time they use a bus. Fares are collected on the honor system. Unscrupulous Jack, who is about to board a bus during the rush hour, thinks to himself, Nobody will notice if I don't pay the fare, and the bus system can easily support my free ride; so I will take a free one this time. Obviously if everyone thought and acted like Jack, the bus system would be bankrupt in short order.

In these situations it is beneficial to all to agree to engage in some form of cooperative action and yet tempting to each to defect and take advantage of the others. How then can rational self-interested agents avoid the conclusion that they ought to cheat whenever they can? Thomas Hobbes, who was the first philosopher to attempt to use cases like the prisoner's dilemma to ground morality, argued that rational self-interested agents will see that it is necessary to build into the cooperative ventures penalties that are sufficiently harsh to make cheating irrational. Since he was seeking the very foundations for civil society in his version of the prisoner's dilemma, he hypothesized that the parties to his cooperative venture would create a sovereign with the power to detect and punish cheaters. Like the solution to the prisoner's dilemma based on the code of silence, this resolves the dilemma by changing the players' utility functions and thus by changing the game.

Recently David Gauthier has addressed the problem again in the hope of showing that rational self-interested agents can come to the conclusion that they should cooperate with their fellows even when there is no sovereign to punish cheaters. The key to Gauthier's approach is that he considers the situation of an agent who knows that in the future he is likely to be confronted with a prisoner's dilemma and chooses now between cooperating or cheating. For Gauthier, this is to choose to develop one of two character traits (or dispositions to behave in certain ways). To decide to cooperate is to decide to be the sort of person who will join a cooperative venture and stay with it so long as the prospects are good that your colleagues will continue to cooperate too. To decide to cheat is to decide to be the sort who will defect from a cooperative venture whenever it is to your personal advantage to do so.

Suppose you are trying to decide whether to become a cooperator or to be a cheater. Gauthier makes the usual decision theoretic assumption that you will make this decision so as to maximize your expected utility. (Thus as of now you are a cheater.) Now if we were all perfect mind readers, when we met you we would know whether you were a cooperative type or a cheater. Furthermore, if we knew that you were a cheater, we would exclude you from our cooperative ventures. (Of course, we might not if we could be certain that we could prevent you from cheating. But Gauthier is trying to avoid such Hobbesian solutions.) You would know that in a prisoner's dilemma you should avoid being excluded from the cooperative venture. You would also know that you cannot even seriously consider joining us and cheating afterward. Thus of the options realistically open to you, you would rather join us and remain faithful. Thus you would see that it is in your self-interest to become the sort of person who cooperates in a prisoner's dilemma.

It follows that each member of a group of rational self-interested agents, who are also perfect mind readers, will separately decide to become the sort of person who cooperates in a prisoner's dilemma. Now we could stipulate that an ideally rational agent is a perfect mind reader. That would not make any difference to zero sum game theory since, whether or not your opponent can read your mind, he knows that if you are rational you will play an equilibrium strategy. It will make a difference to the theory of nonzero sum games in which *no* communication is possible; for there will be no such games unless we limit mind reading—for instance, to face-to-face confrontations. In any case, resolving the prisoner's dilemma by introducing perfect mind readers has little real-life fallout. So Gauthier introduced a refinement to make his solution more realistic.

Suppose again that you are trying to decide whether to remain a cheater or to become a cooperative type. Although we will not assume that anyone can read minds, we will assume that there is a chance that cheaters will be recognized and thus excluded from cooperative ventures. Hence if you decide to remain a cheater, you might find an occasion to negotiate a cooperative venture with some cooperative types. If you do, you might not be recognized as a cheater, and if you are not, you will be able to exploit your partners. Of course, if you are recognized, you will be excluded from the cooperative venture. On the other hand, if you decide to become a cooperative type, you too might meet some fellow cooperators. If you do and you recognize each other, you will be able to benefit from the cooperative venture.

Suppose the utility of not cooperating is u, that of cooperating with other cooperators is u', that of exploiting a group of cooperators is 1, and that of being exploited by a cheater is 0. Also suppose that $0 < u < u' < 1$; that is, it is best to cheat, next best to cooperate, next best not to cooperate, and worst to be exploited. Finally, suppose the probability of meeting a cooperative type is p, that of being able to exploit one is q, and that of being able to recognize and cooperate with a fellow cooperator is r. Then we may represent your decision by means of the following tree (figure 5-2).

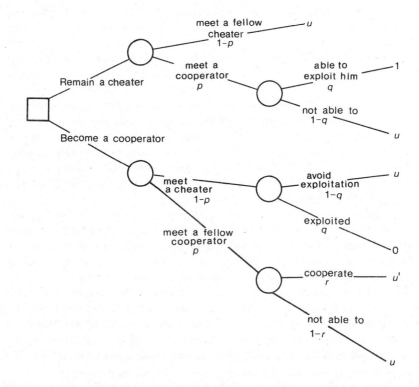

Figure 5-2

If you now calculate the expected utilities of your two choices, you will find that remaining a cheater has an expected utility of

(1) $u + pq(1 - u)$,

while becoming a cooperator has one of

(2) $u + pr(u' - u) - q(1 - p)u$.

Before we proceed any further let us try to assign some meaning to these numbers. The first term of both (1) and (2), u, is the utility you can expect as things now stand. If you remain a cheater and manage to exploit a cooperator, you will gain an additional amount. Instead of receiving the utility u you will get the utility 1. Thus your gain will be $(1 - u)$. However, you cannot be certain of achieving this gain, so in (1) $(1 - u)$ is weighted by the probability of meeting a cooperator (p) and also being able to exploit him (q). If you become a cooperator, you might gain some utility too; you might go from u to u'. However, a cheater might exploit you, leaving you with 0. The second term of (2) contains your potential gain, $(u' - u)$, weighted by the probability of meeting a cooperator (p) and cooperating with him (r). Your potential loss is $-u$ and the probability of suffering it is that of meeting and being exploited by a cheater, $(1 - p)q$. This yields the third term of (2).

We still do not know whether you will realize more utility by remaining a cheater or becoming a cooperator. You have a chance for a gain if you cheat, and you have a chance at a lesser gain and a potential loss if you do not. But clearly that is not enough information for you to decide. It will depend on the particular values of u, u', p, q, and r, and this is as far as Gauthier's solution in its general form goes.

However, let us look at a special case. Suppose you are certain to meet only cooperators. Then $p = 1$ and we have

(1) $= u + q(1 - u)$
(2) $= u + r(u' - u)$.

Hence you can make your decision by comparing the gains $q(1 - u)$ and $r(u' - u)$. The first is smaller than the second just in case,

$q/r < (u' - u)/(1 - u)$

that is, just in case the ratio of the probability of exploiting to that of cooperating is smaller than the ratio of the gain from cooperating to that of exploiting. Thus if your chance to cooperate is high, your chance to exploit is low, and the gain from cooperating is relatively close to that from cheating, you should become a cooperator. For example, if $u = 1/8$, $u' = 3/4$, $q = 1/4$ and $r = 3/4$, then $q/r = 1/3$ and $(u' - u)/(1 - u) = 5/7$; so you should become a cooperator. On the other hand, if your chance to exploit is high in comparison to that to cooperate and the gain from the former is high in comparison to the latter, you should remain a cheater. For example, if $u = 1/2$, $u' = 5/8$, $q = 3/4$, and $r = 1/16$, then $q/r = 12$ and $(u' - u)/(1 - u) = 1/4$; so you should remain a cheater.

It is clear that we cannot prove that it is rational to choose to cooperate in every prisoner's dilemma situation. However, Gauthier's analysis shows that when the benefits to be derived from cooperating approach those to be derived from exploiting and the probability of successfully cooperating exceeds that of exploiting, it can be rational to cooperate. This opens the way for citizens to *make it* rational to cooperate without having to erect a Hobbesian sovereign.

First, citizens who want to discourage defection by potential cheaters should make the payoffs from cooperating as equitable as possible. Suppose you own a tractor, but only I know how to drive it. By cooperating we can use it to farm our lands, and if we do not cooperate, neither of us can grow a crop worth harvesting. If you manage to get me to take just enough of the crop to sustain myself while you grab the lion's share for yourself, I will be sorely tempted to cheat you whenever I can. Thus if you intend to keep my cooperation, it makes sense for you to raise my share. But if you raise it too much, we will simply switch our positions and it will no longer be rational for you to remain a faithful cooperator. Striking the proper balance leads us to the question of rational bargains—a topic to be treated in the next section.

Second, citizens can discourage cheaters by developing methods for identifying potential cheaters and fellow cooperators. Failing that they should enter prisoner's dilemma situations only when they are confident that their partners are true cooperators. Of course, we do that in real life. Governments and certain corporations run security checks on their employees before trusting them with important secrets. You and I would not volunteer our house keys or credit cards to a perfect stranger, and even those close to us must earn our trust before we expose ourselves to great risks at their hands.

As the tractor example hints, a promising step to take next in trying to derive a basis for morality from game theory is to examine cooperative games, in particular bargaining games. We will turn to them shortly. We must stress, however, that despite our talk of cooperative strategies and cooperation, the prisoner's dilemma is not a cooperative game, technically speaking. The players in a game cooperate when they *intentionally coordinate* their strategies. In the cases we have considered so far the players do not coordinate; rather, each decides independently to implement a strategy that eventuates in a so-called cooperative outcome—their seeming to cooperate is really a coincidence. This applies even to prisoner's dilemmas that arise after one has formed a partnership. Suppose, for example, that Joe and Moe happen to solve a cooperative game when each deposits $1,000 in a joint bank account. This plunges them into a noncooperative game for each has a chance to double his investment by cheating on the other.

If we are to base morality on bargaining games it is thus crucial to show that it can be rational to stick with one's bargains—even when more immediate utility can be gained by breaking them.

This underscores the importance of Gauthier's reasoning. For, if it is correct, it establishes that rational agents will *sometimes* abide by an agreement to cooperate when they find themselves in a prisoner's dilemma. It does not show that no one can gain more utility *in those instances* by breaking his agreement, for then there would be no prisoner's dilemma. Rather it shows that it is rational (in the sense of maximizing one's expected utility) to choose to *live by a policy* that requires one to cooperate faithfully when presented with a cooperative venture in which (1) one may obtain more utility than by continuing on one's own, and (2) one has a reasonable expectation that one's partners will remain faithful to their commitments too.

PROBLEMS

1. Are the outcomes $(-25, -1)$ and $(-1, -25)$ of the prisoner's dilemma Pareto optimal?
2. Can there be Pareto optimal outcomes in a zero sum game?
3. Here is a two-person version of the free rider problem. Hank and Ike own a mule that they both use for plowing their gardens. They have agreed to help each other feed the mule every day. The job requires moving a heavy sack of grain that the two men can handle with ease. Each fellow knows that the other could move the sack by himself if necessary. Thus each thinks to himself, It's not necessary for me to go there every day. Hank [Ike] will be there if I am not and he can get the job done, and I'd rather do something else. Suppose both Hank and Ike would prefer that the mule be fed by someone to its not being fed at all and that both would prefer that the other do it to doing it alone or together. Show that this game is a version of the clash of wills.
4. Here is another version of Hank and Ike's situation. Each would still rather that the other fellow feed the mule but now each so resents the prospect of doing it by himself that he prefers that the mule not be fed at all if he has to do it alone. Furthermore, each prefers that they feed the mule together to letting it starve. Show that this is a version of the prisoner's dilemma.
5. Verify that the expected utilities for remaining a cheater and becoming a cooperator are respectively (1) and (2).
6. Where $p = 1/2$, $q = 3/4$, $r = 1/4$, $u = 1/4$ and $u' = 3/4$, determine whether it is more rational to remain a cheater or to become a cooperator.

5-5. Cooperative Games

Until now we have assumed that communication between the players in a game is impossible. Thus although their interests might overlap—that is, the game might not be zero sum—they have had no opportunity to coordinate their strategies and realize together what neither can obtain on his own. Let us now give them that opportunity.

To see what a difference this can make, let us return to the clash of wills. Intuitively the fair solution was for the players to toss a coin and go skiing together on heads and to the festival on tails. But since they could not coordinate their strategies, this solution was out of the question. Now it is open to them. To see how this works out numerically, consider this game (table 5-33). First, suppose Col and Row cannot communicate but each decides separately to flip a coin and play his first strategy on heads and his second on tails.

5-33	(1, 2)	(0, 0)
	(0, 0)	(2, 1)

Then the utility to Row is that of the pair of mixed strategies

$$(1/2 \ R_1, \ 1/2 \ R_2); \ (1/2 \ C_1, \ 1/2 \ C_2),$$

i.e., $1/4(1) + 1/4(0) + 1/4(0) + 1/4(2) = 3/4$. This is also the utility to Col of his half of the pair. Now, let us suppose Row and Col can communicate and that they agree to flip a coin and play R_1 and C_1 together on heads and R_2 and C_2 on tails. Then they will have adopted a *coordinated* strategy. Their particular coordinated strategy can be represented by

$$1/2(R_1, \ C_1); \ 1/2(R_2, \ C_2)$$

and yields Row a utility of $1/2(1) + 1/2(2) = 3/2$. A similar calculation shows that Col also receives a utility of 3/2 from this pair. Obviously, Row and Col do better with their coordinated coin toss than they do with their separate ones.

In general if Row and Col play a coordinated strategy pair

$$x(R_1, \ C_1); \ (1-x)(R_2, \ C_2),$$

where $0 < x < 1$, their utilities are

$$x(1) + (1-x)2 = 2 - x \quad \text{(for Row)}$$
$$x(2) + (1-x)1 = 1 + x \quad \text{(for Col)}.$$

For there is chance of x that they will achieve the outcome (1, 2) and one of $1 - x$ that they will achieve the outcome worth (2, 1).

Suppose we think of each pair of Row's and Col's utilities as determining a point in the plane whose horizontal axis is Row's scale and whose vertical axis is Col's scale. Then when $x = 0$, their coordinated strategy yields the point (2, 1). When $x = 1$, it yields the point (1, 2), and when x falls between these values, it yields a point on the line joining (2, 1) and (1, 2). It can be shown that Row and Col can achieve no utility points better than the points on this line. Thus each of these points is Pareto optimal. Yet, of course, those toward the (2, 1) end of the line are better for Row and those toward the (1, 2) end are better for Col. The problem for game theory, then, is to determine which point or points on this line to recommend as the solution for the game.

Putting the problem more generally, in a cooperative game the players can usually achieve outcomes with coordinated strategies that they cannot achieve on their own. In the game we have been considering, the outcome (3/2, 3/2) is a case in point. Furthermore, by playing coordinated strategies the players can guarantee that they avoid outcomes that are worse for both of them. (They can avoid the (0, 0) outcomes in our game.) Let us call the set of outcomes they can achieve by playing either coordinated or individual strategies the *achievable set*. We can limit our attention to the Pareto optimal members of the achievable set.

For if an outcome is not Pareto optimal, there is some other achievable outcome in which one or both of the players can do better. If only one does better, he does so at no cost to the other — not even in psychological terms since the utilities already reflect the psychological aspects of the other player's doing better. Thus no player could prefer an outcome that is not Pareto optimal to one that is.

Some game theorists think that all strategies that produce Pareto optimal outcomes in a cooperative game should count as solutions to that game. But that does not distinguish the apparently "fair" outcome (3/2, 3/2) of our recent game from the "biased" ones (2, 1) or (1, 2), nor in a cooperative version of the prisoner's dilemma would it distinguish $(-1, -25)$ and $(-25, -1)$ from the "cooperative" outcome $(-2, -2)$, since all three outcomes are Pareto optimal.

Furthermore, this broad conception of a solution often leaves the players with many outcomes yielding many different values to each. Unlike the case with multiple equilibrium pairs in a zero sum game, there is no solution to the coordination problem this generates. Thus the situation will quickly degenerate into a competitive game in which the players vie for Pareto optimal outcomes favorable to themselves. One way to deal with this is to have the players bargain for Pareto optimal outcomes. This leads us to bargaining games.

PROBLEMS

1. Plot the achievable set of utility points for the game presented at the beginning of this section. (They will form a triangle.)
2. Plot the achievable set for the prisoner's dilemma. (Start by plotting the four points achieved by playing pure strategies, connect these to form a polygon, and fill in the region.) Describe the game's Pareto optimal points in geometrical terms.
3. The points of the achievable set for a two-person game always form the boundary and interior of a polygon. (Can you explain why?) Prove that the set of Pareto optimal points constitute the northeastern boundary of the polygon.

5-5a. Bargaining Games

A natural suggestion for resolving the problem posed by cooperative games with several achievable Pareto optimal outcomes is that the players select a single outcome by bargaining with each other. Since it is certainly more rational to end disputes by negotiation than to leave them festering or to resolve them by force, bargaining games merit the attention not only of pure-game theorists but also of those interested in a rational basis for morality.

A bargaining game is specified in terms of the achievable set of a cooperative game. Using the graphing approach introduced earlier, the set of achievable outcomes will be called the *bargaining region* of the game. We will assume that the region contains at least two Pareto optimal points for otherwise there would be nothing to contest. We will also assume that the region contains a non-Pareto optimal point, called the *failure point* of the game, which marks the

GAME THEORY

payoffs to the players in case they fail to cooperate. In the prisoner's dilemma the failure point is the point $(-10, -10)$, in the game given in the last section it is $(0, 0)$. The problem for the game theorist is to specify a point within the bargaining region that would be selected by rational bargainers. Let us call such a point *the negotiation point* of the game. We will examine first a solution proposed by John Nash.

Let us designate the failure point of a bargaining game by (f_1, f_2), where f_1 is the utility received by Row and f_2 that achieved by Col. Now suppose we have been given a cooperative game that generates a bargaining region R and a failure point (f_1, f_2). By assumption there are some Pareto optimal points in R. Let (u_1, u_2) be one of them. Consider the numbers $u_1 - f_1$ and $u_2 - f_2$. These represent the amount of utility to be gained, respectively, by Row and Col in case they agree on the point (u_1, u_2). Clearly, rational bargainers will agree on a Pareto optimal point if they agree on any point at all. But there is more than one Pareto optimal point in the bargaining region. Row will prefer some and Col will prefer others.

Nash proposed taking the negotiation point as that point of the bargaining region R for which the product

$$(u_1 - f_1)(u_2 - f_2)$$

is the largest. For future reference we will call this the *Nash point*.

Why should we count this point as a solution? First, the Nash point is certain to be Pareto optimal. For if a point is not Pareto optimal, one or both of the utility gains associated with it will be smaller than those associated with some other point and none of the gains will be larger than those associated with any other point. Thus its associated product will not be maximal and it cannot be a Nash point.

Second, there will be only one Nash point. For suppose there are two Pareto optimal points, (u_1, u_2) and (u'_1, u'_2), whose products $(u_1 - f_1)(u_2 - f_2)$ and $(u'_1 - f_1)(u'_2 - f_2)$ are equal. Let "g_1" abbreviate "$u_1 - f_1$," and let "g_2," "g'_1," and "g'_2" abbreviate the other factors of the two products. Since the points are distinct Pareto optimal points, there is one in which the gain for Row is greater and that for Col is less. Let us suppose that this happens in the first point. Then $g_1 > g'_1$ while $g_2 < g'_2$. However, from this it follows that

$$g_1 > (g_1 + g'_1)/2 > g'_1$$
$$g_2 < (g_2 + g'_2)/2 < g'_2.$$

But then

$$g_1 g_2 < g_1(g_2 + g'_2)/2.$$

But since the product on the left equals $g'_1 g'_2$, we have

$$g'_1 g'_2 < g_1(g_2 + g'_2)/2.$$

From which it follows that

$$g'_1 g'_2 < (g_1 + g'_1)/2 \times (g_2 + g'_2)/2.$$

160

However, the product $(g_1 + g'_1)/2 \times (g_2 + g'_2)/2$ corresponds to another Pareto optimal point in the bargaining region. This is the point halfway between the points (u_1, u_2) and (u'_1, u'_2). (See exercise 4 in the following Problems section.) This contradicts our assumption that these two points are Pareto optimal points with maximal Nash products.

More can be said for Nash's proposal than just that it selects a unique Pareto optimal point from the bargaining region. There are four plausible conditions for any solution to the bargaining problems to satisfy, and it turns out that Nash's is the *only* solution to the bargaining problem that satisfies all four. After I state the conditions and show that Nash's proposal meets them, I will discuss their appropriateness. The four conditions are as follows:

(1) *Pareto optimality*: The negotiation point must always be a unique Pareto optimal point.

(2) *Invariance under utility transformations*: If two bargaining games can be obtained from each other by positive linear transformations of the players' utility scales, their negotiation points can be obtained from each other by the same transformations.

(3) *Symmetry*: If a bargaining game is symmetrical in the sense that (a) a point (u, v) belongs to the bargaining region if and only if (v, u) does, and (b) $f_1 = f_2$, the negotiation point assigns the same value to each player.

(4) *Irrelevant expansion/contraction*: If (a) the bargain region of one game is contained within that of another and (b) the two games have the same failure points, then if the negotiation point for the game with the larger region happens to fall within the smaller region, the two games must have the same negotiation point.

We have already shown that Nash's proposal meets the Pareto optimality condition. I will let you establish that it meets conditions (2) and (3). (See exercises 5 and 6.) So let us now show that it meets condition (4).

Suppose that G and G' are bargaining games with the same failure points, that the G region contains the G' region, and that the negotiation point for G falls within the G' region. Since, according to Nash's proposal, the negotiation point is the Nash point, we must show that the Nash point for G is also the Nash point for G'. By definition, the Nash point for G is the point of the bargaining region of G whose associated product is maximal. Since G and G' have the same failure points, the product associated with any point in the bargaining region of G' will be identical to that associated with the point under G. Since the Nash point, N, for G falls within the bargaining region of G' and every G' point is also a G point, the point N will also yield the product that is maximal for the points of G'. Thus N will be the negotiation point of G'.

Having established that Nash's proposal meets conditions (1)–(4), we must also show that it is the only solution that does so. Let us suppose then that we have a method M for solving bargaining games that satisfies (1)–(4) and prove that M must always yield all and only Nash points. Then M will coincide with Nash's proposal.

161

To do this, let us assume we are given an arbitrary bargaining game with the failure point (f_1, f_2) whose Nash point is (n_1, n_2). We must show that this is M's solution to the game as well. We first create a second game by applying the positive linear transformations

$$u_1' = u_1/(n_1 - f_1) - f_1/(n_1 - f_1)$$
$$u_2' = u_2/(n_2 - f_2) - f_2/(n_2 - f_2)$$

to Row's and Col's utility scales, respectively. As a result the failure point is transformed to $(0, 0)$, and the Nash point is transformed to $(1, 1)$. (See exercise 7.) Next we create a third game by cutting the bargaining region for this second game back to a symmetrical region whose axis of symmetry is the line $y = x$. Of all the Pareto optimal points of this third game the point $(1, 1)$ is the only one that satisfies the symmetry condition. So it must be M's solution of the third game. However, by the expansion/contraction condition it must be the solution to the second game as well. Finally, by the invariance-under-utility-transformations condition, the Nash point of the first game must be its solution by M too. Furthermore, M cannot produce more than one negotiation point for the first game, since the third game had just one negotiation point.

PROBLEMS

1. In some games one player may stand to gain more at every Pareto optimal point; that is, the number $u_1 - f_1$ for Row, say, will be greater than $u_2 - f_2$ for every Pareto optimal point. Propose a way for defining "favorable" that is independent of the absolute amount gained by the players and according to which some Pareto optimal points will favor Row and others Col.

2. Show that in every bargaining game there must be at least one outcome with respect to which Row and Col have opposite preferences.

3. Find the Nash solution to the bargaining games corresponding to the prisoner's dilemma and the clash of wills.

4. Show that the point generating the product

$$(g_1 + g'_1)/2 \times (g_2 + g'_2)/2$$

lies between (u_1, u_2) and (u'_1, u'_2).

5. Suppose G' is a bargaining game that can be obtained from the game G by replacing every point (u_1, u_2) of G's bargaining region with $(au_1 + b, cu_2 + d)$ where both a and c are positive. Show that if (n_1, n_2) is the Nash point of G, $(an_1 + b, cn_2 + d)$ is the Nash point of G'.

6. Suppose G is a symmetrical bargaining game. Prove that if $u_1 < u_2$, the product of the gains associated with (u_1, u_2) is less than that associated with (u_2, u_2).

7. Verify that the positive linear transformations used in the proof of the uniqueness of the Nash solution do transform the failure point to $(0, 0)$ and the Nash point to $(1, 1)$.

Now that we have seen that Nash's solution is the only one to satisfy conditions (1)–(4), we should examine the conditions themselves. For their reasonableness is the main case to be made for Nash's proposal—other than its mathematical elegance.

There is little to dispute in the Pareto optimality and utility transformation conditions. Our previous examination of cooperative games pointed to the desirability of having a method for selecting a single Pareto optimal point as the solution to a cooperative game, and condition (1) does no more than codify that. Furthermore, solutions to games should be invariant under positive linear utility transformations, since utility scales themselves are fixed only up to positive linear transformations. A method for solving games that permitted solutions to change when utilities are varied by those transformations would respond to more information than utility scales represent.

The symmetry condition is both an informational condition and a fairness condition. If the players in a bargaining game occupy completely symmetrical positions, it seems only fair that the solution should allocate the same amount of utility to both. It is difficult to imagine rational negotiators not insisting on that. On the other hand, since the players' positions are entirely symmetrical, there is no information—other than the players' names—on which to base a non-symmetrical solution. Since favoring one player over the other would mean arbitrarily choosing one, the symmetrical solution has the strongest claim to rationality. (I am ignoring considerations of justice or rights and the players' histories.)

The controversy begins when we turn to the expansion/contraction condition. We encountered a condition much like it when discussing decisions under ignorance. You will recall that there we considered several conditions decision theorists have proposed for the purpose of identifying the most rational rule to use for making decisions under risk. One condition that turned out to be quite controversial was the condition that the ranking of two acts should remain unchanged when a new act is introduced, so long as the new act is ranked below the original acts. We may give condition (4) a parallel formulation: When the bargaining region is expanded, the negotiation point should remain the same—so long as none of the new points is taken as the negotiation point and the failure point remains the same. Given this parallel, we should not be surprised that there is controversy concerning condition (4).

One might argue in favor of the condition that an expansion of a bargaining situation that introduces only new prospects that are not possible negotiation points and leaves the failure point fixed does not really change the situation. The new points are merely distractions, which smart negotiators will cast aside in order to focus on the heart of the matter at hand.

Unfortunately, this argument is based on a misinterpretation of condition (4). Condition (4) does not say that the new prospects are not possible negotiation points. It simply says that if none of the new prospects is chosen, their presence should not change the point chosen from among the old prospects. We can make a better case for the condition by considering contractions rather than expansions. For the condition may also be paraphrased as stating that if we contract a bargaining region while retaining both the failure and negotiation points, the latter should be the negotiation point for the new game. For if the point was an acceptable point of agreement when there were more points to choose from, it should remain acceptable when there are fewer and the consequences of failing to reach an agreement are the same.

This argument for condition (4) neglects the role of additional points in determining the aspiration levels of the players. Consider this somewhat fanciful example. The pilots' union and High Flyer Airlines had been negotiating a new wage contract. The union began the negotiations by demanding a 15% raise for the pilots, knowing full well that they would be forced to settle for 10% or less, since 15% would bankrupt High Flyer. The airline and union were about to settle on 8.5%, when the president announced a wage hike ceiling of 10%. This caused the airline to demand that the union accept 7%, the union protested that the airline had been negotiating in bad faith, the negotiations collapsed, and a general sympathy strike by all airline pilots ensued. Since this happened in the midst of the Christmas travel season, the public and press angrily blamed the president for his untimely announcement. The president called a press conference to explain his position. "You see," he said, "I had no reason to expect such irrational behavior from the airline or union. My announcement didn't change anything, since they never expected to settle for a raise above 10% anyway." If you find the president's explanation plausible, you sympathize with condition (4). If not—if you think his restrictions changed the bargaining context enough to make one or both parties see that a lower raise was now in order—you can see why some game theorists doubt the condition.

Let us approach the matter more abstractly and consider a game with a bargaining region bounded by the points (0, 0) (the failure point), (0, 5), (5, 5) and (10, 0). The bargaining region is a trapezoid with the line from (5, 5) to (10, 0) marking the Pareto optimal points. (See exercise 1 in the next Problems section.) This line has the equation

$$y = 10 - x.$$

The Nash point for the game is (5, 5). (See exercise 2.) Now consider a game with the bargaining region that is the triangle bounded by (0, 0) (again the failure point), (0, 10), and (10, 0). This game is an expansion of the first. Its Pareto optimal points are again on the same line, except that it now extends to (0, 10). The Nash point is once again (5, 5), which accords with condition (4) and the symmetry of the game. Yet one can surely argue that the new game has strengthened Col's bargaining position and that the solution should reflect this. Or one could argue that the solution to the first game is unfair to Row in picking a symmetrical negotiation point when the shape of the bargaining region gives an advantage to Row. From the point of view of Nash's solution, however, there is no essential difference between the two games.

In view of the objections to condition (4) and Nash's solution it is worth looking at some other proposals. Notice that in the first (trapezoid) game the point (5, 5) yields Col 100% of the maximal utility available to him in the game whereas it yields Row only 50% of the maximum available to him. In the second (triangle) game, however, both players are allocated the same percentage of their maximums. We can also view this in terms of concessions: In the first game Row is forced to concede 50% of what he would want under ideal circumstances whereas Col makes no concession. Thus it might be worth approaching bargaining games through the concepts of proportional gain and proportional concession.

Putting matters more formally, let us call the *ideal point* of the game that point (i_1, i_2) in which i_1 (i_2) equals the maximum utility afforded to Row (Col) at any point of the bargaining region. Ordinarily the ideal point will not be in the bargaining region or identifiable with a possible outcome of the game. In the trapezoid game it is (5, 10) and in the triangle game it is (10, 10). The *potential gain* for a player is the difference between his value at the ideal point and his value at the failure point. In the trapezoid game Row has a potential gain of 5 while Col has one of 10. The *same* formula defines a player's potential concession, since in each case we are concerned with the amount of utility between the failure point (where the player "concedes" everything) and the ideal point (where he gains everything). The *proportional gain for a player at a point* may now be defined as the ratio of the player's actual gain at the point to his potential gain. For any point (u_1, u_2) in a game the *proportional gain* for Row is given by the formula

$$(u_1 - f_1)/(i_1 - f_1).$$

(By interchanging the subscripts we get a similar expression for Col's proportional gain.)

We will also define a player's *concession at a point* as the difference between his value at the ideal point and that at the point in question. His *proportional concession at a point* is then defined as the ratio of his concession at that point to his potential concession. For the point (u_1, u_2), Row's proportional concession is given by the formula

$$(i_1 - u_1)/(i_1 - f_1).$$

As one might suspect, there is a simple relationship between proportional gains and concessions. The proportional gain and concession at a point for a player must sum to 1. (See exercise 5.) Letting "*PG*" and "*PC*" stand for proportional gain and proportional concession, respectively, and suppressing the phrases "for a player" and "at a point," this yields:

$$PG = 1 - PC$$
$$PC = 1 - PG.$$

Notice that as a player gains more (proportionally) he concedes less (proportionally), and conversely. Thus in defining solutions for bargaining games we may use either of these concepts and dispense with the other.

A simple approach to bargaining solutions using proportional gains (concessions) is to specify the negotiation point as the point at which the proportional gains are identical for each player and as large as possible. Let us call this the *equitable distribution point*. This picks (5, 5) in the triangle game since each player obtains a proportional gain of 1/2. However, it prevents (5, 5) from being the negotiation point in the trapezoidal game, since Col obtains a proportional gain of 1 whereas Row's is only 1/2. Instead it picks the midway Pareto optimal point (20/3, 10/3) in which each player has a proportional gain of 2/3.

We can also describe this solution in terms of concessions. For the point at which the proportional gains are maximal and equal is also the point at which the proportional concessions are minimal and equal. Thus the equitable distribution point is the same whether we think of the solution as distributing gains or concessions. In either case we can see the appeal of the proposal: Each player knows that the other is bearing the same burden (or has been given the same advantage) and that this has been reduced (or maximized) as much as possible compatible with its being distributed equitably. Furthermore, in a symmetrical game the equitable distribution point and the Nash point are the same. (See exercise 6.)

This solution also satisfies the invariance-under-utility-transformation condition (exercise 7) and the Pareto optimality condition (exercises 8–10). We have already seen that it does not satisfy the expansion/contraction condition. Instead it meets the following *monotonicity condition*: If one bargaining region contains another and they have the same failure and ideal points, the negotiation point in the larger region affords each player at least as much as he receives from the negotiation point of the smaller region. It can be proved that conditions (1)–(3) plus this new condition uniquely characterize the equitable distribution solution. We will omit that proof here.

Unfortunately, when we apply the solution in terms of equitable distribution points to bargaining games with three or more players we obtain unsatisfactory results. Consider the three-person game with a triangular bargaining region determined by the points (0, 0, 0) (the failure point), (0, 1, 1), and (1, 0, 1). The Pareto optimal points for this region lie on the line connecting (0, 1, 1) and (1, 0, 1). But the third player receives a proportional gain of 1 at every point on this line. Thus there is no point on the line at which all three receive the same proportional gain. Thus the equitable distribution point cannot be a Pareto optimal point. Worse, the only point in this region at which the players' proportional gains are the same is the failure point (0, 0, 0). Hence in this game the equitable distribution solution declares the failure point as the negotiation point.

David Gauthier has proposed an alternative solution for dealing with cases of this sort. Instead of requiring that the proportional gains be identical, he proposes that we require that the minimum gains be maximized and pick the point allocating the most to each player consistent with this requirement. This sets the negotiation point for the last game at (1/2, 1/2, 1)–the midpoint on the Pareto optimal line. It can be shown that Gauthier's maximin proportional gains solution satisfies the Pareto optimality, invariance-under-utility-transformations, and symmetry conditions. Furthermore, in the two-person case it is equivalent to the equitable distribution solution. (See exercise 11.)

PROBLEMS

1. Draw the bargaining region bounded by (0, 0), (0, 25), (5, 25), and (10, 0). Do the same for the region bounded by (0, 0), (0, 50), and (10, 0).

2. There are several methods for verifying that the Nash point of the trapezoidal game is (5, 5). One is to plot the gain products for Pareto optimal points and use the graph to locate the greatest of these. Since the products have the form xy with $y = 10 - x$, this is the same as plotting the graph of the function $f(x) = 10x - x^2$. Plot this for the values of x between 0 and 10, inclusively. (If you know how to calculate derivatives, you can calculate the critical point for $f(x)$ by solving $f'(x) = 0$. You will find that x must equal 5.)

3. What are the ideal points for the prisoner's dilemma and the clash of wills?

4. Show that in any bargaining game Row's percentages of potential gain and concession range between 0 and 1.

5. Show that $PC + PG = 1$.

6. Prove that in a symmetrical game the Nash point and the equitable distribution point coincide.

7. Prove that if two bargaining games can be obtained from each other by applying positive linear transformations to the player's utility scales, the equitable distribution points of the games can be obtained from each other by applying the same transformations.

8. Prove that if Row's utility at a point (x, y) in the bargaining region is greater than it is at the point (x', y'), Row's proportional gain (or concession) is greater (less) at the first point than at the second.

9. Prove that if (x, y) is a Pareto optimal point and (x', y') is not, at least one player has a greater proportional gain at (x, y) than at (x', y') and neither player has less.

10. Since the players have a finite number of pure strategies, the set of Pareto optimal points in the bargaining region forms a broken line running from the point where Col's proportional gain is 1 and Row's is 0 to one where Row's is 1 and Col's 0. It follows that there is exactly one point on this line at which their proportional gains are identical. Show that this is the equitable distribution point for the game.

11. Show that in a two-person bargaining region Gauthier's maximin proportional gains point is the equitable distribution point.

5-6. Games with Three or More Players

In this section I will present a brief and incomplete discussion of n-person game theory. The theory itself suffers from many loose ends, and there is little agreement among game theorists about the proper way to define the concept of a solution to an n-person game. Perhaps this will excuse my cursory treatment of the subject.

To begin, we should note that some two-person games have analogs with three or more players. The oil cartel case is a generalized instance of the prisoner's dilemma, as we have already mentioned. As should be obvious, the free rider problem also comes in many-person versions. The clash of wills does too. Suppose Alice, Mary, and Sally are three friends who always prefer being a threesome to being a couple and that in turn to being alone. Then suppose they might go to any one of three places A, B, or C. Alice prefers A to B to C, Mary C to A to B, and Sally B to C to A. Then we have all the ingredients for a three-person clash of wills. (If you want to try working this out, note that there are 27 possible pure strategy combinations, ranging from AAA, AAB, AAC, to ABA, ABB, ABC, and on to CCA, CCB and CCC.) There are also n-person versions of bargaining games. For instance, in negotiating a real estate sale, a broker might offer to reduce her commission for the sake of concluding the deal. Then what is ordinarily a two-person bargaining game would become a three-person one. In the three-person case, however, the bargaining region is usually not a polygon in a plane but rather a solid in three-dimensional space. In the general case it is a hypersolid in n-dimensional space.

There are even n-person versions of zero sum games. They are the *constant sum games*, so-called because the total amount of utility available under each outcome always sums to the same number. By appropriately transforming the players' utility scales this number can be made to equal zero. Consider, for example, a game with four players in which each outcome results in placing each player as first, second, third, or fourth, with ties being excluded. Suppose each player assigns a first the utility of 4; a second, 3; a third, 2; and a fourth, 1. Then the utilities always sum to 10. But by subtracting 5/2 from every utility number, we can convert the game to a zero sum game.

Unfortunately, the maximin theorem does not extend to n-person constant sum games. If we allow mixed strategies, there will be equilibrium points for each game. However, as in the clash of wills, there may be several equilibrium points, each yielding different values to the players. Thus we have little reason to hope for elegant, simple, and compelling solutions in n-person game theory.

The bulk of the theory is not concerned with the n-person analogs of two-person games, which we have just reviewed. Rather the theory focuses on *coalitions* formed by some of the players to take advantage of the others or "the system." Coalitions are familiar from everyday life. Soldiers or students will gang up to put down the barracks or locker room bully. Political parties band together to form parliamentary majorities. State governors form coalitions to put pressure on the federal government or Congress. Citizens organize to combat drug abuse or drunk drivers or whatever. Thus n-person game theory promises to yield analyses of a variety of complex everyday phenomena. (Although coalitions are impossible in two-person games, some multiperson games can be reduced to two-person games between coalitions.)

Many questions can be raised about coalitions. Who will join with whom to form one? (Will the moderates join the liberals or the conservatives?) Does a given coalition have sufficient strength to secure a given outcome? (Can the coalition against drunk drivers get the drinking age raised?) How much utility will accrue to it? How much utility can a player expect from joining a coalition?

Is a given coalition stable, that is, are its members unlikely to defect and seek new alliances with other players? It is no wonder then that there are many different approaches to n-person games.

I will not attempt to show you how game theorists have tried to answer all these questions about coalitions. However, I can give you some flavor for how game theory handles some of them by working through one example. So let us turn to that now.

Hank, Ike, and Ned farm wheat, and Fred buys wheat for resale abroad. Fred has a rush order for at least 10,001 but no more than 16,000 bushels of wheat. Hank's crop comes to 10,000 bushels, Ike's to 7,500, and Ned's to 5,000. Thus no farmer can fill the order by himself. So Fred makes the following proposal: "I will pay each of you or any group of you $1 per bushel for any sales totaling 10,000 bushels or less. I will pay $2 per bushel for any sale totaling more than 10,000 bushels but no more than 16,000 bushels. And I will pay $1.25 per bushel for the excess over 16,000." Will the farmers deal with Fred directly by themselves? Or will some of them form a coalition? If so, who will join with whom and how will they split the proceeds? By addressing these questions formally we can cover some of the more fundamental ideas of n-person game theory.

First, let us make the simplifying assumption that dollar amounts indicate the utility received by the farmers. In other words, they are EMVers. Now let us look at the proceeds accruing to all the possible coalitions our three players can form. These are presented in table 5-34. Game theory allows for one-player

5-34	Coalition	Value (Proceeds)
	(Hank)	10,000
	(Ike)	7,500
	(Ned)	5,000
	(Hank, Ike)	33,875
	(Hank, Ned)	30,000
	(Ike, Ned)	25,000
	(Hank, Ike, Ned)	40,125

or unit coalitions, so these are included in the table. Their values are computed on the basis of sales at $1 per bushel. The (Hank, Ned) and (Ike, Ned) coalitions are paid at the rate of $2 per bushel, since their sales fall between 10,000 and 16,000 bushels. The other coalitions have more bushels to sell, so they are paid $2 per bushel for the first 16,000 bushels and $1.25 for the excess.

In mathematical terms, table 5-34 presents a function whose arguments are coalitions and whose values are utilities accruing to coalitions as wholes. Each is called the *value of the coalition* for the game, and the function itself is called the *characteristic function* of the game. (In conforming to the abstractive spirit of mathematics, most game theorists have tried to answer the questions we posed earlier about coalitions by using just the information contained in the characteristic function while disregarding the particular rules and circumstances of the game. Thus from the game theoretic point of view our particular example is just one of infinitely many equivalent three-person games, all of which have the same characteristic function. Furthermore, as one might expect, game theory will even allow us to perform certain positive linear transformations on the values for the coalitions and still count the results as equivalent to the original game.)

With the concept of the value of a coalition and the characteristic function of a game in hand, let us return to our example. Will two or more farmers form a coalition? It certainly seems likely that they will, since each coalition of two or more farmers has a higher value than any coalition consisting of just one farmer. Thus it would seem rational for some of them to combine and make a bargain to divide the profits they obtain by doing so. For example, by combining, Hank and Ned can make 30,000. If we subtract from that what each can make alone (10,000 + 7,500), there is a balance of 12,500 for them to share. Similar calculations indicate that each of the other coalitions containing two or more farmers provides potential individual profits.

At first sight it seems likely that all three farmers will form a coalition since that would produce more proceeds to split than any other. Suppose for the moment that they do this and have 40,125 to divide. How should they divide it? One suggestion is that they divide according to the amount of wheat each has contributed. Since Hank has contributed roughly 44%, Ike roughly 33%, and Ned roughly 22%, this would yield a distribution of 17,655 to Hank, 13,241 to Ike, and 8,827 to Ned. Everyone would have reason to be dissatisfied with this. For if Hank and Ned were to form a coalition and divide the proceeds according to their contributions (2 to 1), Hank would receive 20,000 and Ned 10,000. Of course, in that case Ike would get only the 7,500 that he can obtain by selling to Fred on his own. Similarly, if Ike and Ned were to form a coalition and divide the proceeds according to their contributions (again 2 to 1), Ike would receive 15,000 and Ned 10,000. This time Hank would receive only 10,000.

In game theory distributions of utility to the players such as we have been considering are called *imputations* and are represented as ordered n-tuple (or vectors) of utility numbers. The theory has a few fundamental postulates concerning characteristic function and imputations that it is appropriate to mention now. The first is called the *superadditivity* condition and may be phrased as follows: *If a coalition is formed by combining the players from two completely separate coalitions, the value of the new coalition is at least as great as the sum of the values of the two earlier ones.* The reasoning behind this is that if two disjoint sets of players would actually do worse in combination than alone, it is pointless for them to unite. This implies as a special case that each coalition of several players must have a value greater than or equal to the sum of the utilities each of its members can achieve on his own. (See exercise 4.) As you can easily verify, the characteristic function for our wheat farmers game satisfies the super-additivity condition. (See exercise 1.)

The next condition—the condition of *individual rationality*—is stated in terms of imputations. It stipulates that *no imputation may result in a player receiving less utility than he can obtain by acting on his own.* This excludes (9,000, 20,000, 6,000), since Hank (who receives the 9,000) can always get 10,000 on his own. Again, none of the distributions we have mentioned so far violate this requirement. Although the condition of individual rationality does not mention coalitions explicitly, it clearly restricts the options for distributing the proceeds of a coalition to its members. By the way, an imputation is a distribution to *all* the players and not just to those within a coalition. However, since the members of a coalition cannot give the proceeds to players who are not members, given the characteristic function and an imputation we can often deduce what coalition has formed and how the proceeds are distributed among its members. (See exercise 5.)

Another condition proposed for restricting imputations is that an imputation be Pareto optimal in the sense that there is no other distribution under which each player does just as well and some do better. Despite the importance Pareto optimality plays in two-person game theory, there are grounds not to endorse it here. We have already seen that there is little reason to expect Hank, Ike, and Ned to unite in one big coalition, since the Hank and Ned and Ike and Ned coalitions are prima facie more desirable from an individual point of view. Yet requiring that imputations be Pareto optimal would exclude all but three-membered coalitions in our farmers game. For given any imputation associated with a coalition of two, there is a Pareto optimal imputation associated with the coalition of all three in which each player does better.

To see this, suppose two of the farmers, A and B, have formed the coalition (A, B) whose value is v. Further suppose that the third farmer, C, receives c while A and B receive a and b, respectively. Then $a + b = v$ and the total value of the imputation equals $a + b + c$. Now if C joins A and B, the new coalition, (A, B, C) will receive the value, v', greater than $v + c$. That means that $a + b + c < v'$. Now let $d = v' - (a + b + c)$. This is positive and so is $d/3$. Thus the imputation yielding $a + d/3$ to A, $b + d/3$ to B, and $c + d/3$ to C can be associated with the coalition (A, B, C). Not only does everyone do better, but the imputation is Pareto optimal. And yet we have seen that there are other Pareto optimal imputations (e.g., 17,655, 13,241, 8,827), which each of the players desires to abandon in favor of a coalition that is not Pareto optimal.

Let us introduce a new term to describe the situation we have just described. We will say that an imputation X *dominates* an imputation Y *with respect to the coalition S* just in case (1) every member of S does better under X than under Y, and (2) the value of S is at least as great as the sum of the utilities its members receive under X. The first clause of this definition simply says that whatever coalitions the members of S may belong to under the imputation Y, they—at least—are better off belonging to S. The second condition says that S receives enough value to make the payoffs to its members required to better those they would receive under Y. In brief, the first condition says that S can make an attractive offer to its potential members, the second that it can pay off. According to our definition, $E = (20{,}000, \ 7{,}500, \ 10{,}000)$ dominates $F = (17{,}655, \ 13{,}241, \ 8{,}275)$ with respect to the coalition formed by Hank and Ned. On the other hand, that imputation is itself dominated by $G = (21{,}000, \ 8{,}500, \ 10{,}625)$ with respect to the coalition of all three farmers.

Let us say that an imputation X *dominates* an imputation Y just in case there is some coalition with respect to which X dominates Y. Despite its similarity to our earlier concept of domination, this new notion must be carefully distinguished from the old one. If one *act* dominates another, the latter does not dominate the former. Not so for imputations: We have just seen two imputations that dominate each other. Furthermore, if one imputation dominates a second and the second a third, it need not be the case that the first dominates the third. The imputation G given earlier dominates F and F dominates E, but G does not dominate E. In fact, E and G are both Pareto optimal imputations associated with the coalition of all three farmers. No imputation of this sort dominates any other of the same kind. (See exercise 6.)

We can now turn to the Von Neumann-Morgenstern treatment of the farmers game. They impose the requirement, which we have questioned, that an imputation must be Pareto optimal. In the case of the farmers game this implies that the only coalition that can form is the one containing all three farmers.

Von Neumann and Morgenstern do not identify a single imputation as *the* solution to our game. Instead, they define a solution to be any class of Pareto optimal imputations with the property that (1) no member of the class dominates any other member of the class, and (2) every imputation outside the class is dominated by some member within it. Their solution to the farmers game is the class of all Pareto optimal imputations associated with the three-farmer coalition. Unfortunately, there are an enormous number of ways for Hank, Ike, and Ned to divide 40,125 while still ensuring that each receives more than he can on his own. Thus this solution tells us very little about the way "rational" or "just" farmers would distribute their proceeds. The situation is even worse for other games. Some games have infinitely many solution classes, and others have none at all.

These drawbacks have prompted game theorists to try other approaches. I will sketch one proposed by R. J. Aumann and Michael Maschler. They focus on distributions of values within coalitions and ask whether the members are likely to remain satisfied or to try to better their payoffs by forming other coalitions. To illustrate their ideas, suppose that Hank, Ike, and Ned have tentatively agreed to form a coalition and distribute their proceeds according to the imputation $G = (21{,}000, \ 8{,}500, \ 10{,}625)$. Then Ike approaches Hank and says, "Look, I want 9,500. You give up 1,000. If you don't, I'll form a coalition with Ned, offer him 15,000 and keep 10,000 for myself." Hank might reply, "Try that, and I'll go to Ned and top your offer. I'll give him 16,000 and keep 14,000 for myself." But, of course, Hank would lose in the process. Aumann and Maschler say that Ike has a *valid objection* to his payoff with respect to Hank's. More generally, one member in a coalition can validly object to his payoff with respect to another member's if he can form a coalition with other players that will pay him and the others more, but the player to whom he is objecting cannot do the same. Aumann and Maschler propose that a solution should consist of out-comes—coalitions and distributions within them—to which no member has a valid objection. Like the Von Neumann-Morgenstern approach this permits a game to have infinitely many outcomes.

We have just seen that not every Pareto optimal imputation need be part of an Aumann-Maschler solution. What about imputations that are not Pareto optimal? Consider the imputation (20,000, 7,500, 10,000), which arises when Hank and Ned form a coalition. Hank can ask for more and threaten to form a coalition with Ike in which he tops Ike's current 7,500 and takes more than 20,000 for himself. But Ned can do this too. Thus neither Hank nor Ned has a valid objection against each other, so their coalition and distribution count as part of an Aumann-Maschler solution. This shows that these solutions need not be Pareto optimal.

What should we make of this? Certainly, there are few morals to draw for morality or rationality from theories as tentative and controversial as the various coalition theories for n-person games. Yet the various concepts that have been proposed may provide useful frameworks for describing and discussing inter-actions between a number of rational agents. Political scientists, economists, and other social scientists have found this to be so, but—with the exception of Gauthier—philosophers apparently have not. Moreover, even Gauthier has not treated coalitions and has concentrated on the n-person prisoner's dilemma and bargain games instead.

Besides this, current coalition theories employ a highly questionable as-sumption about the "transferability" of utility. Most of our discussion about Hank, Ike, and Ned makes sense only if they can divide the values accruing to their multiperson coalitions. Since they are EMVers and the values accruing to their coalitions have been defined in terms of the money accruing to them, the case posed no pressing problem. But serious problems do arise when we turn to games in which the players are not EMVers or in which the value of a coali-tion is determined by some intangible or indivisible gain. If, for example, Fred paid the farmers with pieces of farm equipment, the problem of distributing the value acquired by a coalition to its members would be much more complicated, although perhaps solvable by awarding the farmers shares of ownership. Matters become all the more difficult when we consider how to distribute the value of a coalition formed to pass a constitutional amendment to ban abortion. Almost certainly there would be no tangible good to distribute after the amendment passed—you cannot distribute feelings of satisfaction. However, in a legislative game it makes more sense to measure the value of a coalition in terms of its power to get things done. This in turn is determined in part by the numbers of its members and in part by their power and influence. Insofar as one can quantify power and influence, there is hope for making sense of distributing the power of a coalition among its members.

Still, the assumption that the value of a coalition can be distributed in various combinations among its members is not one that we should accept lightly. The numbers assigned to individual players are utilities—not dollars, shares of ownership, or bits of power. We have seen that interpreting numbers in game tables as utilities is essential to making sense of two-person game theory. And the same reasoning applies to the n-person theory as well, for it too uses mixed strategies. (If Hank, Ike, and Ned were involved in bidding for a contract to provide Fred with grain, it would not be utterly fantastic for each to consider joining coalitions that would implement coordinated mixed strategies calling for various bids.) Thus we are really dealing with an assumption to the effect that *utility* can be distributed among players more or less at will. This raises a very serious issue when we remember that utility scales simply reflect agents' preferences for various outcomes. Thus when we speak of three players moving from a utility distribution of, say, (1/3, 1/2, 3/5) to another, say, (1/4, 3/5, 1), we must remember that the players are not exchanging some *commodity* called utility, but rather are passing from a prospect having a ranking at the 1/3 spot on the first player's utility scale, at the 1/2 spot on the second's, and at the 3/5 spot on the third's to another prospect ranking at the 1/4, 3/5, and 1 spots on the scales of the first, second, and third player, respectively. It is not clear that in a typical application the prospects required are always on hand. Witness the case of coalitions to ban abortions.

(Note: The transferability of utility does not entail its interpersonal comparability, that is, that we can draw conclusions from the utilities about how much more one player prefers a given prospect than another does. However, we would make interpersonal utility comparisons if we argued that certain distributions are unfair or unjust because they satisfy the preferences of one player more than those of another.)

PROBLEMS

1. Verify that the characteristic function for the Hank, Ike, and Ned game satisfies the superadditivity condition.
2. Suppose Fred refuses to buy wheat from any single farmer, but that otherwise the Hank, Ike, and Ned game remains the same. Give its new characteristic function.
3. Verify that the new game satisfies the superadditivity condition.
4. Taking the superadditivity condition as given, prove that each coalition S of several players must have a value greater than or equal to the sum of the values of the one-member "coalitions" formed from each member of S.
5. Show that given an imputation for the game of exercise 2, we can easily determine which coalition has formed and how its value has been distributed among its members.
6. Prove that in the original farmers game no Pareto optimal imputation dominates any other Pareto optimal imputation.

7. The Aumann-Maschler solution allowing the coalition of Hank and Ned does not take into account that Ned can actually make a larger offer to Ike without cutting into his current payoff. Explain how Ned can do this. Explain how this demonstrates how a "weaker" player could be at a bargaining advantage with respect to a "stronger" one.

8. The following is a well-known n-person game taken from *The Calculus of Consent* by James Buchanan and Gordon Tullock. In a certain rural county in a certain state there are 100 farms, each with a county-maintained road running to it. There are no official standards for deciding whether a road should be repaired; rather each farmer applies his personal standard and a road is repaired when and only when a majority of the farmers of the county vote to repair it. Buchanan and Tullock consider four possibilities:

   (1) Everyone votes on principle: Each farmer votes to repair a road when and only when it meets his standard for repair.
   (2) Everyone votes selfishly: Each farmer votes to repair his and only his road.
   (3) A majority vote on principle, the rest selfishly.
   (4) Farmers form coalitions and vote to repair all and only members' roads.
      (a) Prove that if (1) obtains, a road is repaired when and only when it meets the standard of more than half the farmers.
      (b) Prove that if (2) obtains, no road is repaired.
      (c) Prove that if (3) obtains, the quality of the unselfish farmers' roads will be lowered whereas those of the selfish farmers will be raised.
      (d) Suppose (4) obtains. Let 0 be the value to a coalition whose members do not have their roads paved. Let 1 be the value to a coalition whose members do have their roads paved. Explain why the only coalitions that will form will be those containing at least fifty-one farmers.
      (e) Suppose the situation in (d) obtains except that the value of a coalition is the number of its members whose roads are paved. Supposing the costs of paving a road do not matter, what coalition(s) will form? (This a question for discussion. I doubt that it has a single "correct" answer.)

9. Consider an n-person game involving voters who have various preferences on legalized abortion and who may or may not form coalitions to pass or defeat constitutional amendments banning abortion. How, if at all, could we make sense of the transferability of utility in this context? (Suggestion: in a real-life context, no outcome will consist of the unadorned passage or defeat of an amendment but will be accompanied by other background events – such as certain members of the coalition becoming politically influential figures. Perhaps the prospects required to underwrite the transferability of utility can be constructed by enlisting possible background events.)

5-7. References

Game theory began with *Von Neumann and Morgenstern*, but I have based my account on *Luce and Raiffa*. *Davis* is rich with examples and contains an exposition of the Aumann-Maschler approach. *Luce and Raiffa* also contains an exposition of Nash's approach to bargaining games, but the reader should consult *Gauthier* for a more detailed exploration of the relevance of games to morals. Although *Buchanan and Tullock* is well known to political scientists, I have not treated that work here. I recommend it to readers who are interested in learning more about multiperson interactions. Finally, the connection between the Predictor and prisoner's dilemma is noted in *Gibbard and Harper* and elaborated on in *Lewis*.

Chapter 6
SOCIAL CHOICES

6-1. The Problem of Social Choice

Groups of individuals—such as clubs, nations, or professional societies—that aim to function as cohesive units cannot depend on the choices made by their members on an individual basis to lead to a collective outcome that furthers the group's interests. A university, for example, that did not fix a schedule of classes and vacation breaks could hardly promote an orderly learning process, because everyone—professors and students alike—has different ideas about the best way to schedule classes. But how should a class schedule be developed? What weight should be assigned to the opinions of the various constituencies affected? Should it be a matter of faculty decision alone? Or should the students be given a voice? And should the higher administration hold the trump card? Is class scheduling a matter of developing a rational plan or a fair plan? More generally, in the social sphere what are the relationships between the demands of rationality and those of justice or fairness? These are some of the problems connected with social choices.

At a more abstract level the problem of social choice may be characterized as follows: A group of individuals has two or more alternative group actions or policies open to adoption. The members of the group (henceforth, called *citizens*) have their own preferences concerning the group choice. The problem is to develop a group choice from these. Social choice theory studies the properties of various methods that have been proposed for solving this problem.

The problem is often specified more fully by using a deeper analysis of the context of social choice. For example, one would expect that were any citizen to make the choice for her society on her own, she would temper her preferences for outcomes by her assessments of the probabilities of the relevant background states. Thus one might approach the problem of social choice as the twofold task of (1) combining the preferences of the citizenry to obtain a social preference ordering and (2) of combining their probability assessments to obtain a group probability function. In fact, very little social choice theory concerns (2); the preponderance of the work in this field has been directed toward the problem of deriving a social ordering from the orderings of the citizenry. And this is as it probably should be; for it is not clear that the notion of a group probability function makes sense—even for the subjectivist. Certainly, a society of objectivists would develop probabilities for group use by methods that are independent of the personal assessments of its citizens. (However, the citizens of any type of society might choose the *method* to be employed in assessing probabilities for use in social choices.) Moreover, since subjectivists identify probabilities with the assessments of particular individuals, it is difficult to understand how they could endorse a probability that belonged to no individual in particular—even if it were derived somehow from individual probabilities.

In view of this we will restrict the problem of social choice to that of obtaining a group choice as an aggregation of the choices of its members. More specifically, we will assume that each citizen has already established a personal preference ranking that satisfies at least the ordering conditions O1–O8 (see chapter 2) used to generate an ordinal utility scale. A set of such individual orderings—one for each citizen—is called a group *preference profile*. For example, consider a society of three citizens—Jackson, Quimby, and Short. Assume that they have four dinners under consideration: beef, chicken, fish, and macaroni. Jackson prefers the dinners in the order given, Quimby has the opposite preferences, and Short is indifferent between chicken and fish but prefers them both to beef and prefers that in turn to macaroni. This describes one preference profile for that society and that set of alternatives. We can represent it using the obvious abbreviations as follows in table 6-1. This is only one of the many

6-1	J	Q	S
	b	m	c, f
	c	f	b
	f	c	m
	m	b	

preference profiles that are possible in this case; another in which all three citizens have the same ordering is shown in table 6-2.

6-2	J	Q	S
	c	c	c
	f	f	f
	b, m	b, m	b, m

A collective choice rule is a method that operates on preference profiles and yields a social ranking of the alternatives. We will always assume that both the number of alternatives and the number of citizens are finite and will concentrate on a special type of collective choice rules known as *social welfare functions* (SWFs). Social welfare functions operate on all the preference profiles possible for a given set of alternatives and citizens, and they yield social orderings that satisfy conditions O1–O8. Many collective choice rules fail to do this. Two-thirds majority rule yields no social orderings for profiles in which no alternative is preferred to another by two thirds of the citizens. Moreover, simple majority rule can yield cyclical social orderings, as table 6-3 illustrates. Since a majority

6-3	1	2	3
	a	b	c
	b	c	a
	c	a	b

prefer *a* to *b* and a majority prefer *b* to *c* and a majority also prefer *c* to *a*, the social preferences generated by simple majority rule would form a circle, violating the condition that requires not *aPc* if *cPa*. This very simple anomaly is known as the *voting paradox*, and it is just a sample of the problems to come.

The voting paradox shows that even so revered a principle of collective choice as majority rule is not a social welfare function. May we not have set our sights too high? No, let us not abandon social welfare functions yet; the high standards set for them are worth aiming for in both theory and practice. For we do not want a method of collective choice that breaks down here and there; and because we cannot count on always getting our first choice, many situations of group choice require preference rankings that satisfy O1–O8.

We will abstract from the mechanisms that are used by social welfare functions to produce social orderings: If two mechanisms of social choice associate the same social orderings with the same preference profiles, they will count as the same social welfare function. For example, let us suppose that Jackson, Quimby, and Short devise the following method for determining a social ordering: First they list all the possible preference profiles; then starting with the first listed they draw straws and take the social ordering for that profile as identical with the preference ordering of the citizen winning the draw on that round; they proceed in this manner until a social ordering is determined for each profile. This defines an SWF, but of course the method might produce any number of other SWFs instead since the drawings could have resulted in different winners. Now let us suppose that Short just happens to win each drawing, and thus, the social ordering always equals his. From our point of view *the same* SWF would have been generated by stipulating *at the outset* that Short's ordering was to be the social ordering. We are purposely abstracting from the very different spirits reflected in the two methods used as examples and focusing only on the fact that they produce the same outputs for the same inputs.

Our concept of social welfare functions even allows for SWFs that no formal rules of collective choice implement. This includes group preferences generated through the action of the marketplace. There our aggregated individual choices, as expressed by the prices we pay for goods and services, determine the options open to society as a whole. Thus if few people buy soyburgers, our economic "votes" will see to it that the local soyburger stand is short lived.

A social welfare function is defined for a specific society and a specific set of alternatives. The requirement that it produces a social ordering for every preference profile (derived from those alternatives and those citizens) is called the *unrestricted domain* condition (condition U). There are a number of other conditions that social choice theorists think a reasonable SWF should satisfy besides condition U. One of them is that an SWF not be dictatorial (condition D). An SWF is *dictatorial* when it always identifies the social ordering with that of one of the citizens—the same citizen being used each time. Thus the SWF in our last example was dictatorial because its social ordering was always the same as Short's. We will discuss later other conditions on SWFs that seem to be just as reasonable as conditions U and D. Once a number of such conditions had been proposed it was only natural for social choice theorists to seek SWFs that satisfy them. We have already seen that majority rule does not satisfy condition U. But, as is to be expected, it satisfies condition D. In 1951 an economist, Kenneth Arrow, proved a theorem that subsequently shaped much social choice theory. Unfortunately, Arrow's theorem is a negative result: It shows that no SWF can satisfy five quite reasonable conditions—two of which happen to be conditions U and D. Because Arrow's theorem is so central to social choice theory the next section will be devoted to formulating and proving it. Subsequent sections will present other approaches to social choice that circumvent his theorem by relaxing one or more of its conditions.

PROBLEMS

1. Does a collective choice rule, which merely selects one alternative from a set of alternatives and declares it to be the first choice, count as an SWF?
2. Suppose there are six citizens and three alternatives and the collective choice rule in use is the following: To decide how to rank a pair of alternatives in the social ordering, roll a die and take the ranking of the citizen whose number comes up as the social ranking of that pair.
   a. Will this method necessarily implement an SWF?
   b. Could this method yield a dictatorial SWF?

6-2. Arrow's Theorem

6-2a. Arrow's Conditions

The first step toward developing Arrow's theorem is to formulate the conditions on SWFs that are treated by the theorem. We have already mentioned conditions

U and D. However, these scarcely narrow the field of social welfare functions to a reasonable class. For example, there are SWFs that associate the same social ordering with *every* preference profile on which they operate. These *constant* SWFs, as one might call them, satisfy both conditions U and D. They satisfy condition U by determining *at least one* social ordering for each preference profile. It is the same ordering for each profile, of course, but that does not disqualify a constant SWF from being an SWF. Because they do not agree with one and the same citizen on each profile, constant SWFs also satisfy condition D. But this hardly qualifies them as satisfactory means of collective choice because no matter how the citizens happen to feel about the alternatives, constant SWFs impose the same social ordering. Constant SWFs illustrate the important distinction between social welfare functions that *impose* an ordering and those that are *dictatorial*. Dictatorial SWFs identify the social ordering with that of one member of society – they make a dictator of that citizen. By contrast, imposed orderings may fail to reflect the preferences of any *citizen*, although they may reflect the preferences of someone who is not a member of the society in question.

There may be a place for imposed social orderings in human affairs. Under certain circumstances it is quite proper for an adult to impose a preference ordering on the options available to a group of young children. And in some religious societies divine revelation imposes the social ordering. For the most part, however, imposed social orderings are unrealistic and unfair. For this reason Arrow considered a condition on SWFs that is designed to exclude them. This is called the *citizens' sovereignty* condition (condition CS) and requires that *for each pair of distinct alternatives x and y there is at least one preference profile for which the SWF yields a social ordering that ranks x above y.* This rules out constant SWFs because they put two alternatives in the same order no matter what their status in a preference profile may be. For example, an SWF that *always* ranked beef above macaroni in the Jackson, Quimby, and Short example would violate condition CS, because CS requires that there be at least one preference profile for which the SWF ranks macaroni above beef. With an SWF satisfying CS, Jackson, Quimby, and Short could guarantee either social ranking of macaroni and chicken by seeing to it that their personal rankings conformed to the appropriate profile. Thus the social ordering could not be imposed on them in a way entirely independent of their own preferences.

Yet with just CS there could be a perverse relationship between the citizens' preferences and the social ordering. An SWF that ranked alternatives oppositely to that of the majority of the citizens would satisfy both conditions D and CS! To exclude this we need another condition called the condition of *positive association between individual and social values* (condition PA). This condition states that *if an SWF ranks an alternative x above an alternative y for a given profile, it must also rank x above y in any profile that is exactly like the original one except that one or more citizens have moved x up in their own rankings.* Consider, for example, the profiles for Jackson, Quimby, and Short presented in tables 6-4 and 6-5. The only difference between these two profiles is that in going from profile 1 to profile 2, Jackson changes his preference for

6-4	J	Q	S
	b	c, f	c, f, m
	c	b	b
Profile 1	m	m	
	f		

6-5	J	Q	S
	b, c	c, f	c, f, m
Profile 2	m	b	b
	f	m	

beef to chicken into an indifference between them. Thus any SWF that satisfied PA and socially ordered chicken above beef for profile 1 would do the same for profile 2.

Today many discussions of Arrow's work replace conditions PA and CS with another one named after the Italian economist, Vilfredo Pareto. The Pareto condition (condition P) states that *the SWF must rank x above y for a given profile if every citizen ranks x above y in that profile*. It could also be called the condition of *unanimity rule*.

The Pareto condition implies the citizens' sovereignty condition. For if it is in force, profiles in which all citizens rank x above y are profiles in which x is above y in the social ordering. Thus there will be profiles for which x is socially ranked above y (meeting condition CS). However, condition P does not imply condition PA. For consider a society with just three citizens, Able, Baker, and Charles, and two prospects to rank, x and y. Let F be an SWF that takes Able's ranking as the social ranking whenever Baker and Charles have the same preference orderings, and when they do not, let F take Baker's ordering as the social ordering. Thus in all cases the social ordering for x and y will equal either Baker's or Able's. When all three citizens prefer one alternative to the other, so will society. Thus F meets the Pareto condition. Next consider the two profiles presented in tables 6-6 and 6-7. In the first profile F ranks x above y, and in going from the first to the second the only change is in Charles's preferences. He has moved x up. Yet F no longer places x above y; so it does not meet condition PA.

| 6-6 | | | | 6-7 | | | |
Able	Baker	Charles	Society	Able	Baker	Charles	Society
x	x, y	x, y	x	x	x, y	x	x, y
y			y	y		y	

In the presence of another condition, still to be introduced, conditions PA and CS together imply condition P. This important fact is crucial to the proof of Arrow's theorem and it is one of the reasons many social choice theorists have bypassed those two conditions in favor of the Pareto one. (Another reason is that the latter is much easier to formulate and explain.) We will prove that implication later, but before we can we must introduce Arrow's last condition.

This is known as the independence-of-irrelevant-alternatives condition (condition I). In rough terms, condition I requires social welfare functions to obtain social orderings by comparing alternatives two at a time taken in isolation from the other alternatives. For example, if Jones's and Smith's preferences for beverages are as given in table 6-8, an SWF satisfying condition I would not respond to the fact that Jones puts tea at the bottom of his list whereas Smith puts

6-8	Jones	Smith
	coffee	tea
	milk	coffee
	water	cola
	cola	water
	tea	milk

coffee in second place. In determining the social ranking of coffee and tea, condition I prevents the SWF from taking into account the information that Jones ranks several alternatives between them. Only the fact that Jones and Smith have opposite preferences for the beverages may be registered. Since the social order is to be constructed by means of pairwise comparisons, the other alternatives have become "irrelevant."

By the same token, an SWF meeting condition I cannot respond to information used in constructing Von Neumann-Morgenstern utility scales since this depends on comparing alternatives with lotteries involving them. Condition I also excludes the popular rank-ordering methods that assign points to alternatives according to their places in citizen rankings and totals these to obtain social rankings; these methods employ entire rankings in obtaining scores.

So far we have described condition I in terms of the types of social choice mechanisms it excludes. However, Arrow's theorem (and social choice theory in general) abstracts from the mechanisms used in deriving social orderings and does not distinguish between SWFs that yield the same outputs for each possible input. Hence we must formulate condition I in terms that do not refer to the mechanisms used to implement SWFs. The following formal statement of condition I meets this desideratum.

> Condition I: If each citizen ranks the alternatives x and y in the same order in the preference profiles P_1 and P_2, x and y must be in the same order with respect to each other in the social orderings that the SWF yields for P_1 and P_2.

The following example illustrates how condition I excludes rank-order methods. Jackson, Quimby, and Short rank alternatives a, b, and c as indicated in table 6-9. They use a rank-order method to obtain social orderings: Alternatives are assigned one point for a first place, two for a second place, and three for a third place; the social ordering is then generated by favoring alternatives with the lowest number of total points. Here each alternative receives six points so they

6-9	J	Q	S	Society
1	a	b	c	a, b, c
2	b	c	a	
3	c	a	b	

are ranked as socially indifferent. However, when their method is applied to the profile in table 6-10, society prefers a to b. Yet notice that a and b stand in the

6-10	J	Q	S	Society
1	a	b	a	a
2	b	a	b	b
3	c	c	c	c

same respective order in both profiles; if c were deleted from both profiles, the profiles would look exactly alike. Condition I requires the SWF to rank a and b alike in both social rankings; thus the rank-order method used to generate these two tables (and any other SWF giving rise to them) fails to satisfy condition I.

Since condition I excludes the rank-order method and Von Neumann-Morgenstern utility functions, one might wonder why anyone would think it a reasonable condition to place on SWFs. Yet there are major conceptual and practical obstacles to using additional alternatives when ranking a single pair — whether the extra ones are deemed relevant or not. Take, for instance, the method of counting the number of alternatives located between two alternatives as a means of measuring preference intensities, which in turn could be used to decide whose preferences to favor. Can we conclude from table 6-8 that Jones's preference for coffee over tea is more intense than Smith's for tea over coffee? Jones ranks many beverages between coffee and tea, but perhaps steps down his ranking indicate only slight changes in preference whereas steps down Smith's indicate great changes. In that case Smith might prefer tea to coffee much more than Jones prefers coffee to tea. But how are we to tell? And if we could tell, would it be just or fair to take such preference intensities into account? What if the introduction of "really" irrelevant alternatives such as preferences for clothes, movies, or books put their preferences for coffee and tea in a new light? And what is really irrelevant anyway? Such questions raise difficult issues that must be faced by anyone using many of the methods that do not satisfy condition I. This is not to say that it is impossible to deal with them satisfactorily. However, they show that, other things being equal, an SWF satisfying condition I is preferable. Thus it was reasonable for Arrow to include it on his list of conditions.

We can now prove the implication that we set aside until the discussion of condition I had been completed. This is done in the following lemma.

THE PARETO LEMMA. *Any SWF that satisfies conditions PA, CS, and I also satisfies condition P.*

PROOF. Assume that the SWF satisfies conditions PA, CS, and I. Next assume that P_1 is a profile in which every citizen ranks alternative x above another, y. To establish that condition P is met we must show that the SWF yields a social ordering for P_1 in which x is ranked above y. Since condition I is in force we can restrict our attention to just the alternatives x and y. Any social ordering of x and y determined by considering just their respective places in a profile cut down to just these two alternatives must hold for all larger profiles containing it. We will suppose for P_1 the SWF does not socially rank x above y and derive a contradiction. Then there must be some profile P_2 different from P_1 for which the SWF socially ranks x above y, because CS is in force. Furthermore, P_1 and P_2 must differ in their placement of x and y. Thus some citizens in P_2 do not prefer x to y. Yet the placement of x and y in P_1 can be obtained from that of P_2 by moving x up in the ranking of one or more citizens. Hence by PA, the social ordering for it must rank x above y. But then by condition I, the social ordering for P_1 must also rank x above y. And that contradicts the assumption that the SWF failed to socially order x above y, for P_1.

PROBLEMS

1. Prove that every dictatorial SWF must satisfy condition P.
2. Explain why we cannot prove the Pareto lemma by applying condition PA directly to P_2 and dispensing, thereby, with the use of condition I.
3. Suppose that in Heaven God keeps a book that lists for each person and for each possible alternative God's assessment of the value of that alternative to that person—on a scale of $-1,000$ to $+1,000$. Now consider an SWF that works as follows: To decide how to rank two alternatives x and y, we first use God's book to find their values for the citizens of the particular society at hand. Then we sum the values for x and y, rank x above y if its sum is greater, y above x if its sum is greater, and rank them as indifferent otherwise. Would this SWF necessarily violate condition I? Condition D? Condition CS?
4. Prove that the following condition implies condition I: If P_1 and P_2 are two profiles and S is any subset of the set of alternatives, then if the citizens' relative rankings of the members of S are the same for P_1 and P_2, the SWF places the members of S in the same relative positions in both P_1 and P_2.
5. Prove that condition I implies the condition of exercise 4. (Hint: Prove [a] that condition I implies it for S with 0, 1, or 2 members and [b] that if condition I implies it for S with n members ($n > 1$), it implies it for S with $n + 1$ members.)

6-2b. Arrow's Theorem and Its Proof

We are at last in a position to state Arrow's theorem.

> THEOREM. *Where three or more alternatives and two or more citizens are involved, there is no SWF that meets all five conditions CS, D, I, PA, and U.*

(The restrictions on the number of citizens and alternatives open to them are necessary for the truth of the theorem. If there is just one citizen or just one alternative, there is no social choice to be made. On the other hand, if there are just two alternatives and two or more citizens, all five of Arrow's conditions are met by simple majority rule [with the added stipulation that alternatives count as socially indifferent provided that no majority favors either]. We will tacitly assume in subsequent discussions of the theorem that there are three or more alternatives and at least two citizens. This will save us from repeating that condition.)

The Pareto lemma established that conditions CS, PA, and I imply the Pareto condition. Hence if no SWF meets conditions D, I, U, and P, neither can any SWF meet conditions CS, D, I, PA, and U. For if it satisfied the latter, it would automatically satisfy the former, given the Pareto lemma. Consequently, we can prove Arrow's theorem by proving its *Pareto version*, namely, that no SWF simultaneously meets D, I, U, and P. Our strategy will be to prove the Pareto version by proving the following theorem that is logically equivalent to it: *If an SWF satisfies conditions U, P, and I, it must be dictatorial.*

Before we begin the proof it will be helpful to introduce several definitions. These now follow:

1. A set of citizens is *decisive for x over y* just in case x is socially preferred to y whenever each member of the set prefers x to y.
2. A citizen is a *dictator for x over y* just in case the set consisting of him alone is decisive for x over y.
3. A citizen is a *dictator* if and only if he is decisive for every pair of distinct alternatives.
4. An SWF is *dictatorial* just in case some citizen is a dictator under it.

We will need another battery of definitions in addition to these, but let us pause for an easy lemma.

LEMMA 1. *For any set of citizens and any pair of distinct alternatives there is at least one decisive set.*

PROOF. The set of *all* citizens is decisive for every pair of alternatives. For if every citizen prefers an alternative x to another one y, then, by condition P, society prefers x to y. So there is at least one set that is decisive for x over y.

Now for the other definitions:

5. A set of citizens is *almost decisive* for x over y just in case the social ordering ranks x above y when (a) all members of the set do and (b) all members outside prefer y to x.
6. A citizen is *almost decisive for x over y* if and only if the set consisting of him alone is almost decisive for x over y.

Notice that every decisive set is also almost decisive for the same pair of alternatives. For if the members of the set can determine the social ordering of x over y with or without the aid of their fellow citizens, they can do so when they are opposed. That is a matter of pure logic. However, not every almost decisive set is also a decisive set, unless both conditions I and PA are in force.

(We could use the equivalence of decisiveness and almost decisiveness—given conditions PA and I—if we were proving the full version of Arrow's theorem directly. However, since we are proving the Pareto version instead, we can establish the additional fact that it implies Arrow's theorem by avoiding the use of condition PA in its proof and keeping the two types of decisiveness separate.)

There is another logical point about decisive sets that must be understood to appreciate the details of the proofs to follow. A set that is decisive for x over y need not be decisive for y over x. For example, under most circumstances each of us is decisive for continuing to live over dying on the spot, in the sense that if we want to continue to live society will not prevent us from so doing. On the other hand, we are not ordinarily decisive on our own for dying on the spot over continuing to live. Society usually intervenes if someone tries to kill himself. The same point applies to almost decisive sets: A set that is almost decisive for x over y need not be almost decisive for y over x.

The proof of Arrow's theorem can now be reduced to two more lemmas. Here is the first.

LEMMA 2. *There is a citizen who is almost decisive for some pair of alternatives.*

PROOF. By lemma 1 there are decisive sets for each pair of alternatives. Thus there must be sets that are almost decisive for each alternative as well. Since the number of citizens and alternatives is finite, there must be at least one nonempty set that is almost decisive for some pair of alternatives but that has no nonempty subsets that are almost decisive for any alternatives. We can find such a set by starting with society as a whole, which we already know to be almost decisive for every pair, and proceed to check all sets obtained from it by deleting one member, and so on, until we find one with the desired property. Let M be such a minimal almost-decisive set and let it be almost decisive for x over y. Since M is nonempty, at least one citizen belongs to it. Let J be such a citizen. We will prove that only J belongs to M. That will show that J is almost decisive for x over y.

Let us assume that more than one citizen belongs to M and derive a contradiction. Let z be any alternative besides x or y and consider the profile in table 6-11. Here M–J is the set of citizens other than J who are

6-11	J	M-J	Remainder
	z	x	y
	x	y	z
	y	z	x

in M, and the Remainder is the set of the remaining citizens in society. There might be no remaining citizens, of course, but the proof can be modified to take care of that case. Since M is almost decisive for x over y, society prefers x to y. Since condition U holds, the social ranking meets the ordering conditions O1–O8 (see chapter 2), and society is either indifferent between x and z or prefers one to the other. If it prefers x to z, it must do so in all other profiles in which x and z are similarly arranged because condition I is in force. But then M–J, whose members favor x over z while everyone else favors z over x, is almost decisive for x over z, contradicting the minimality of M. If society is indifferent between x and z, then by the ordering condition society prefers z to y (since society already prefers x to y). But J prefers z to y while everyone else prefers y to z, and since condition I is in force, this holds for all other profiles in which y and z are similarly arranged; hence J is almost decisive for z over y. This again contradicts the minimality of M. Thus the only alternative left is that of society preferring z to x, and that again leads to the contradictory conclusion that J is almost decisive for z over y. (See exercise 3.) Thus we have derived a contradiction from our assumption that M did not consist of J alone.

PROBLEMS

1. Verify that simple majority rule (supplemented as in the preceding text) does satisfy all of Arrow's conditions when there are just two alternatives. What can happen when there are three alternatives and three citizens?
2. Establish that when conditions PA and I are not in force, some almost-decisive sets are not decisive.
3. Establish the step missing at the end of the proof of lemma 2, namely, that the assumption that society prefers z to x leads to the conclusion that J is almost decisive for z over y.
4. Carry out the proof of lemma 2 for the case when there are no citizens in the Remainder. (Hint: In that case the last column of the profile can be deleted.)

One of the puzzling features of Arrow's proof is its inference from the social ordering obtaining for a particular profile to general conclusions concerning the behavior of the social welfare function. (We have just seen it at work in the proof of lemma 2, where we have concluded that J is almost decisive for x over y on the basis of one profile containing x and y.) This seems to go against the standard mathematical and logical injunctions against drawing general conclusions from specific instances. Condition I is what makes this possible in Arrow's proof. It tells us that the social ranking of two alternatives is the same for every profile in which each citizen places the alternatives in question in the same relative positions. Thus one can look at a particular profile and at the social ranking of two alternatives for that profile in order to determine how those alternatives will be ranked in other profiles. Arrow's genius consisted in combining this fact about condition I with a selection of profiles from which he could infer the general conclusions requisite to his theorem.

A citizen who is almost decisive for a pair of alternatives x and y would seem to be a far cry from a dictator, since according to our definitions, the citizen in question determines the social choice for x and y only when he prefers x to y and no one else does. We cannot say how society will rank x and y when he fails to have that preference—much less how it will rank other alternatives. Our final lemma will show that there is much more here than meets the eye.

LEMMA 3. *Any citizen who is almost decisive for a single pair of alternatives is decisive for every pair of alternatives.*

PROOF. Assume that J is a citizen who is almost decisive for x over y. We will show that he is decisive for all pairs of distinct alternatives. These pairs may be divided into seven cases: x over y, y over x, x over a, a over x, y over a, a over y, and a over b, where a and b are alternatives distinct from each other and from x and y. Our proof will take the somewhat tedious course of demonstrating, one pair at a time, that J is decisive for that pair. Fortunately, the treatment of several of the cases is the same, and this will permit us to abbreviate the proof.

Case: x over a. Assume that a is an alternative distinct from x and y and consider the profile in table 6-12.

6-12	J	Remainder
	x	y
	y	$x\mid a$
	a	

Notice that here I have written "$x\mid a$" rather than "x,a." This is to indicate that no information is given about the relative ordering of x and a in the rankings of the remaining members of society. Also "$x\mid a$" has been written in the column below "y" to indicate that y ranks above both x and a. In short, each citizen but J ranks y above both x and a, but each might place the latter two in any order independently of his fellow citizens. J ranks x above y and y in turn above a.

Since J is almost decisive for x over y and he ranks x over y while the others rank y over x, society must rank x above y. But since everyone—J included—ranks y over a and condition P holds, society ranks y over a. But because the ordering condition holds, society must also rank x over a. Now consider how society dealt with x and a for this profile: J ranks x over a, the remainder rank them in any way possible; yet society ranks x over a. What holds for this profile holds for all others in which x and a are similarly arranged, since condition I is in force. Thus whenever J prefers x to a, society does. In short, *J is decisive for x over any alternative a that is distinct from both x and y.*

Case: a over y. Consider the profile in table 6-13. Since every citizen

6-13	J	Remainder
	a	$a\mid y$
	x	x
	y	

ranks a over x, society does (by condition P). Society must also rank x over y, because J is almost decisive for x over y. Then by the ordering condition it follows that society ranks a over y. Next we apply condition I to this profile to conclude that whenever J prefers a to y, so does society. In other words, *J is decisive for a over y*.

Case: y over a. Consider this profile (table 6-14). By condition P

6-14	J	Remainder
	y	$a\|y$
	x	x
	a	

society prefers y to x. Since we have already established that J is decisive for x over a, we can conclude that society prefers x to a. But then by the ordering condition, it must prefer y to a. Condition I then lets us conclude that *J is decisive for y over a*.

Case: a over x. Take the first of the three previous profiles and interchange a and x in J's column alone. The a-over-y case permits us to infer that society prefers a to y; condition P results in its preferring y to x. The argument then proceeds as in the previous cases to conclude that *J is decisive for a over x*.

Case: x over y. Let a be any alternative distinct from x and y and consider any profile in which J prefers x to a and a to y. By the x-over-a case, society prefers x to a. By the a-over-y case, society prefers a to y. We then proceed as usual to infer that *J is decisive for x over y*.

Case: y over x. Interchange "x" and "y" in the last proof.

Case: a over b. We know that J is decisive for a over x where a is any alternative distinct from x and y; we also know that he is decisive for x over b where b is any alternative distinct from x and y. Thus we may consider a profile in which J prefers a to x and x to b and argue as in the x-over-y case to establish that *J is decisive for a over b*.

We have now established that J is decisive for any pair of alternatives. Since the ordering conditions are in force, the social ordering is fully determined once the order of each pair of alternatives is fixed. Thus J determines the entire social ordering and must be a dictator.

PROBLEMS

1. Write the complete proof for the y-over-x case.
2. Do the same for the a-over-b case.

6-3. Majority Rule

Arrow's theorem is discouraging only to the extent that one is attached to his conditions. By relaxing some of them we may be able to show that reasonable social choice rules are possible. In this section we will show that we can do better than that by proving an important theorem about majority rule. This theorem tells us that by dropping condition U and *strengthening* Arrow's other conditions, we arrive at a set of conditions satisfied by majority rule alone. This gives us reason to be more optimistic about the problem of social choice than we were when confronted with Arrow's result alone. For we have a trade-off of conditions—relaxing one, tightening the others—that, arguably, leads to conditions just as reasonable as Arrow's.

Before we proceed any further we should specify precisely what majority rule is to mean in the discussion to follow. Thus we define it as follows:

> *An SWF is a case of majority rule* if and only if it socially ranks x above y just in case more citizens prefer x to y than prefer y to x, and it ranks x and y as socially indifferent just in case as many citizens prefer x to y as prefer y to x.

Majority rule, as we mentioned before, does satisfy Arrow's conditions when there are only two alternatives. It continues to satisfy all of Arrow's conditions except condition U when more than two alternatives are under consideration. Here is a quick proof of this. By definition it ranks pairs of alternatives by examining citizen preferences for them alone, so it satisfies condition I. An option x is socially preferred by it to y only if a majority of citizens prefer x to y, and a majority will still prefer x to y if one or more citizens move x up in their orderings; thus it satisfies condition PA. Citizens can force society to prefer x to y by arranging for a majority to prefer x to y; so it satisfies condition CS. Finally, a majority will overrule the preferences of any single citizen; so it satisfies condition D too.

On the other hand, majority rule does not satisfy condition U; we cannot depend on it to yield a social ordering satisfying conditions O1–O8 (chapter 2) when applied to all preference profiles. The voting paradox showed that. Yet even this difficulty can be obviated if we place restrictions on the forms preference profiles can take. Suppose all the citizens classify the alternatives along the same "objective" continuum and base their personal preferences on determining how close an alternative comes to a certain point on the continuum (the point may vary from citizen to citizen). For example, suppose all citizens classify candidates for a public office on the same liberal, moderate, conservative continuum, and also identify themselves with certain locations along that continuum, the liberal citizens identifying with the liberal end, the moderates with the middle, and so forth. Then liberals will rank highest the candidates whom *everyone* considers liberal, moderates will rank moderate candidates at the top and will put both extreme conservatives and extreme liberals at the bottom, and so on. If we were to graph the preferences of any single citizen using the liberal-conservative continuum as the x-axis and ordinal utilities as the y-axis, the graph would take the form of either a straight line or a broken line with only one change of direction. In figure 6-1 the graph for liberals is represented by a solid line, that for moderates by a dashed line, and that for conservatives by a dotted line.

Preference orderings such as these are called *single-peaked*. It can be proved that if majority rule is restricted to preference profiles in which all the

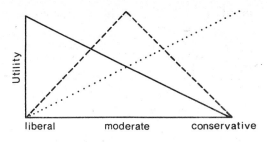

Figure 6-1

preferences are single-peaked, it not only satisfies conditions SC, D, I, and PA but also produces social orderings that meet conditions O1–O8. There are several other results like this but we will not prove them here.

Instead let us turn to an easier and possibly more interesting theorem by K. O. May, which shows that majority rule is the only SWF that satisfies certain strengthened versions of Arrow's conditions. The first of these conditions is the *anonymity condition* (condition A). It states that the *SWF produces the same social ordering for two profiles P_1 and P_2 if one can be obtained from the other by exchanging the preference orderings among the citizens.* For example, suppose that in profile 1 a citizen, Smith, prefers eggs to grits whereas in the same profile another citizen, Brown, is indifferent between them. Next suppose profile 2 is exactly like profile 1 except that now Smith is indifferent between eggs and grits and Brown prefers eggs to grits. Then any SWF that satisfies condition A will assign the same social ordering to both profiles. This means that the SWF cannot favor any citizen (since it can respond only to their orderings, not to their identities), and thereby rules out dictators. Condition A is thus a stronger version of condition D.

The next condition is called the *neutrality condition* (condition N) and requires the SWF to disregard the nature of the alternatives under consideration. An SWF that always favored conservative alternatives over liberal ones, while disregarding the identities of those who voted for them, would satisfy condition A while violating condition N. We need the following more formal statement of condition N for our theorem: *Let P_1 and P_2 be two profiles (not necessarily distinct ones) and suppose that x and y occupy the same relative positions in P_1 as z and w occupy in P_2.* (That is, for each citizen i, i prefers x to y, is indifferent between them, or prefers y to x in P_1 if and only if he prefers z to w, is indifferent between them, or prefers w to z in P_2.) *Then x and y must occupy the same relative positions in the social ordering for P_1 as z and w do for P_2.* For example, consider a society with three citizens, A, B, and C, and five alternatives, u, w, x, y, and z. Let P_1 and P_2 be the two profiles given in tables 6-15 and 6-16. Then condition N will require an SWF to rank x and y in the same order for profile 1 as it ranks z and w for profile 2. This implies, for instance, that if all citizens prefer x to y and society ranks x above y, it must also rank z above w if every citizen prefers z to w. An SWF that satisfies condition N ranks x above

6-15	Profile 1			6-16	Profile 2		
	A	B	C		A	B	C
	x	x, y	u		z	z, w	u
	u, w	z	x, z, w		u, y	x	x, z, y
	y, z	u, w	y		w, x	u, y	w

y (x indifferent to y, y above x) for profile 1 if and only if it ranks z above w (z indifferent to w, w above z) for profile 2.

The political systems of most countries do not satisfy this strong form of neutrality. Suppose, for example, that a majority of 51% of the U.S. Senate and a majority of 51% of the U.S. House of Representatives vote to pass (rather than defeat) a new bill. Then the bill will pass. But now suppose that Congress considers a bill the president has vetoed and that everyone who voted in favor of the first bill votes for the second and everyone who voted against the first bill votes against the second. Then the bill will be defeated.

If we replace "z" with "x" and "w" with "y" in the preceding statement of condition N, we get: *If x and y occupy the same relative positions in P_1 and P_2, they must also occupy the same relative positions in the social orderings for P_1 and P_2.* This is condition I. Thus condition N implies condition I.

The last condition we need is a stronger form of condition PA. It is called the *positive responsiveness condition* (condition PR) and reads as follows: *If society regards x as at least as good as y for P_1 and the only difference in the rankings of x and y between P_1 and P_2 is that some citizens have moved x up in their orderings, then society must prefer x to y for P_2.* Thus if x and y are socially indifferent under P_1 and some citizens switch in favor of x and that is the only change made in going to P_2, then society must favor x over y under P_2. Notice that if society already favors x over y, it must continue to do so under such changes. Accordingly, condition PR implies condition PA.

We are now ready for the theorem relating majority rule and the preceding conditions.

THEOREM. *The only SWF that satisfies conditions A, N, and PR is majority rule.*

PROOF. The reader may check that majority rule does indeed satisfy the conditions in question. Given this, our proof will be complete if we establish that any SWF that satisfies the conditions is a case of majority rule. So let us assume that F is an SWF that satisfies conditions A, N, and PR. Since it satisfies N it must also satisfy condition I, and thus the social ranking it determines for two alternatives x and y will depend on the citizens' rankings for these alternatives alone. Moreover, since it satisfies condition A its ranking cannot depend on the rankings of any particular citizen or citizens. Therefore, in ranking any pair of alternatives x and y, F must depend on only those features of a profile that are invariant under all rearrangements of the columns and that involve no other alternatives. But this means that F can only consider the number of citizens who are indifferent between x and y or prefer one to another. Now suppose that exactly as many citizens regard x as at least as good as y as do conversely. Then F must rank x and y as indifferent, because it satisfies condition N. Moreover, if we move from a profile of this sort to one in which a majority of the citizens prefer, say, x to y, then condition PR requires F to socially rank x above y. In sum, F operates by counting the number of those who prefer one of two alternatives. If the numbers are equal, the alternatives are ranked as socially indifferent. Otherwise the one with the greater number of citizens in favor of it is socially preferred. Thus F is a case of majority rule.

What, then, should we make of majority rule? The last theorem says much in its favor, but it still fails to meet condition U. This might pose no practical problems. Many social choices are made in contexts that do not require a well-behaved ranking of the social options. They demand only that we specify a first choice or a first choice among any pair of options, and one can count on majority rule to do the latter—at least. But practical difficulties lurk in the voting paradox, and that casts a further cloud over majority rule. Consider the voting paradox again (table 6-17). If a and b are compared, a is preferred; if b and c are com-

6-17	1	2	3
	a	b	c
	b	c	a
	c	a	b

pared, b is preferred; and if a and c are compared, c is preferred. This creates a cycle; no alternative can be first choice. Worse than that, suppose the preferences are as given in table 6-17, but the first choice is to be obtained by pitting one alternative against another and the winner against the remainder. Then if a and b are compared first, c will win in the second round; if a and c go first, b will win; and if b and c go first, a will win. Thus citizen #1, for instance, can get his first choice by having his fellow citizens agree to pit b against c first. The social choice will not be made here by the citizens' preferences but rather by a fluke of parliamentary procedures. But, of course, no skilled politician would be surprised by an outcome like this.

PROBLEMS

1. Prove that condition A implies condition D.
2. Describe a social choice method that satisfies condition I but fails to meet condition N.

6-4. Utilitarianism

A view with considerable appeal is that social choices should attempt to maximize the well-being of the citizenry. Stated thus none but misanthropes can fail to accept it. But that is due as much to the many interpretations our formulation permits as to its forthright appeal. There is too little content to the present doctrine to make it worthy of debate. In the last century Jeremy Bentham and John Stuart Mill attempted to remedy that defect by identifying well-being with happiness, itself characterized in terms of pleasurable feelings. They coined the name "utilitarianism" for their view.

The doctrine of Bentham and Mill yielded a method for ordering social options: Place at the top those that produced the greatest amount of pleasure for the citizenry as a whole; continue on downward, putting options yielding lesser amounts of total pleasure below those yielding greater amounts. Of course, this still is not as precise as we might wish. For it is not clear how we are to measure the amount of pleasure available under each social option. Are we to pass a pleasure meter over society as a whole — if only hypothetically — much as an applause meter measures an audience's enthusiasm for a contestant at an amateur hour? Or should we measure the pleasure obtained by each citizen and sum pleasures? Or calculate averages? Nobody has ever taken the first alternative seriously, but adherents of the latter two have generated two versions of utilitarianism — sum utilitarianism and average utilitarianism. The former ranks options in terms of the sums of individual pleasures they produce, the latter ranks them in terms of average amounts. If the number of citizens is kept fixed, there is no difference between the social policies the two versions favor. However, if the number of citizens is allowed to vary, sum utilitarianism will favor options that increase the population (the more to be merrier) — provided natural resources permit the citizenry to enjoy minimal amounts of pleasure. For little amounts of pleasure enjoyed by many people can sum to a larger total than that produced by a smaller number of citizens, each one enjoying a large amount of pleasure. Because modern social choice theory has tended to view the problem of social choice as one in which the number of citizens remains fixed, the distinction between sum and average utilitarianism has not been of much moment to it.

One may design all sorts of pleasure meters in fantasy, but that is what they are likely to remain — pure fantasy. Modern utility theory, however, may be just what is needed to make utilitarianism reputable. For the well-being enjoyed by a citizen under a given social option can be identified with his or her utility for the option, and the total or average amount of utility can be identified with the total or average obtained using the individual utility numbers.

We are treading on dangerous ground here and must not be hasty. As we have noted several times, utility numbers in modern utility theory represent relative positions in individual preference orderings; in no sense do they represent commodities or measurable quantities that can be combined, transferred, added, or averaged. So the simpleminded sum and average approaches of the last paragraph are based on a misconception about the nature of utility.

Despite these misgivings, there is a remarkable theorem of Harsanyi's that can be used to underwrite social orderings specified in terms of the total utility available per option. Harsanyi avoids the fallacy of treating separate person's utilities as additive by identifying total social utility with the utility of a single individual, whom I will call *the Planner*. Very roughly, his theorem states that the Planner's preferences for social options can be so represented numerically that they appear *as if* they were obtained by ordering options according to the total amount of citizen utility they yield.

Another important feature of Harsanyi's theorem is that it is based primarily on assumptions about the rationality of the citizens and the Planner, and its additional ethical assumptions are quite minimal. Thus one could plausibly use Harsanyi's theorem to argue that utilitarianism is simply the result of approaching the problem of social choice rationally.

6-4a. Harsanyi's Theorem

Let us take a closer look at this important theorem. It is concerned with a finite number of citizens and a finite number of social options. There is also the Planner, who may or may not be one of the citizens. If the Planner is a citizen, he is required to have two (but not necessarily different) preference orderings — his personal ordering and his moral ordering. The latter is subject to more constraints than his ordering qua citizen (if he is one). Henceforth, when we speak of the Planner's ordering, we will mean his moral ordering.

The citizens' and the Planner's preference orderings must satisfy certain conditions of rationality: Each must rank not only the social options but also all lotteries involving social options. (For the remainder of our discussion of Harsanyi's theorem we will use the term "option" to include these lotteries as well as the original social options.) Furthermore, these rankings must meet all the assumptions of the expected utility theorem. Following Harsanyi, let us call these requirements on the citizens' and the Planner's preferences the *conditions of individual and social rationality*. From these conditions it follows immediately that each citizen's preference ordering can be represented by means of a Von Neumann-Morgenstern utility function. Let $U_i(x)$ be the utility the ith citizen assigns to the option x. Similarly, the Planner has a utility function, and we will let $W(x)$ be the utility he assigns to x. For convenience we will assume that all citizens use 0 to 1 utility scales and that 0 marks the lowest point on the Planner's scale. (His highest point might exceed 1.)

Now for the ethical conditions. First, we will need a principle, which we will call the *strong Pareto principle* since it implies condition P of Arrow's theorem. This reads: *(1) If each citizen is indifferent between two options, so is the*

Planner; (2) if no citizen prefers x to y and at least one prefers y to x, the Planner prefers y to x too. The only other ethical condition needed is the anonymity condition from the theorem on majority rule; this will guarantee that the Planner assigns the same weight to each citizen in ordering social options.

Harsanyi's theorem can now be stated as follows: If the citizens and the Planner satisfy the conditions of individual and social rationality and the Planner meets the anonymity and strong Pareto condition, then for each prospect x,

$$W(x) = U_1(x) + U_2(x) + \ldots + U_n(x).$$

To start our proof of this theorem, let us note that we can represent each option by means of the vector (i.e., finite sequence) of utility numbers the citizens assign to the option. This is because each citizen assigns utility numbers to every option and uses the same number for all options that are indifferent to him or her. For example, suppose a society consists of four citizens. The first assigns the option x a utility of 0, the second assigns it 1/2, the third 1, and the fourth 3/4. Then the option x can be represented by the vector

(0, 1/2, 1, 3/4).

If each citizen is indifferent between x and some other option y, then the same vector will be used to represent y as well.

The Planner's utility function assigns numbers to options as well. The following lemma states how these numbers are related to the citizens' vectors.

LEMMA 1. *One and only one of the Planner's utility numbers corresponds to each citizens' vector.*

PROOF. Given the way in which the citizens' vectors are obtained, each corresponds to an option. Because utility numbers for the Planner are assigned to each option as well, at least one Planner number corresponds to each citizens' vector. Suppose that u and v are two Planner numbers corresponding to the citizens' vector A. Then, since several options may be represented by the same vector, u and v may be assigned by the Planner's utility function to different options. However, each citizen must regard the options as indifferent; otherwise they would have been represented by different vectors. Then by the strong Pareto principle, the Planner must be indifferent between the two options, and thus u and v must be the same utility number.

Lemma 1 allows us to represent the Planner's utility function as a function of the citizens' utilities. This justifies the following equation:

(1) $W(x) = f[U_1(x), U_2(x), \ldots, U_n(x)].$

Here $W(x)$ is the Planner's utility function, $U_1(x)$, $U_2(x)$, $\ldots$, $U_n(x)$ are the utility functions of the citizens (who number n), and f is the as yet unknown functional relationship between $W(x)$ and the $U_i(x)$. We will eventually prove that f is the summation function. Since for each alternative x, $U_i(x)$ and $W(x)$ are particular numbers, we can deal with utility numbers directly and write (1) as

(2) $w = f(u_1, u_2, \ldots, u_n)$,

where w is the value of $W(x)$ and each u_i is the value of $U_i(x)$. In view of this, to prove Harsanyi's theorem it suffices to prove

$$w = u_1 + u_2 + \ldots + u_n.$$

Consider any option represented by the vector $(0, 0, \ldots, 0)$. It must be ranked lowest by all citizens, and by the Pareto principle must be so ranked by the Planner too. But 0 is the lowest number on his utility scale, hence

(3) $W(0, 0, \ldots, 0) = 0$.

On the other hand, since the Planner's ranking meets the anonymity condition he must assign the same utility to all prospects represented by the unit vectors, $(1, 0, 0, \ldots, 0)$, $(0, 1, 0, \ldots, 0)$, $(0, 0, 1, \ldots, 0)$, $\ldots$, $(0, 0, \ldots, 0, 1)$. Let us stipulate that this utility number is 1, thus we have

(4) $W(A) = 1$, for each unit vector A listed above.

Next we turn to another major lemma.

LEMMA 2. *The function f of equations (1) and (2) satisfies*

(5) $af(u_1, u_2, \ldots, u_n) = f(au_1, au_2, \ldots, au_n)$,

where a is any real number with $0 \leq a \leq 1$.

PROOF. To simplify our notation we will prove this for the case of two citizens. The general proof uses completely parallel reasoning. Let u_1 and u_2 be given and let a be any real number such that $0 \leq a \leq 1$.

Let L be a lottery that yields the social option (u_1, u_2) with a chance of a and yields the option $(0, 0)$ with a chance of $1 - a$. The two citizens and the Planner assign L utilities in accordance with the expected utility theorem, thus

(6) $U_1(L) = aU_1(u_1, u_2) + (1 - a)U_1(0, 0)$
(7) $U_2(L) = aU_2(u_1, u_2) + (1 - a)U_2(0, 0)$
(8) $W(L) = aW(u_1, u_2) + (1 - a)W(0, 0)$.

But the first citizen values (u_1, u_2) as u_1, the second values it as u_2, and both value $(0, 0)$ as 0. By equation (3) we have

(9) $U_1(0, 0) = U_2(0, 0) = W(0, 0) = 0$.

Using this with (6), (7), and (8) we obtain

(10) $W(L) = aW(u_1, u_2)$
(11) $U_1(L) = au_1$
(12) $U_2(L) = au_2$,

and then by (1) we get

(13) $aW(u_1, u_2) = f(au_1, au_2)$,

from which the lemma follows by an application of (2) to the left side of (13).

With lemma 2 at hand we can now prove the Harsanyi theorem.

THEOREM. $W(u_1, u_2, \ldots, u_n) = u_1 + u_2 + \ldots + u_n$.

PROOF. Again for convenience we will restrict our attention to two citizens. Let u_1 and u_2 be given, and consider the lottery L', which yields an equal chance at $(u_1, 0)$ and $(0, u_2)$. Using the expected utility theorem we obtain

(14) $W(L') = 1/2 W(u_1, 0) + 1/2 W(0, u_2)$

(15) $U_1(L') = 1/2 U_1(u_1, 0) + 1/2 U_1(0, u_2) = 1/2 u_1$

(16) $U_2(L') = 1/2 U_2(u_1, 0) + 1/2 U_2(0, u_2) = 1/2 u_2$,

where the last parts of (15) and (16) are due to the fact that the first citizen values $(u_1, 0)$ as u_1, $(0, u_2)$ as 0, whereas the second values the former as 0 and the latter as u_2. From (15), (16), and (2) we obtain

(17) $W(L') = f(1/2 u_1, 1/2 u_2)$,

and then by (5)

(18) $W(L') = 1/2 f(u_1, u_2)$.

But by (2), (4), and (5),

(19) $W(u_1, 0) = u_1 W(1, 0) = u_1$

(20) $W(0, u_2) = u_2 W(0, 1) = u_2$.

Then substituting in (14), we obtain

(21) $1/2 f(u_1, u_2) = 1/2 u_1 + 1/2 u_2$.

Then algebra and (2) yield our theorem.

This theorem is important for decision theory as a whole. For as the proof shows, it bridges individual decision making and group decision making. The key link consists in embodying the group decision in an impartial (via the anonymity condition) and "benevolent" (via the strong Pareto principle) planner. This scheme seems to exclude citizen participation in favor of imposed decisions, but a little reflection should allay that fear. First, the citizens' preferences determine the social ordering, since the Planner's utility function is a function of citizen utilities. Second, the Planner's utility function satisfies the citizens' sovereignty condition. Finally, any citizen in the Planner's shoes would produce the same ranking.

PROBLEMS

1. Prove that the strong Pareto principle implies condition P.
2. Is the social choice rule yielded by Harsanyi's theorem an SWF?
3. Does Harsanyi's version of utilitarianism violate condition I?
4. Show that it does not violate conditions CS, PA, and D.

6-4b. Critique of Harsanyi's Theorem

The preceding proof is a shortened version of Harsanyi's own proof. This has been accomplished by restricting the citizen utility scales to 0 to 1 scales and the Planner's to a nonnegative scale. Despite this, both Harsanyi's original proof and the one given here employ an implicit assumption that casts doubt on the applicability of the theorem to many important contexts of social choice. I want to turn to that matter now.

If you reread the proof carefully, you will observe that at crucial junctures in the proof of both lemma 2 and the main theorem, lotteries among certain social options were introduced. Such lotteries exist only if the options to which they lead exist. The options were represented via vectors of utility numbers, so their existence amounts to the existence of options in which the utility distributions match those of the vectors in question. Reviewing the proof for the two-citizen case we find the following vectors used in the lotteries L and L':

$$(0, 0), (0, 1), (1, 0), (u_1, 0), (0, u_2), (u_1, u_2).$$

The last vector was introduced entirely hypothetically as a representative of an arbitrary option whose social utility was to be shown to be the sum of the citizen's utilities. The others, however, are assumed to exist categorically or at least conditionally on the existence of (u_1, u_2). Yet *none of Harsanyi's assumptions guarantee the existence of these options*. Indeed, in many instances their existence is not even logically possible. For example, suppose in a two-citizen case the "social" options consist in giving a scholarship to one citizen but not to the other. Suppose further that each citizen is concerned about himself alone. Then $(1, 0)$ corresponds to the first citizen getting the scholarship, $(0, 1)$ corresponds to the second getting it. But what of $(0, 0)$? It is not among the original options, nor is it equivalent to a lottery involving them. Thus given the original description of this situation of social choice, an option corresponding to $(0, 0)$ is not even logically possible. Of course, an option corresponding to $(0, 0)$ seems easy enough to introduce in this case; it is simply the option of awarding the scholarship to neither citizen. But that changes the situation of social choice, and it does not obviate the need for an existence assumption to support the constructions used in Harsanyi's proof.

The general problem is this: The proof given earlier and Harsanyi's original proof both depend on the introduction of social options that yield utility distributions conforming to certain patterns; yet the assumptions of the theorem fail to guarantee the existence of such options. We can remedy this defect by adding additional assumptions to the theorem, but then this will restrict the application of the theorem to cases where those conditions obtain.

One assumption that is more than adequate to the task of repairing the proof of the theorem is the following:

> For every vector of numbers $(u_1, u_2, \ldots, u_n)$ with $0 \leq u_i \leq 1$, there is at least one social option for which the distribution of citizens' utilities equals that of the vector in question.

I will call this the *distributable goods assumption*, because the only social situations in which it is certain to hold are ones in which each citizen's utility is determined solely by the amount of a distributable good or goods that he or she receives under an option. Here a distributable good is one, such as income, food, health, education, talent, friendship, for which all distributions throughout a society are at least logically possible. For example, if, in a two-citizen case, the good in question is food, the vector $(0, 0)$ could correspond to the prospect in which neither citizen receives sufficient food, $(1, 0)$ could correspond to that in which the first was adequately fed but the second was not, and so forth. For many situations of social choice the distributable goods assumption is easily met, and, perhaps, from the economist's viewpoint those are the only situations of interest. On the other hand, philosophers also look to social choice theory for help in resolving problems in which interests conflict—situations, for example, in which citizens gain only at the expense of others, or ones in which the citizens envy each other, or prefer to sacrifice for each other. These are situations in which we cannot count on the distributable goods assumption to hold. These are more matters of ethics and justice than of economics. Thus it would appear that the philosophical applications of Harsanyi's theorem are limited.

(The distributable goods assumption is equivalent to coalition theory's assumption that utility is transferable from player to player. Thus it is not surprising that the objections raised against the former in the context of game theory also threaten the use of the latter in the context of social choice theory.)

The story is not complete yet. Because Harsanyi assumes that in addition to the basic social options the citizens rank all lotteries constructed from them, many utility vectors have options answering to them in the form of lotteries. For example, starting from the options $(0, 0)$ and $(1, 0)$ and using lotteries that yield the latter with a chance of u_1, we obtain all options corresponding to $(u_1, 0)$, but they take the form of lotteries.

By extending this line of reasoning it can be shown that all the options required for the two-person case of Harsanyi's theorem can be obtained as lotteries constructed from options corresponding to $(0, 0), (1, 0)$, and $(0, 1)$. Using 0 to 1 utility scales, $(0, 0)$ would represent the worst prospect for both citizens, $(1, 0)$ a prospect best for the first and worst for the second, and $(0, 1)$ one best for the second and worst for the first. In many applications such prospects may be exceedingly hard to find. The fate of the two citizens may be so closely linked that it is impossible for one to achieve his best possible outcome while the other suffers the worst. Obviously, matters are even worse when we consider real-life examples involving hundreds, thousands, or even millions of people.

We can alleviate this problem by using the fact that utility scales are unique only up to positive linear transformations. This will allow us to use utility scales in which 0 and 1 need not represent the worst and best prospects. Then we can derive the theorem from the following *special prospects assumption* (stated here for the two-person case alone): There are three social options a, b, and c, such that (1) the first citizen prefers b to a and is indifferent between a and c; and (2) the second citizen prefers c to a and is indifferent between a and b. Then a can be represented as $(0, 0)$, b as $(1, 0)$, and c as $(0, 1)$. Furthermore, the three special prospects, a, b, and c, can be very similar or "close" to each other, so that the first citizen's preference for b over a is just a slight one—as is the second's for c over a. Where there are n citizens, the special prospects assumption postulates the existence of $n + 1$ prospects related to each other as a, b, and c are. I will skip the proof that the special prospects assumption provides a sufficient repair for Harsanyi's theorem.

(It is also possible to prove a weakened version of Harsanyi's theorem that requires as its only additional assumption that there is one prospect to which all the citizens are indifferent. This prospect will then play the role of $(0, 0, \ldots, 0)$. In this weakened version, which happens to be the version Harsanyi first stated,

$$W(x) = a_1 U_1(x) + a_2 U_2(x) + \ldots + a_n U_n(x),$$

where a_i is the weight assigned to the ith citizen. Unfortunately, this allows the Planner to satisfy Harsanyi's conditions of rationality and morality and still assign a negative weight to each citizen. The resulting SWF would be just the opposite of utilitarianism as ordinarily understood. For this reason I will continue to focus on the strong version of Harsanyi's theorem.)

From the purely mathematical point of view, the special prospects assumption is much weaker than the distributable goods assumption. Not only does the latter logically imply the former but the former postulates a finite number of options whereas the latter postulates infinitely many. Thus it seems likely that the special prospects assumption imposes only a minor restriction on the Harsanyi theorem and in no real way limits its applications to ethical situations. Returning to the scholarship case, just as an example, we see that two of the three options required for the assumption to hold are already present; clearly, in any real-life situation there will be social options that both citizens find worse than the scholarship being given to the other. It seems quite likely that similar factors will also be at work in other applications of the theorem to real-life cases.

Before evaluating this defense of the application of Harsanyi's theorem to ethics, a necessary condition for any adequate defense should be noted. Throughout the proof of Harsanyi's theorem we deal with a preference profile that is held fixed. Thus we cannot defend the theorem by introducing the possibility that one or more citizens have changed their preferences, for that would change the profile. For example, in the scholarship example we cannot stipulate that the first citizen prefers for the second to have the scholarship and then argue that awarding the scholarship to the first corresponds to $(0, 0)$. Thus one must defend the theorem by arguing either that a "true" representation of the citizens' preferences will give rise to the appropriate vectors or that there is a set of "background" options sufficiently rich to support the same vectors, or that certain profiles, such as those in which considerations of envy or altruism are operative, should not be considered.

Given this understanding of the logic of the defense of the theorem, it seems to me that the applicability of the theorem must be decided on a case-by-case basis. For although the prospects required by the special prospects assumption appear quite minimal, I see no way of constructing a *general* argument for the universal applicability of the theorem unless strong assumptions about human nature and the human condition are introduced. Even in the scholarship example we cannot be sure that there will be a background prospect corresponding to $(0, 0)$. Perhaps one citizen is a masochist; anything that horrifies his fellows he enjoys, even if it happens to him too.

Establishing the special prospects assumption on a case-by-case basis allows us to use facts concerning the circumstances of the case, such as the personalities of the citizens and their stations in society. In trying to prove that the assumption always holds, we must abstract from such particulars and make use of general premises. But the sort of general premises for such a proof that come to mind seem quite implausible. Thus we would probably need to assume that the citizens' preferences for social options were based on an indifference to the fate of others. For how else can we cover cases like the scholarship example? And we would need to assume that the various distributions of goods are economically, physically, and biologically, as well as logically independent. Otherwise we could not be certain of the existence of options, say, to which each citizen but one assigns the utility 0 while the one remaining citizen assigns it 1. Such independence assumptions may be objectionable even when the incremental differences between the distributions in the various options are quite small. In any case, their legitimacy must be examined before we can rest assured that the conditions for the application of Harsanyi's theorem hold in general.

Even if this problem is resolved, there is also the question of the relevance of the "background" options introduced to underwrite Harsanyi's proof. Suppose, for instance, a social planner is attempting to develop a social policy for a group of citizens whose interests seriously conflict, and suppose there is no option under consideration that every citizen regards as minimal. To be more specific, suppose the planner must rank prospects involving government support of in vitro human fertilization, and that the citizens have the usual spectrum of moral attitudes concerning methods of conception and fertilization. Would it be moral or rational for the planner to reach a ranking by introducing the option of abolishing human fertilization in all forms, hoping thereby to have a prospect minimal for all? I suspect that in many cases involving deep moral issues a social planner would be forced to such devices in order to apply Harsanyi's theorem.

(Actually, the special prospects assumption does not require that there be a prospect that is minimal in the set of all prospects but only one that is minimal with respect to others that can play the role required by the assumption. Despite this, social planners are unlikely to find the requisite prospects already on hand.)

These considerations are not decisive against Harsanyi's approach to utilitarianism, because they are too indefinite. But they do detract from the purity of his approach. The theorem promised to furnish a substantial logical underpinning for utilitarianism by avoiding such poorly defined notions as happiness and pleasure and by eliminating questionable moral and empirical assumptions about preferences. On the first count it appears reasonably successful. However, the need for special prospects and the problems encountered in establishing their existence show that on the second count the theorem is not much of an advance over the earlier versions of utilitarianism.

PROBLEMS

1. Explain how, given a prospect, P, valued by two citizens as $(0, 0)$ and one, Q, valued as $(1, 0)$, we can construct prospects valued as $(u, 0)$, for every u between 0 and 1.
2. Harsanyi's proof introduces $(0, 0)$ in equation (3) and $(0, 1)$ and $(1, 0)$ in equation (4). The former was grounded on the fact that $(0, 0)$ represented the worst prospect for each citizen, the latter on the anonymity condition. How can we ground (3) and (4) if we use the special prospects assumption to prove Harsanyi's theorem?
3. Prove that the distributable goods assumption implies the special prospects assumption.
4. Explain how the distributable goods assumption postulates infinitely many options.
5. Suppose that the social planner in the fertilization example could introduce new prospects by promising to give the citizens small amounts of money. Could he construct the special prospects by (1) selecting one of the original prospects, A, to be $(0, 0, \ldots, 0)$ and (2) introducing a new prospect, B, that is just like A except that the first citizen receives enough money in B to prefer it to A, introducing a prospect, C, that is just like A except that now the second citizen receives enough money to ensure that she prefers C to A, and so on? What empirical assumptions would have to be true for this to work?

6-4c. Interpersonal Comparisons of Utility

Although utilitarianism has had and continues to have many adherents among economists and philosophers, there are several major problems with the view that must be considered by anyone seriously concerned with the problem of social choice. The one I will address here—the problem of interpersonal comparisons of utility—is closely tied to our previous discussion of utility. Although this difficulty arises most acutely with respect to utilitarianism, it affects several other approaches to social choice as well.

Mary and Sam are trying to choose a joint vacation. They have been considering going to the seashore, camping in the local mountains or visiting the museums in a nearby city. It turns out that these all cost about the same, so monetary considerations are not relevant. Mary prefers going to the seashore to going to the museums and that in turn to camping. Sam's preferences are the exact opposite. However, going to the seashore is the only alternative that Mary finds bearable, although she feels more negative about going to the mountains than to the museums. Each choice is fine with Sam, although he would much prefer going to the mountains. Mary and Sam know all this. Were they an ordinary couple with a modicum of mutual respect and goodwill, one of them would suggest going to the seashore, since the gain in happiness for Mary would more than offset Sam's slight disappointment. If Sam resisted this suggestion, Mary would rightly resent his selfishness.

But *this* Mary and Sam are not an ordinary couple for they have been to business school and have learned about utilities. They note that although it appears that Mary has stronger preferences concerning the three options under consideration than Sam does, it does not follow that more *total* utility will be achieved by opting for her first choice. So Mary and Sam decide to develop utility scales to measure their preferences more accurately. Instead of restricting themselves to just the three options under consideration they rank a very wide range of alternatives, so that they can see how their preferences for the three particular items fit into the general scheme of their likes and dislikes. For ease in computation they both use 0 to 100 scales. The amounts of utility scored by each option under this system are shown in table 6-18. Upon seeing this Sam

6-18	Mary	Sam	Total
Seashore	20	86	106
Museums	10	93	103
Mountains	9	100	109

insists on having his first choice—camping in the mountains. This turn of events causes Mary to become quite irked. Sam is a songwriter who spends much of his time in activities he finds enjoyable. She works in the complaints office of a large department store; her customers are aggressive and nasty. This is her annual vacation, and for her the difference between the seashore and the mountains crosses the threshold between the bearable and the intolerable. She feels that her "right" to an emotionally recuperative vacation will be violated by following this utilitarian scheme.

Mary believes she knows Sam well. Despite the fact that he spends most of his time in activities he enjoys, he never enjoys *anything* very much. Nor for that matter does he dislike anything much. His moods are so constant that Mary sometimes wonders if he is really human. Fortunately for her, he is open to reason, and she reasons with him as follows: "Look, Sam. We shouldn't have used the same units on our utility scales. My preferences are so intense in comparison with yours that my scale should range between 0 and 1,000, if yours ranges between 0 and 100. If that change is made, the total utilities become seashore 286, museums 193, and mountains 190, and it is clear that we should go to the seashore."

Sam responds in a quiet but unrelenting tone: "Your reasoning, Mary, is correct but it is based on a false premise. You think that my preferences are rather weak, but the fact is I feel things quite deeply. I have been brought up in a culture very different from yours and have been trained to avoid emotional outbursts. In my family it was considered unseemly to jump with joy or to scream with anger or to weep when sad. But I have strong feelings all the same. And even if I did not, I do not think that extra weight should be given in a utilitarian calculation to those who are capable of more intense preferences. After all, each person is due as much consideration as any other."

Unable to resolve their dispute, Mary and Sam visit their business school professor, a man of great wisdom and wealth. He ponders their problem for a while and tells them that they need to talk with a philosopher. Mary and Sam leave him in utter despair and later agree to make their choice as most other couples would. They go to the seashore.

This parable illustrates most of the difficulties raised by interpersonal comparisons of utilities. These include epistemological, metaphysical, and ethical issues. For instance, are such comparisons based on an objective reality? Is Mary's preference for the seashore *really* stronger than Sam's for the mountains? Or is she just a more vocal person, as Sam suggests? If some people's preferences are in fact stronger than others', how could we *know* this? Does it make any more sense to compare Sam's preferences with Mary's than it does to compare a dog's preference for steak bones with a horse's preference for oats? Finally, even if we answer all these questions affirmatively, is it morally proper to respond to such information in making social choices?

Some utilitarians have argued that such problems will dissolve once psychology develops an adequate theory of the emotions. In particular, if as recent neurophysiology suggests, our emotional life can be explained in terms of brain processes, there is an underlying reality at which interpersonal comparisons hint and eventually it will be known. Furthermore, the argument continues, there can be no question that we do make such interpersonal comparisons in our daily lives. Anyone who bases a decision on the varying preference intensities of the people affected implicitly makes such comparisons by his or her very choice. Thus we should not raise artificial philosophical quibbles against a practice that is so well entrenched in human affairs.

But this does not end the matter. Let us grant that a neurophysiological account of the emotions is possible and that we do react to preference "intensities" in making certain choices. This still does not advance the cause of utilitarianism. For compare the neurophysiological account of perception with the hoped-for account of the emotions. Neurophysiology tells us quite a bit about perception: how the eye works, what parts of the brain are concerned with sight, what one can or cannot see under certain conditions, and so on. However, in discussing perception, this science speaks entirely in terms of neurological phenomena or observable human behavior. When neurophysiologists tell us that under certain conditons people suffer from double vision, their criterion for double vision is given in terms of patients' responses to questions and tests, and, possibly, measurements of the behavior of the patients' brains. But no one who thinks there is more to perceiving than responding to external stimulations in certain ways or having certain brain waves will take the neurophysiologists' account as the complete account of perceiving. Similarly, a neurophysiological account of the emotions will tell us about laughing, crying, fighting, or kissing, and, perhaps, brain patterns associated with them; but it will have nothing more to add for those who believe that joy, sadness, anger, and love are not totally reducible to our behavioral displays and bodily states. And that will leave us right in the midst of Mary and Sam's debate over whether there is more to emotions than our displays of them.

The second part of the utilitarian argument focused on our choices made in response to preference "intensities." Consider the case of an employer who must choose between two equally qualified employees to promote. Let us assume that everything about their contributions to the firm, their length of service, personal financial needs, and so forth, is the same, and that the employer favors neither one on purely personal grounds. He summons both employees to his office for separate conversations. The first is an impassive type who allows that he would be pleased to be promoted. The second, on the other hand, effusively tells the employer how long he has hoped for the promotion, how he and his family have discussed it many times. The employer promotes the second employee and later explains to a friend that he did so because "it meant so much more" to the second.

Next consider the case of a politician who must decide whether to demolish a block of old houses to make room for a new library. The residents of the houses are old and feeble, and the sponsors of the library are young and quite vocal. The politician studies the matter and finds that the case for either side is equally compelling. Then delegates from both sides visit him. The old are so weak that it is all they can do to speak, but the young forcefully plead their case and indicate how grateful they will be if he decides in their favor. The politician finds it politically expedient to favor the young.

Those who believe in the interpersonal comparison of utilities will grant that the two cases have been correctly described: The employer weighed the utilities of his two employees; the politician simply responded to political pressure. But to those who are skeptical about interpersonal comparisons of utility, the difference between the two cases will appear chimerical. In both cases, they will argue, the decision maker is simply behaving in accordance with cultural conditioning to respond in certain ways to the actions of others; the second employee's effusiveness is just as much a form of pressure as the political activists'. Both forms of behavior are intended to manipulate the persons at whom they are directed. Thus the claim that we make interpersonal comparisons of utility in making our everyday social choices has no substance for we merely respond to pressures in making these choices.

Let us turn from this general philosophical debate, which is likely to remain unresolved for some time, to examine the more technical aspects of interpersonal comparisons of utility. It will be useful for us to distinguish interpersonal comparisons of utility *levels* from interpersonal comparisons of utility *increments*. Mary's resentment of the utilitarian choice that favored Sam's preferences was based on her current utility level being lower than Sam's. Despite the greater overall utility gains to be obtained from going to the mountains, she felt raising her utility level should be given priority. Social planners influenced by Rawls would also want to compare the utility levels of various citizens in order to identify the worst off. On the other hand, those concerned with how much additional utility one prospect affords in comparison with another are concerned with utility *increments*. Sam's case for going to the mountains was based on comparing the incremental utility it gave him with that yielded by the other alternatives. So long as we rank alternatives by simply asking which one yields more utility, we are concerned with utility increments rather than utility levels.

The utilitarian SWF produced by Harsanyi's theorem—call it H—deals with incremental utilities and ignores utility levels. To see this, recall that H ranks a prospect x above another y just in case the sum of the citizens' utilities for x is greater than that for y. That numerical relationship will be preserved if we add the same number to x and y. Indeed, it will be preserved if we add different numbers to the individual citizens' utilities for x and y, so long as we add the same numbers to their utilities for both x and y. Adding these numbers is tantamount to changing the zero points or *origins* of the citizens' utility scales. These are the reference points by which utility levels can be measured. Consequently, adding different numbers to the scales of different citizens is to shift their origins independently and, hence, to shift independently the basis for measuring their utility levels. But shifts of origins, whether in concert or independently, do not register with H at all. Thus it neither responds to individual utility levels nor presupposes interpersonal comparisons of them.

On the other hand, H does respond to changes in the units used to measure individual utility increments. Mary hoped to use this to turn the tables on Sam. She tried to force him to use a 0 to 100 scale (with 100 units) while she used a 0 to 1,000 scale. In effect, she wanted to multiply her original scale by one number (10) while multiplying Sam's by another (1). Since this would place a different item at the 1 spot on her scale, it would change the item that marks the *unit* of her scale.

We fix the origin of a utility scale when we fix its 0 point; we fix its unit when we fix its 1 point. As we have just seen, we change the origin of a scale when we add the same number to every value on the scale, and we change its unit when we multiply each value by the same positive number. It follows that an arbitrary positive linear transformation may shift both the origin and unit of a scale. A social choice method that responded to any (nonidentical) positive linear transformation of a citizen's utility scale would thus respond to both utility levels and utility increments. The following SWF, G, is an illustrative example. G ranks x above y if and only if (1) the utility level of the best-off person in x is greater than that of the best-off person in y, or (2) (in case x and y tie according to (1)) the total utility afforded by x exceeds that afforded by y. In case x and y tie on both counts, G ranks them as socially indifferent.

All the social choice methods we have discussed so far respond only to changes in utility scales that alter the positions of the citizens with respect to one another—either by moving the origin of one with respect to that of another or by changing the ratio of the number of units of one to that of another. None of these social choice methods responds to uniform changes affecting every citizen's scale in the same way. Thus we need not worry about whether we have found the "real" origins or the "real" units for our citizens' utility scales, so long as we have properly calibrated their scales *with respect to one another*.

Moreover, when using a social choice method that responds only to utility levels, we need concern ourselves only with whether the origins of our citizens' scales are properly aligned, that is, with the *interpersonal comparison of utility origins*. On the other hand, when using a social choice device, such as Harsanyi's *H*, which responds to utility increments, we must concentrate instead on the proper alignment of the scale units, that is, on the *interpersonal comparison of utility units*. Summing up, some social choice methods respond only to changes in utility origins, these presuppose the interpersonal comparability of utility origins. Other social choice methods respond to changes in utility units and presuppose interpersonal comparisons of utility units. Finally, some respond to both sorts of changes and, accordingly, presuppose both sorts of comparisons.

Returning to Mary and Sam, we now know that the problem of comparing their utilities may be reduced in their case to the problem of comparing their units. Mary believes she has a greater preference interval separating the seashore and the mountains than Sam has. Thus she objects to their both being assigned 0 to 100 scales, which represents her interval as eleven units long when Sam's is represented as fourteen units long.

Mary bases her complaint on the following interpersonal comparison of *preferences*:

Mary's preference for the seashore over the mountains is stronger than Sam's for the mountains over the seashore.

This has the general form

A's preference for *x* over *y* is greater than B's for *z* over *w*.

Now if we can make a case for such comparisons, we can solve the problem of the interpersonal comparison of utility units. For we can stipulate that

A's preference for *x* over *y* is exactly as great as B's for *z* over *w*

is to hold just in case neither one's preference is greater than the other's. Then we can select the distance between two items on some citizen's scale as our standard unit. Having done this we can rescale his utilities so that the item he most prefers of the two selected marks his 1 point and the other his 0 point. Then we can recalibrate everyone else's scales by picking items that are separated by the same preference interval and use them to mark their 0's and 1's. Two items *x* and *y* are separated on A's scale by the same preference interval as *z* and *w* are on B's scale just in case A's preference for *x* over *y* is exactly as great as B's for *z* over *w*.

However, now everything turns on our ability to compare one person's preference for one item over another with another person's preference for one item over another. In trying to come to grips with this, it is useful to turn to the problem of comparing one and the same person's preference for an item *x* over *y* with his preference for *z* over *w*. It turns out that Von Neumann-Morgenstern utility theory already provides a basis for such comparisons. For a person marks a greater preference interval between *x* and *y* than he does between *z* and *w* just in case $u(x) - u(y) > u(z) - u(w)$. But that in turn holds if and only if

$u(x) + u(w) > u(z) + u(y)$. That holds—as you can show in exercise 4—if and only if the person prefers the lottery L to L', where

$L = L(1/2, L(u(x), B, W), L(u(w), B, W))$
$L' = L(1/2, L(u(z), B, W), L(u(y), B, W))$.

We now have placed the problem of the *intra*personal comparison of preference strengths on as firm a basis as that of utility theory. Unfortunately, there seems to be little hope for doing this for *inter*personal comparisons. We cannot extend our lottery trick to the interpersonal case, because it presupposes that one and the same agent is choosing between lotteries. What is more, we can draw the interpersonal comparisons however we wish without affecting the intrapersonal ones. That is because no matter which positive linear transformation we use to draw interpersonal comparisons and convert one person's u-scale into his new u'-scale, $u(x) - u(y) > u(z) - u(w)$ holds if and only if $u'(x) - u'(y) > u'(z) - u'(w)$ does.

Thus we must take "A's preference for x over y is greater than B's for z over w" as a primitive notion that cannot be explicated in terms of our single-person utility theory. As we have indicated, we can use it to make enough interpersonal comparisons of preference to allow us to compare the utility units of different agents. Having compared their units, we can derive new interpersonal comparisons of preferences and check these for consistency with our initial judgments. To see how this works, suppose Mary and Sam have ranked a, b, c, d, e, and f and all lotteries constructed from them on 0 to 100 scales.

	0	10 11	15	20	30	35		88	100
Mary	a	b c	d			e			f
Sam	f	d	b					c	e

Now suppose we take Sam's preference for b over d as our standard unit. Also suppose we decide that Mary's preference for the lottery $L(1/2, c, b)$ over b is exactly as great as Sam's for b over d. That means that, according to the scales given above, 5 units of Sam's is actually the same as half a unit of Mary's. Suppose that to reflect this we transform Mary's scale by multiplying it by 10. Having done this, the distance on her scale between e and f is now 650 standard units whereas the distance between b and e on Sam's scale remains 85 standard units. An immediate consequence of this is that Mary's preference for f over e is greater than Sam's for e over b. If this consequence agrees with our independent comparisons of their preferences, our rescaling is confirmed. On the other hand, if it fails to agree with our comparisons, the comparison by which we standardized the two scales is inconsistent with our new one. In this case we must try to bring our comparisons in line with each other. If doing so happens to be very difficult or impossible, we should conclude that we do not know enough about Sam and Mary to compare their preference intensities and give up our attempt.

Although our procedure prevents us from using totally blind and irresponsible interpersonal comparisons of utility units, it makes sense only if it makes sense to compare the preference intensities of different persons in the first place. If you are skeptical about that, nothing we have done will be of much assurance. One might try to respond to you by proposing links between interpersonal comparisons of preference intensities and overt behavior just as we forged a link between intrapersonal comparisons and choices between lotteries. However, as our parable illustrated, behavior is not always a reliable indicator of preference intensities. Thus the problem of the interpersonal comparison of utilities remains unresolved, and that is how we will leave it here.

PROBLEMS

1. Prove that if x yields more total utility than y, it continues to do so if we add different numbers to the individual citizens' utilities for x and y, so long as we add the same numbers to both x and y.
2. Show that the SWF G responds to both changes of origins and changes of units.
3. Explain why when we are concerned only with comparing the utility units of different persons, we can select any two items on any citizen's scale to serve as our standard unit and any other two separated by the same preference interval on each other citizen's scale to serve as his unit.
4. Calculate the expected utilities for L and L' and show that L is preferred to L' if and only if $u(x) - u(y) > u(z) - u(w)$.
5. Take Mary's preference for c over b as the standard unit, assume that her preference for c over b is exactly as great as Sam's for e over c, and transform his utility scale to bring it in line with Mary's.

6-5. References

An excellent treatment of most of the matters touched on in this chapter is to be found in *Sen*. *Arrow* is also valuable and contains the first proof of Arrow's theorem. *Luce and Raiffa* also cover most of the material of this chapter. *Smart and Williams* is a fine introduction to utilitarianism and its non-decision theoretic problems. For Harsanyi's theorem see *Fishburn*, *Harsanyi*, and *Resnik*. *Harsanyi*, *Sen*, and *Weirich* are good sources for material on the interpersonal comparison of utility.

BIBLIOGRAPHY

BIBLIOGRAPHY

||||||||||||

Allais, M. "Le comportement de l'homme rationnel devant le risque: critiques de postulates et ax-
iomes de l'ecole Americane." *Econometrica* 21(1953):503–46.

Arrow, K. J. *Social Choice and Individual Values*. New York: Wiley, 1951.

Bernoulli, D. "Exposition of a New Theory on the Measurement of Risk." Trans. L. Sommer.
Econometrica 22(1954):23–26. Original published in 1730, 1731, and 1738.

Buchanan, J. M., and G. Tullock. *The Calculus of Consent*. Ann Arbor: University of Michigan
Press, 1962.

Carnap, R. *Logical Foundations of Probability*. 2d ed. Chicago: University of Chicago Press, 1962.

Chernoff, H., and L. Moses. *Elementary Decision Theory*. New York: Wiley, 1974.

Davis, M. *Game Theory*. New York: Basic Books, 1973.

DeFinetti, B. "Foresight: Its Logical Laws, Its Subjective Sources." Trans. H. Kyburg. (Original
published in 1937.) In H. Kyburg and H. Smokler, eds., *Studies in Subjective Probability*. New
York: Wiley, 1964.

Eells, E. *Rational Decision and Causality*. Cambridge: Cambridge University Press, 1982.

Ellsberg, D. "Risk, Ambiguity and the Savage Axioms." *Quarterly Journal of Economics*
75(1961):643–69.

Fishburn, P. "On Harsanyi's Utilitarian Cardinal Welfare Theorem." *Theory and Decision*,
17(1984):21–28.

Gauthier, D. *Morals by Agreement*. Oxford: Oxford University Press, 1985.

Gibbard, A., and W. Harper. "Counterfactuals and Two Kinds of Expected Utility." In W. Harper,
R. Stalnaker, and G. Pearce, eds., *Ifs*. Dordrecht: Reidel, 1981.

Harsanyi, J. *Essays on Ethics, Social Behavior, and Scientific Explanation*. Dordrecht: Reidel,
1976.

Jeffrey, R. *The Logic of Decision*. New York: McGraw-Hill, 1965.

———. "Savage's Omelet." In F. Suppe and P. Asquith, eds., *PSA 1976*. Vol. #2. East Lansing,
Mich.: Philosophy of Science Association, 1977.

Kyburg, H. *Epistemology and Inference*. Minneapolis: University of Minnesota Press, 1983.

Kyburg, H., and H. Smokler, eds., *Studies in Subjective Probability*. New York: Wiley, 1964.

Levi, I. *The Enterprise of Knowledge*. Cambridge, Mass.: MIT Press, 1980.

Lewis, D. "Prisoners' Dilemma Is a Newcomb Problem." *Philosophy and Public Affairs* 8
(1975):235–40.

Luce, R. D., and H. Raiffa. *Games and Decisions*. New York: Wiley, 1957.

Nozick, R. "Newcomb's Problem and Two Principles of Choice." In N. Resher et al., eds., *Essays
in Honor of Carl G. Hempel*. Dordrecht: Reidel, 1969.

Raiffa, H. *Decision Analysis*. Reading, Mass.: Addison-Wesley, 1970.

Ramsey, F. "Truth and Probability." (First published in 1929.) In H. Kyburg and H. Smokler, eds.,
Studies in Subjective Probability. New York: Wiley, 1964.

Rawls, J. *A Theory of Justice*. Cambridge, Mass.: Harvard University Press, 1971.

Resnik, M. "A Restriction on a Theorem of Harsanyi." *Theory and Decision* 15(1983):309–20.

BIBLIOGRAPHY

Savage, L. *The Foundations of Statistics*. 2d ed. New York: Dover, 1972

Sen, A. *Collective Choice and Social Welfare*. San Francisco: Holden-Day, 1970.

Skyrms, B. *Choice and Chance*, 2d ed. Belmont, Calif.: Dickensen, 1975.

——. *Causal Necessity*. New Haven, Conn.: Yale University Press, 1980.

Smart, J. J. C., and B. Williams. *Utilitarianism: For and Against*. Cambridge: Cambridge University Press, 1973.

Von Neumann, J., and O. Morgenstern. *Theory of Games and Economic Behavior*. Princeton, N.J.: Princeton University Press, 1944.

Weirich, P. "Interpersonal Utility in Principles of Social Choice." *Erkenntnis* 21(1984):295–317.

INDEX

INDEX

Disutility, 88
Dominance principle, 9–10, 46, 110
Domination: by acts, 9, 25; by imputations, 171–72; by strategies, 128
Dutch Book theorem, 71–74, 75–76

Eells, Ellery, 117–18
Ellsberg, Daniel, 106, 109
Ellsberg's paradox, 105–7
Equilibrium, 129–30, 144–50
Equilibrium pairs, 129
Equilibrium value, 130
Equitable distribution point, 165–66
Exhaustiveness, 50
Expected monetary values (EMVs), 46, 85–88
Expected utility property, 90
Expected utility theorem, 90, 93–100, 125

Failure points, 159
Fairness, 42, 172
Free rider problem, 152
Functions: characteristic, 170

Gains: proportional, 165
Gambles, 87–88, 143
Games: defined, 5, 121–25; bargaining, 159–67; constant sum, n-person, 168; cooperative, 126, 157–59; n-person, 167–76; strictly competitive, 126–43; two-person, 126; two-person nonzero sum, 144–67; values, 129; zero sum, 128
Game tables, 124
Game theory, object of, 126
Game trees, 122–23
Gauthier, David, 173; on Prisoner's dilemma, 153–57; on bargaining, 166–67
Group choice, 178
Group decisions, 5

Harsanyi, John, 40–43, 197
Harsanyi's theorem, 197–204, 209
Hobbes, Thomas, 152
Hume, David, 115–16, 118

Ideal agents. See Rationality
Ideal points, 165
Ignorance, 14
Imputations, 170
Independence, 15, 49
Independence-of-irrelevant-alternatives condition, 183–85, 189
Indifference classes, 24
Information: imperfect, 122; value of, 57–59

Insufficient reason, principle of, 35–37, 42, 68
Interval utility scales, 30, 81–85
Inverse probability law, 53–54
Irrelevant expansion/contraction condition, 39, 161, 163–64

Lotteries, 89, 91
Lottery trees, 92

Majority rule, 38, 179, 191–95
Maschler, Michael, 172
Maximax rule, 32
Maximin rule, 26–27, 43
Maximin theorem, 136–42, 168
May, K. O., 193
May's theorem, 194–95
Mill, John Stuart, 41, 196
Minimax equilibrium test, 130
Minimax regret rule, 28–32
Mixture condition, 39
Monetary values, 85–88
Monotonicity condition, 106
Morality, 144, 151–57
Morgenstern, Oskar, 88
Multiattribute utility scales, 103
Multidimensional utility scales, 103
Mutual exclusiveness, 49

Nash, John, 160
Nash point, 160
Nash solution, 161–64
Neutrality condition, 193
Newcomb's paradox. See Predictor paradox

Odds, 70–71
Optimism index, 33
Optimism-pessimism rule, 32–34, 39
Ordering condition, 22–24, 91, 178
Ordinal scales, 81–83, 145
Ordinal transformations, 25, 29, 81, 82, 145
Outcomes, 6–7, 15, 16

Paradoxes: effects on decision theory, 119
Pareto, Vilfredo, 151, 182
Pareto condition, 182
Pareto lemma, 185
Pareto optimality, 151, 159, 160, 161, 163, 166
Pareto principle: strong, 197–98
Payoff, objection to, 173
Positive association condition, 181

Michael D. Resnik received his M.A. and Ph.D. in philosophy from Harvard University. He is now a professor of philosophy at the University of North Carolina at Chapel Hill, where he has taught since 1967. Resnik serves on the editorial board of *History and Philosophy of Logic*. He has contributed articles to numerous journals, including *NOUS, Theory and Decision*, and *Journal of Philosophy*. Resnik is author of *Elementary Logic* and *Frege and the Philosophy of Mathematics*.